# Transforming Scholarship

*Transforming Scholarship* is a user-friendly work of practical guidance and inspiration for supporting a student's interest in a Women's and Gender Studies degree. Berger and Radeloff use empirical evidence to help students with the major barriers they face when exploring Women's and Gender Studies: the negative response a student often faces when announcing to the world that he or she is interested in Women's and Gender Studies; and the perceived lack of employment and career options that supposedly comes with graduating with a Women's and Gender Studies degree. This book will support students to think critically about what they know, how to demonstrate what they know, and how to prepare for life both personally and professionally after the degree. *Transforming Scholarship* is a practical guide for students interested in Women's and Gender Studies that targets advanced undergraduates who have a firm connection to the discipline. This book is ideal for Women's and Gender Studies capstone courses, and for those who have finished their degree and need a resource to assist in conceptualizing the answers to the question "What's next?"

This second edition of *Transforming Scholarship* focuses on areas that undergraduates might want integrate into their Women's and Gender Studies education: study abroad, civic engagement projects, internships, independent studies, and honors theses. It includes exercises to help flesh out talents, passions, and skills, and how to link them to employment, information about the diversity of employment opportunities (and further professional training) available, and a plan to help prepare for graduation. It also delves into how to live a feminist life after graduation, including activism after college, building and sustaining feminist communities, and feminist parenting. The authors have also added new "Point of View" boxes throughout the book, where scholars focus on contemporary issues and deepen a student's understanding of the organizations and individuals fighting to end sexist oppression.

**Michele Tracy Berger** is Associate Professor in the Department of Women's and Gender Studies at the University of North Carolina at Chapel Hill. She holds adjunct appointments in the Department of Political Science and the Department of City and Regional Planning.

**Cheryl Radeloff** is a Disease Investigation and Intervention Specialist II with the Southern Nevada Health District. She is also an Adjunct Professor of Women's Studies at the College of Southern Nevada.

# Contemporary Sociological Perspectives

Edited by **Doug Hartmann**, University of Minnesota, and **Jodi O'Brien**, Seattle University

This innovative series is for all readers interested in books that provide frameworks for making sense of the complexities of contemporary social life. Each of the books in this series uses a sociological lens to provide current critical and analytical perspectives on significant social issues, patterns, and trends. The series consists of books that integrate the best ideas in sociological thought with an aim toward public education and engagement. These books are designed for use in the classroom, as well as for scholars and socially curious general readers.

## Books in the Series

**Published:**

*Political Justice and Religious Values* by Charles F. Andrain

*GIS and Spatial Analysis for the Social Sciences* by Robert Nash Parker and Emily K. Asencio

*Hoop Dreams on Wheels: Disability and the Competitive Wheelchair Athlete* by Ronald J. Berger

*The Internet and Social Inequalities* by James C. Witte and Susan E. Mannon

*Media and Middle Class Mom: Images and Realities of Work and Family* by Lara Descartes and Conrad Kottak

*Watching T.V. Is Not Required: Thinking about Media and Thinking about Thinking* by Bernard McGrane and John Gunderson

*Violence Against Women: Vulnerable Populations* by Douglas Brownridge

*State of Sex: Tourism, Sex and Sin in the New American Heartland* by Barbara G. Brents, Crystal A. Jackson, and Kate Hausbeck

*Social Statistics: The Basics and Beyond* by Thomas J. Linneman

*Sociologists Backstage: Answers to 10 Questions About What They Do* by Sarah Fenstermaker and Nikki Jones

*Gender Circuits* by Eve Shapiro

*Surviving the Holocaust: A Life Course Perspective* by Ronald Berger

*Transforming Scholarship: Why Women's and Gender Studies Students are Changing Themselves and the World* by Michelle Berger and Cheryl Radeloff

*Stargazing: Celebrity, Fame, and Social Interaction* by Kerry Ferris and Scott Harris

*The Senses in Self, Society, and Culture* by Phillip Vannini, Dennis Waskul, and Simon Gottschalk

*Who Lives, Who Dies, Who Decides?* by Sheldon Ekland-Olson

*Surviving Dictatorship* by Jacqueline Adams

*The Womanist Idea* by Layli Maparyan

*Social Theory Re-Wired: New Connections to Classical and Contemporary Perspectives* by Wesley Longhofer and Daniel Winchester

*Religion in Today's World: Global Issues, Sociological Perspectives* by Melissa Wilcox

*Life and Death Decisions: The Quest for Morality and Justice in Human Societies* by Sheldon Ekland-Olson

*Understanding Deviance: Connecting Classical and Contemporary Perspectives* by Tammy L. Anderson

# Transforming Scholarship

## Why Women's and Gender Studies Students are Changing Themselves and the World

### Second Edition

**Michele Tracy Berger**
University of North Carolina at Chapel Hill

**Cheryl Radeloff**
College of Southern Nevada

NEW YORK AND LONDON

Second edition published 2015
by Routledge
711 Third Avenue, New York, NY 10017

and by Routledge
2 Park Square, Milton Park, Abingdon, Oxon, OX14 4RN

*Routledge is an imprint of the Taylor & Francis Group, an informa business*

First edition published by Routledge 2011

*Library of Congress Cataloging in Publication Data*
  Berger, Michele Tracy, 1968–
  Transforming scholarship: why women's and gender studies students
  are changing themselves and the world/Michele Tracy Berger,
  University of North Carolina, Chapel Hill, Cheryl Radeloff,
  College of Southern Nevada.—Second edition.
    pages cm.—(Contemporary sociological perspectives)
  Includes bibliographical references and index.
  1. Women's studies—United States. 2. Feminism—United States.
  3.Women college graduates—United States. 4. Vocational guidance—
  United States. I. Radeloff, Cheryl. II. Title.
  HQ1181.U5B47 2015
  305.40973—dc23
  2014006854

ISBN: 978-0-415-83652-4 (hbk)
ISBN: 978-0-415-83653-1 (pbk)
ISBN: 978-0-203-45822-8 (ebk)

Typeset in Adobe Caslon, Trade Gothic, and Copperplate Gothic
by Florence Production Ltd, Stoodleigh, Devon, UK

# TABLE OF CONTENTS

# DETAILED TABLE OF CONTENTS

**Introduction**: Transform Yourself: An Invitation to Deepen Your Commitment to Women's and Gender Studies

This chapter covers what the book is about, who it is designed for, and why this book will serve students who have embarked on an academic career in Women's and Gender Studies (WGST). We share our experiences as professors intimately working with the challenges of students seeking to understand and use their Women's and Gender Studies training. We signal to students that they are embarking on a great intellectual and experiential journey, and need specific skills and competencies to prepare for it. They must take their journey with this book.

**Chapter 1**: Claiming an Education: Your Inheritance as a Student of Women's and Gender Studies

This chapter deepens the reader's knowledge about the vibrant interdisciplinary arena of Women's and Gender Studies. This chapter explores the past and present field of Women's and Gender Studies and its connection to social movements. It makes an argument that Women's and Gender Studies students are part of an intellectual tradition and legacy, one that produces a student with a particular set of skills, ways of problem-solving, and worldview. That intellectual tradition, as with others, has produced a distinct set of ideas and concepts that students learn through coursework and other learning experiences.

**Chapter 2**: Developing the Core of Your Academic Career: Coursework, Internships, Study Abroad, and More

This chapter explores the advanced curricular building blocks that students may pursue during their Women's and Gender Studies training, including internships, study abroad programs, praxis, assignments and capstone projects. An interview with Dr. Katherine Brooks provides critical information about working with a career counselor in helping students to identify their talents and interests.

**Chapter 3**: How *You* Can Talk About Women's and Gender Studies Anytime, Anywhere, and to Anyone

The ability to communicate complex ideas to others is heralded as a skill that Women's and Gender Studies graduates possess, yet seldom are students prepared to deal succinctly and powerfully with the stereotypes and misconceptions surrounding Women's and Gender Studies. Not only will we directly address common misconceptions of Women's Studies, but this chapter will provide models for students to use in developing their own "scripts" of what Women's and Gender Studies is, and why it is a useful, desirable, and marketable area of study.

**Chapter 4**: Discovering and Claiming Your Internal Strengths and External Skills

What are the tangible and intangible skills that one develops through Women's and Gender Studies training? In this chapter, we begin with a discussion of the top concepts that graduates identified in our survey as important to their professional work. These concepts emerge from the feminist classroom and also through applied learning opportunities. We also demonstrate how these concepts are used in their professional lives.

This chapter focuses on supporting the student in assessing where they are in their academic career. We suggest how a student might begin to organize what he or she learns in Women's and Gender Studies (e.g. concepts, theories, frameworks, etc.) through the framework of "internal strengths" and "external skills." Internal strengths and external skills evolve out of students' experiences inside and outside the classroom.

**Chapter 5: So, What *Can* You Do With Your Degree? Exploring Various Employment and Career Pathways**

In this chapter, we introduce students to the rich survey data that show the multitude of employment paths that Women's and Gender Studies graduates have taken. We supplement this data with an exploration of the many different kinds of employment opportunities that await students in the health and medical, legal, science and technological, academic, government, and information professions.

**Chapter 6:** Women's and Gender Studies Graduates as Change Agents: Seven Profiles

In this chapter we present the idea of Women's and Gender Studies students as *change agents*. We have developed three categories of "change agent" types in relation to future career pathways: sustainers, evolvers, and synthesizers. We then explore the experiences of seven people who are exemplars of the three categories. Students can use this typology to initially identify themselves, discover new career options, and investigate further skill development.

**Chapter 7:** Transform Your World: Preparing to Graduate and Living Your Feminist Life

This chapter attends to two themes: helping students who are poised to graduate think about the transition from college to professional life, and how to cultivate a vision of social change and transformation.

The chapter gives suggestions on developing or expanding one's feminist community outside the safe environs of the college campus.

# SERIES FOREWORD

"What are you majoring in?" Most college students are familiar with this ubiquitous question uttered in the midst of family gatherings, and most also know that some academic disciplines are easier to take home for the holidays than others. Business Administration, Engineering, Psychology. Mention of these venerable college majors is usually met with nodding approval. But students who announce that they are pursuing degrees in areas such as Women's and Gender Studies are often greeted with the discrediting cry of, "What are you going to do with *that*?"

Berger and Radeloff have written a book guaranteed to give pause to even the most dismissive of skeptics. *Transforming Scholarship* is a tour de force not only of reasons why students thrive in Women's and Gender Studies, but why, as a society, we need these scholars among us. The aim of the book is twofold: to demonstrate the rich content of contemporary Women's and Gender Studies programs, and to situate these programs within the larger context of a university education and its potential to cultivate the next generation of civic and cultural leaders.

The authors present extensive empirical research on Women and Gender Studies programs throughout the United States and include detailed examples of the multiple and impressive paths that graduates of these programs have embarked on. They also revisit higher education's mandate to train students for the public good and provide compelling evidence that Women's and Gender Studies programs are stepping up to this challenge in unique and effective ways. Berger and Radloff make the case that students of Women's and Gender Studies are developing the skills and insights necessary to navigate an increasingly complex global society; they are crafting new visions and putting these into action; they are change makers. This book is for anyone interested in a multi-disciplinary approach to transforming oneself and transforming the world.

Jodie O'Brien
Douglas Hartmann

# PREFACE

Our goals in the first edition of *Transforming Scholarship* were multi-faceted. We wanted to create a user-friendly, accessible guide that supported Women's and Gender Studies students early in their college careers, as well as declared majors and minors. The first edition was originally born out of a desire to change the question and skeptical conversation that Women's and Gender Studies students often face: "What can you do with that degree?" We wanted to write a book that spoke to the progress and aspirations of Women's and Gender Studies students, and provided strategies for how to communicate that interest effectively. We wanted to give students the tools to encourage them to be proactive in thinking about their education and their careers. We wanted to create a book that grappled with the messiness of living one's Women's and Gender Studies and/or feminist values after leaving college.

We were also responding to a significant gap, in the field of Women's and Gender Studies, of texts that supported and prepared graduates for their role as feminist thinkers, workers, activists, and leaders. And we wanted to try to empirically answer the question, "What *can* you do with an interest in Women's and Gender Studies?" We, Women's and Gender Studies professors, and friends, with a combined 15 years in the field, took on the challenge of answering this question by first surveying over

900 graduates at 125 colleges and universities across the world to find out how the major shapes life paths after graduation, as well as interviewing Women's and Gender Studies professors, former students who had graduated with a degree in the field. We scoured the academic literature on Women's and Gender Studies students' post-graduation (which is scant) and followed debates and trends in the blogosphere, such as on popular feminist websites (e.g. Feministing), but also in social media spaces such as Facebook.

*Transforming Scholarship* incorporated unique features that included creative self-assessment and self-discovery tools. Drawing on our rich and persuasive data (and the largest global database of Women's and Gender Studies graduates), we made graduates' career journeys come alive for readers and hopefully provided a guide for those finishing their degrees, as well as those who were considering career changes.

The response to the first edition of *Transforming Scholarship* has been powerful. We have heard from students, faculty members, parents, and administrators that *Transforming Scholarship* has been useful in a variety of ways. Faculty found ways to integrate it into the curriculum; some used it for introductory courses, others as part of a capstone or internship course, others in feminist theory. Deans also found *Transforming Scholarship* helpful in articulating the value of Women's and Gender Studies and its contribution to fulfilling an institution's academic mission. Along with critical acclaim, there also came questions: "Why didn't you include more focus on feminist lawyers?" "Why did you focus so much on the difference between departments and programs?" "Why doesn't this book reflect concerns of students who are already committed to Women's and Gender Studies?" After hearing from colleagues (informally and through the reviews), teaching the text, and also conducting national workshops, we have welcomed the opportunity in this new edition to strengthen current material and fill in missing gaps.

The second edition of *Transforming Scholarship* offers three substantive changes. The most important of the three is that this edition is aimed at and addresses students who have proceeded in their academic trajectory past the introductory Women's and Gender Studies course and have a firm connection to their major/minor, or concentration. This assumes that readers will have committed to Women's and Gender Studies and have taken two to three courses prior to reading the book. We assume also that these readers are looking for ways to deepen their training in Women's and Gender Studies. We assume also, that they will also be interested in all of the features offered in the second half of the book—exercises to help flesh out talents, passions, and skills, and how to link them to employment, information about the diversity of employment opportunities (and further professional training) available, a plan to help prepare for graduation, and how to create a feminist community after graduation. This overall emphasis on advanced undergraduates makes this book appropriate for advanced Feminist Theory courses and all Women's and Gender Studies capstone courses, but also for those who have finished their degree and need a resource to assist in conceptualizing the answers to the question, "What's next?"

Practically, this change means that much of the Introduction and Chapters 1 and 2 are condensed and revised to reflect a more knowledge-able audience. Chapter 1 focuses on the centrality of Women's and Gender Studies in the mission of liberal arts and higher education, and helps students understand the value of this rich intellectual tradition. It also addresses contemporary changes in the field (such as names changes of departments and degree programs within the discipline) and the profes-sionalization of the discipline through organizations such as the National Women's Studies Association (NWSA). The chapter also explores how Women's and Gender Studies is organized in other countries, such as the Lebanon, Switzerland, New Zealand, the West Indies, and the UK.

In our revised Chapter 2, we spend less time attending to the composi-tion of degree programs, and instead spend more time on areas in which juniors and seniors might want to consider as part of their Women's and Gender Studies education: internships, study abroad, and activism projects. We provide examples of how students use their training to create compelling learning experiences, often outside the classroom. Moreover, we focus some on the politics and culture of student life (e.g. activism).

How should a student majoring in Women's and Gender Studies respond when people say, "You can't find a job majoring in that!" Chapter 3 provides students with critical communication tools to gain confidence in responding to family members, peer and the general public about the value of a WGST degree.

In Chapter 4, we highlight the concepts and skills that WGST graduates possess by the time of graduation and how students can assess where they are in their own skill development. In the last edition, we packed a lot into Chapter 5—both information about career pathways and substantial profiles of six graduates. In this edition, Chapter 5 is completely revised and provides readers an in-depth look at an exciting and diverse array of employment opportunities. Chapter 6 is also updated, and we have added another profile, bringing the total to seven. Chapter 7 includes new topics about activism after college, building and sustaining feminist communities, and also feminist parenting.

The second substantive change is that throughout the text, we showcase how the debates over political, social, and cultural issues involve the theoretical insights and conceptual tools developed in Women's and Gender Studies classes. In this edition, we have worked with a talented group of scholars to help us produce "Point of View" materials. In these POV pieces, scholars focus on contemporary issues and deepen a student's understanding of the organizations and individuals fighting to end sexist oppression. To be clear, this is not a Feminist Theory text (as there are many wonderful ones already on the market), but materials suitable for a more sophisticated audience. Areas that we pay particular concern, in developing cases, include: GLBTQQA issues, global issues, immigration, secularity, and reproductive rights. We have kept the tone similar to the rest of the personal and intimate feel of *Transforming Scholarship*, so often these pieces are written in the first person.

The third substantive change is that the profiles that we featured in our rubric of career pathways (evolver, synthesizer, and sustainer) have been expanded, and we have updated the life and career changes of many of the graduates who shared their experiences in the first edition.

We give thanks here to the many people who helped us along the way.

*Michele would like to thank*: As always to my partner, Timothy Dane Keim, who supports me in every way imaginable in all the diverse facets of my life. I am always truly thankful for your unending kindness and love.

I would also like to thank my writing group, composed of two dedicated sociologists: Lisa Pearce and Karolyn Tyson. They are amazing scholars and friends who have provided me with support, nurturance, and critical feedback through both editions.

Periodically, I asked Daiysha Smith, my research assistant for another project, to assist on this project. She did terrific work, and I am thankful for her assistance. I also wish to thank the students in my Fall 2013 "Feminist Principles of Inquiry" class who gave helpful feedback on Chapters 4–7, especially Kevin Claybren.

And, lastly, to a brilliant conspirator of all things Women's Studies-related and to my cherished collaborator—Cheryl. I love that we made one of our dreams real. I look forward to seeing what we will create next! I hope to always call you friend and collaborator.

*Cheryl would like to thank*: During the course of transforming oneself in order to transform the world, I met many folks who not only inspired the book, but gave me support as well. I will always be indebted to all the Women's and Gender Studies students, who I wo-mentored or tormented as students at University of Nevada, Las Vegas, Minnesota State University, Mankato, and College of Southern Nevada, who participated in our survey, but also those who took the time to be interviewed and also gave their insight into the chapters of the book. I am in awe of Adriane Brown, Judi Brown, Caryn Lindsay, Jennifer Pritchett, and Diana Rhodes for their contributions to the world. I also want to thank my friends and activists in the HIV/AIDS community in Las Vegas for providing me with inspiration on a daily basis. Your creativity, grace, ability to organize events and work with ever-changing funding sources, and educate the public amazes me, and I feel blessed every day to work with such amazing people.

I also want to thank my fellow graduates from the Elizabeth Kearney Women's Leadership Program, my colleagues from the Mankato American Association of University Women (AAUW), the FIRS (faculty-in-residence), and participant of New Leadership Nevada and Tri-State, as well as my mentors Avra Johnson and Anne Ganey for giving me the encouragement and strength to follow my vision for leadership, as well as reviving my belief in sisterhood when I was questioning it. I also want to thank John Alesio, the Department of Gender and Women's Studies at Minnesota State, Mankato, and Provost Scott Olsen for approving my leave of absence in order to explore different career and research opportunities. I also want to thank my peer mentors, in particular Jaime Phillips, Becky Bates, Anne Lascamana, Gina Winger, Sarah Sifers, Caryn

Lindsay, Laura Yavitz, Lori Andrews, Crystal Jackson, Nicole Rogers, DeAnna Beachley, Lois Helmbold, Barbara Brents, Kathryn Hausbeck Corrigan, Rebecca Boulton, Aliya Buttar, my colleagues, past and present, at Southern Nevada's Health District, those students who I fe-mentored (and was schooled by as well) at MSU Mankato and in Las Vegas (such as Saswair Sakar, Jennifer Macken, and Christal Lustig), my colleagues and mentors at AASECT and SSSS, and everyone else at UNLV and MSU who helped make me the feminist I am today. In between the first edition of this book and the current edition, I lost one of my intellectual as well as personal mentors, Dr. Ellen Cronan Rose. Your willingness to work with me and support me was unwavering, and I hope to become the terrifyingly passionate and smart role model that you were for me. I also want to thank my colleague Dr. Maricela DeMirjyn who was instrumental in her support of me and Women's Studies while we were colleagues at MSU Mankato and regularly was able to help remind me of intersectionality issues, the interconnections between Women's and Gender Studies, and other area studies, as well as the importance of making connections with the community. I would be remiss for neglecting to thank Mark Rauls and Troy McGinnis for their continued support either through listening to my endless questions, giving advice on survey question construction, or lending their perspectives on academia and Women's Studies. I always thank my mother Betty and my brother Carl for their unwavering love and support and, of course, to my colleague Michele—from the minute we met, we knew it was the beginning of a beautiful, long, personal, and professional friendship. Michele is not only my co-author, but I consider her my friend, colleague, creative coach, and sounding board. Thanks for putting up with me and always being there. Finally, I want to thank my father Robert for his love and support. My father's influence on my feminism is immeasurable.

*We both would like to thank*: Shawn Shulte, our primary research assistant, for this edition. He assisted in the research and reading of drafts. Shawn's fresh perspective, as well as his candor, in discussing the field of Women's and Gender Studies, disclosing and questioning gender and sexuality norms, and his eagle eye in terms of editing and recommendations was truly inspiring. The production of this new edition was helped by the supportive group of readers and informal editors, including

Kim Anichowski, Catherine "Katie" Cashett, Chelsi Cheatom, Lindsey Dermid Gray, and Susan Lee.

We also would like to thank many of our current and former students who generously gave their impressions and feedback in informal and formal ways throughout the development of this idea to book. Your collective enthusiasm and sense that you would have used this book spurred us on.

Our sincere thanks also go to the many program and curriculum directors, and department chairs and administrative staff of Women's and Gender Studies worldwide who forwarded our request about our survey to their alumni lists. We also have to thank the hundreds of participants who took our survey and the many people whom we had the pleasure of interviewing for this book. We continue to draw on this database.

There are many new contributors in this edition, and we believe their insights and analyses make the book stronger. We are appreciative of the people who wrote the new "Point of View" (POV) pieces for this revised edition, including (in the order they appear): Mel Michelle Lewis, Gabrielle Griffin, Adriane Brown, Jennifer Fish, Carol Mason, Jo Reger, Karlyn Crowley, and Anita Tijerina Revilla. Thanks goes to Saswati Sarkar, Brad Freihoefer, Catherine Cashett, Lindsey Dermid Gray, Sarah "Tucker" Jenkins (our amazing research assistant for the first edition!), and Kim Anichowski for their contribution of new Spotlights. We also wish to thank DeAnna Beachely for her piece on community colleges in Chapter 1 and our interview with Katharine Brooks in Chapter 2.

Thanks are also due to the reviewers of this revised edition:

Elizabeth Berila          St. Cloud State University
Danielle DeMuth           Grand Valley State University
LeeRay Costa              Hollins University
Patti Duncan              Oregon State University
Heather Palmer            University of Tennessee, Chattanooga
Nancy Theriot             University of Louisville
Jennifer Reed             California State University, Long Beach
Harriet Hartman           Rowan University
Celeste Montoya           University of Colorado
Stacey Parks              Old Dominion University

| | |
|---|---|
| Kathleen Fine-Dare | Fort Lewis College |
| Melinda Marie Jette | Franklin Pierce University |
| Don Romesburg | Sonoma State University |
| Jacqueline R. deVries | Augsburg College |
| Maxine Weisgrau | The New School |
| Elizabeth A. Kissling | Eastern Washington University |
| Jennifer Fish | Old Dominion University |
| Patricia Pedroza | Keene State College |
| Mary Zeiss Stange | Skidmore College |
| Kim Case | University of Houston, Clear Lake |

We found your suggestions thoughtful, imaginative, and useful. We wish to thank the production team at Routledge for the care the manuscript received from beginning to end. And finally, our editors at Routledge were outstanding to work with during the past two years. We especially thank Samantha Barbaro. Your presence on both editions of *Transforming Scholarship* has been profound. You were always there to answer questions and provide support for us (whether it was answering basic questions and keeping us on task or helping to organize our book reception at NWSA). We could not have welcomed our second edition into the world without you.

# INTRODUCTION
## TRANSFORM YOURSELF
### AN INVITATION TO DEEPEN YOUR COMMITMENT TO WOMEN'S AND GENDER STUDIES

I have told people, and would continue to say, that to choose a course of study or degree in gender and/or women's studies is probably the best foundation one can have from which to grow as a critical thinker and life-long learner. Choosing to do a degree in women's and gender studies takes confidence and a willingness to be challenged academically, politically, and personally. I consider it a tremendous privilege to have earned this degree, and with it comes the responsibility to make a contribution to your piece of the world, whether in the field of women's and gender studies, in law, health, arts, community activism and beyond, or in my field, education.

(2007, WMST major, Queen's University, Ontario, Canada)

The quote above is from a student who participated in our study of Women's and Gender Studies students who graduated from undergraduate institutions from around the world between 1995 and 2010. We will say more about our study later in this chapter. We think this student's quote captures the range of challenge, complexity, and possibility that is involved in pursing an education in Women's and Gender Studies, both inside and outside the classroom. As a Women's and Gender Studies student, you may find yourself outside the classroom talking to peers, friends, family, coworkers and the general public about topics ranging from same-sex marriage and pay equity to whether or not Beyoncé is a feminist. The challenges of navigating and responding to the external perceptions of a Women's and Gender Studies student is, what kind of skills they possess and what kind of careers are possible is not always apparent to students when they first start taking courses in Women's and Gender Studies. We, however, believe that when a student knows and claims his or her intellectual inheritance of Women's and Gender Studies and is empowered to communicate effectively about the field and their employment prospects, a student can truly take ownership over his or her academic career, which is powerful. We want this for you, dear reader. We will return to these insights. For now, consider the following scenarios.

Kendra is a second-year student, attending a large, public, four-year university, and is taking "Gender and the Economy"—her third Women's Studies course and her favorite class of the semester. She is talking on the phone with her mother.

*Kendra*: Mom, I am loving my Women's Studies course! We just finished a section on women and work. It was fascinating! Did you know that on average, women who work full-time earn 77 cents for every dollar that men earn?

*Kendra's mother*: What? No I didn't, honey. I would have thought things were more equal now with so many women in the workplace.

*Kendra*: Yeah, you'd think that, but it's definitely not. African American and Latina women earn even less than the 77 cents. Can you believe it? I was so upset when I read that statistic. My class really dove into the material. Anyway, I just talked with my academic advisor and declared my major in Women's Studies.

*Kendra's mother*: Whoa, wait a minute. What exactly *is* Women's Studies? I've never heard of that major . . . aren't you interested in Political Science anymore?

*Kendra*: Women's Studies puts women's concerns and experiences at the center of academic study. And, Mom, that's the great thing about this major, I can take all sorts of courses that are cross-listed between the Women's Studies department and the Political Science department. For example, I can study women's political participation in Latin America or in the US. Or I could take a Political

Theory class that focuses on what women have considered important about democracy and citizenship.

*Kendra's mother*:   And you can major in that? Can you get a job in
that? What kinds of work do people with a Women's Studies major
actually do? We're not paying all that money for you to come and
live with us after graduation. And why is it, as you say, "putting
women at the center" is something that is so important?

Kendra hesitates and is flustered. "Well . . . I don't know about the job
part."

Later, Kendra thinks to herself, "I don't know why I froze when talking
with my mother about Women's Studies. Of course, I know what
Women's Studies *is*. But I guess I haven't ever really practiced talking
about it with someone other than one of my professors and the other
Women's Studies majors. And I guess I haven't really thought about what
I would do with my interest in Women's Studies. I know it's the right
choice for me, but how do I reassure my mother and the rest of my family?"

Delia is a double major in Women's and Gender Studies and Journalism,
and is beginning her senior year at a private college. She is talking to a
career counselor at the Career Services Office about her future goals.

*Delia*:   I just don't know how I'm going to combine all of my interests
when I leave school. I've never really thought about what I would
do after I graduate. I've just been enjoying learning so much.

*Career counselor*:   Tell me a little about what you've done so far and
how you think it's preparing you for the next step.

*Delia*:   My internship last spring with the local rape crisis center was
great, but I don't think I want to pursue nonprofit work. And
I think I'd like to keep volunteering at a rape crisis center, but I'm
not interested in getting more training in the area of sexual assault.

*Career counselor*:   [*nodding*] What else in your coursework has been
of interest to you that might give us a clue about directions you
can pursue after graduation?

*Delia*:   [*pauses for a moment and says*] For my feminist praxis class, I
ended up creating a project in which I designed an informational,
women's resource website from scratch. I worked long hours on it.
That was a great experience. I got to use my technical skills from

> Journalism, and I focused on the importance of positive body image for women, which grew out of what I learned in some of my classes. I think maybe I want to create feminist content for the Web.
>
> *Career counselor*:   Do you mean as a freelance writer?
>
> *Delia*:   No, not exactly. I think I'd like to build something from scratch and run it.
>
> *Career counselor*:   [*shaking his head*] Well that seems a bit ambitious. What about counseling—you could counsel people either who were victims of domestic violence or even eating disorders?

Delia shook her head. That suggestion did not feel right at all. "I'm really not interested in counseling. Do you have any contacts with magazines like *Bust* or *Bitch*?"

The career counselor replies, "No, I don't."

The career counselor comes up with some additional ideas, but none of them seem to fit Delia's interdisciplinary interests. She leaves feeling unsure about what she wants to do. She visits her department's website and rereads some of the interesting pathways Women's Studies alumnae have taken. She asks herself, "How do I get from here to there?"

Miguel is on a plane back to his home in Argentina for spring break. He is a junior and a Spanish major with a minor in Gender and Sexuality Studies at a research-intensive university. He has great news for his family, and is practicing what he wants to say in his mind:

> I can't believe my independent study project "Masculine Textualities: The Discursive Practice of Gender in Hispanic Writings" has been nominated by my advisor for the best undergraduate research project on gender and sexuality in the department. I so enjoyed researching the ways that masculinity has been produced through popular Spanish texts in the last 40 years. If I win, not only do I receive $250 (US), but this paper could help me get into graduate school. I know that you worry about me and what I want to do with my life, but continuing my education in Gender and Sexuality Studies can open doors for me that would not have been opened if I had stayed at home or in a traditional college minor. So you want to know what I can do with my degree? And, am I gay?

Miguel's internal scripting has come to a screeching halt.

Added to Miguel's internal dialogue are some issues that he knows he has to deal with. Although he is eager about sharing the news with his family, he knows that he will face difficult questions from his grandparents and his maternal aunt and uncle. They do not understand why studying sexuality is intellectually worthwhile or a legitimate subject. Last year, his uncle accused him outright of being gay, which he had to deny strenuously. He loves them and wants them to understand how important this work is to him. He knows he needs to come up with a different way of framing the importance of this work to them.

Between the positive script Miguel is composing in his head and the negative responses he fears he will get from some of his family members, Miguel thinks to himself:

> I wish I had a book or some other sort of reference that would help me. While my classes have taught me how to think critically and analyze texts, I wish I had a class that would help me deal with my family and my decision to get a minor in Gender and Sexuality Studies. We have talked about homophobia and sexism on systemic levels, and I've talked to my friends about how to deal with gay and lesbian baiting on campus, but it's tough telling my family about my studies at school and having constantly to tell them that I am not gay. Every time I discuss my minor, I am troubled . . . not only by the homophobia in my family, but that I feel like I am dishonoring my friends who are queer.

And, one final one: Shane is a second-semester senior attending a job fair and is talking to an employer at a large not-for-profit healthcare organization. So far, things are going well as the employer talks primarily about the internship at the women's health policy think tank that Shane did last year. Shane has listed several skills on ze's resume, including "critical thinking." In the interview, the employer says, "Well, how is critical thinking in Women's Studies any different than other majors? I would expect someone with a liberal arts degree to have critical thinking skills. Does that mean you're a good systems thinker?"

Shane appears flustered and unprepared for this question. Shane thinks, "I've heard from the beginning of my training that Women's Studies helps to develop critical thinkers. But I guess I've never been asked to articulate what that means for me or how to distinguish myself to an employer from all the people who list critical thinking as a skill."

You may be a recent major or minor in Women's and Gender Studies (WGST) and have discovered this book. Or, you may have been given this book by your mentor. Or, you may be graduating soon and suddenly find yourself terrified of the prospect of life after college. You may be wondering how to pursue your dream job or practically engage feminism principles after college. Are the above scenarios familiar to you and speak to your experience? While you were reading them, did you find yourself imagining how you might respond? These scenarios come from real-life experiences that students pursuing an interest in Women's and Gender Studies encounter. We will return to these scenarios soon.

Whether you have had these experiences or not, you have landed in a place where you can explore all the dimensions of deepening your interest in Women's and Gender Studies. This book is about helping you fulfill your potential as a student in Women's and Gender Studies. We are committed to developing students' capacities to learn, lead, and thrive during *and* after their major, minor, or concentration in Women's and Gender Studies, or one of the many related fields that have formed in association with this area of study.[1] It is a user-friendly handbook of practical guidance and inspiration for your interest in pursuing a degree in Women's and Gender Studies.

This book will help you to think critically about what you know, how to demonstrate what you know, and how to prepare for life personally and professionally after graduation.

## Why *This* Book?

We wrote *Transforming Scholarship* to offer students a useful guide to navigating one of the most richly rewarding, yet often underappreciated and frequently misunderstood, academic majors—Women's and Gender Studies. Women's and Gender Studies (WGST) is a vibrant, interdisciplinary field of study. Scholars work on a wide variety of subjects, including lesbian, gay, bisexual, and transgender (LGBT) and sexuality studies, marriage and the family, the state and politics, the environment, science and technology, sports, religion, gendered violence, international relations, education, art, theater, literature, and urban planning. In your classes, you have most likely been exposed to the exciting scholarship in the field.

This is a singular and original book, the first book of its kind—one geared for Women's and Gender Studies students. By writing this book, we affirm that students pursuing questions in Women's and Gender

Studies are part of an important and emergent community of educational pioneers in the US and globally. Students in Women's and Gender Studies are trained to consider how their efforts in the classroom can be translated to affect the status of women and men (and anyone outside the gender binary) beyond the borders of their college or university.

Women's and Gender Studies is a leading stand-alone major and minor on many college and university campuses, or exists on a programmatic level (i.e. as a concentration) in concert with other fields of study. In the United States, there are Women's and Gender Studies programs in over 700 academic institutions, including two- and four-year colleges, public and private universities, women's colleges, historically black colleges and universities (HBCUs), and community colleges. According to Beverly Guy-Sheftall, a leading scholar in Women's Studies, globally, more than 40 countries offer Women's and Gender Studies curricula or research opportunities (Guy-Sheftall 2009). At the undergraduate level, students taking Women's and Gender Studies classes are able to study subjects that span the arts and humanities, social sciences, education, the natural and hard sciences, engineering, and business. Women's and Gender Studies programs offer students training in how to think critically and recognize the importance of how interlinked oppressions and privileges shape both women's and men's experiences. Additionally, as scholar Janell Hobson (2012, emphasis in original) notes, what makes Women's Studies so "unique, intellectually enriching and appealing to diverse students is that more than any other academic discipline, it places at the *center* of learning not just women but marginal groups of all persuasions (the poor, people of color, sexual minorities, immigrant communities, etc.). By taking seriously the lives and struggles of those deemed 'not culturally' important, women's studies encourages students to critically rethink the values they've been taught and that societal institutions justify."

In increasing numbers, students are graduating with degrees that have a concentration in Women's and Gender Studies, and they naturally seek to apply what they have learned to the outside world (Levin 2007). During 2010–2011, there were 1,432 Women's Studies degrees awarded. Moreover, 584 degrees were awarded under the term "Ethnic, cultural minority, gender, and group studies, other." Student demand for these classes and training has increased every year (National Center for Educational Statistics 2012).

The continued success of Women's and Gender Studies has been 40 years in the making, with the first program in Women's Studies, specifically, established in 1970 at San Diego State University (Guy-Sheftall 2009: 57). Although Women's and Gender Studies is a well-established and thriving academic interdisciplinary field of study, students in Women's and Gender Studies still face unique challenges, as we read in the opening scenarios.

In the first scenario, Kendra was excited about the possibilities of Women's Studies, and was trying to find support for her interest as a newly declared major. But she was unprepared for the leap her mother made from declaring a major to thinking about future employment. The first scenario also indicates, surprisingly, that many people in the general public do not realize that Women's and Gender Studies is an academic pursuit and that you can major in it. Nor do many people know that you *can* find employment using your Women's and Gender Studies training!

The second scenario demonstrates the kinds of questions you may face when you are at the very end of your academic journey: "How do you take what you know out into the marketplace?" Delia was trying to figure out how to take what she had already learned in Women's and Gender

## DATA SUPPORT ECONOMIC VALUE OF A WOMEN'S AND GENDER STUDIES DEGREE

Our global research study suggests that a Women's and Gender Studies degree can help you in *any* job. Whether you share your knowledge of the politics of gender, race, sexuality, and class with clients when you are filling out demographic questions for official forms, or you subtly challenge the gendered descriptions of Halloween costumes through your job as a copyeditor for a corporation, a Women's and Gender Studies education makes you a valuable asset to any organization. Participants report using many WGST skills, including using gender as a category of analysis, critical thinking, considering an issue from multiple perspectives, and the ability to communicate effectively, in their professional lives. They reported high satisfaction with their degree, despite encountering some skepticism and resistance from others. Research on college graduates consistently demonstrates that over one's life, holders of liberal arts degrees are successful, especially for those that pursue a graduate degree (which many in our study did), and do well financially.

Studies classes and use it professionally. Unfortunately, her career counselor was not as helpful as she had hoped in showing her how she could fulfill her desire to create feminist Web content. Although it would have helped Delia to come to the meeting with a stronger sense of what her interests were, the career counselor should be expected to do better, given that Women's and Gender Studies is no longer a brand new major. Nor did the career counselor help her assess her strengths and skills developed through her coursework and internship.

Although Women's and Gender Studies remains one of the fastest-growing majors and minors on campuses and universities, students cannot always envision or articulate the real-world benefits of their degree (Luebke and Reilly 1995; Dever 2004; Stewart 2007). Thus, like Delia, students can be bogged down by the persistent question of "What does one do with an interest and/or a degree in Women's and Gender Studies?"

A 2007 article in *Ms.* magazine, "Transform the World: What Can You Do with a Degree in Women's Studies?," beautifully captured the tension between the lingering popular ignorance of Women's and Gender Studies as a field, and the dynamism and enthusiasm of the undergraduate Women's Studies experience. The truth is that Women's and Gender Studies graduates go on to become professionals in many areas, including politics, medicine, and higher education administration, and secure employment in the private, public, and government sectors. They also become practitioners in the trades, as well as independent business owners. Many Women's and Gender Studies graduates also remain committed to the pursuit of gender equality as lifelong advocates and activists. However, there is no single employment path for Women's and Gender Studies graduates, nor is there an easily recognizable cookie-cutter model to emulate.

In the third scenario, Miguel is clearly feeling elated at being chosen as a finalist for a prestigious award, but he is also worrying about how to talk with his extended family about his strong interest in gender and sexuality. If you express an interest in Women's and Gender Studies, you may find yourself faced with personal questions and assumptions about your political beliefs and sexual identity. This might seem daunting, but it comes with the territory, and once you are prepared for it and have responses for when and if it comes up, you will be prepared to engage in a confident and straightforward way. You may have already experienced this issue or know close friends who have.

Shane's scenario represents how students can struggle translating some of their skills when they talk with employers. It takes reflection and practice to confidently respond to employers' questions.

Given the range of educational choices available and the expansion of Women's and Gender Studies globally, we believe there is no better time to be an undergraduate doing work in WGST than now. A central aim of this book is to help students take advantage of the opportunities and challenges in pursuing intellectual work in Women's and Gender Studies.

*Transforming Scholarship* is ambitious in scope and goes further than the few short articles or previous books about Women's and Gender Studies students (Luebke and Reilly 1995; Magezis 1997; Garrett and Rogers 2002; Dever 2004). Our goal is to give you concrete information so you can confidently answer the question, "What can you do with a Women's and Gender Studies degree?" To do so, we did extensive research for this book. We surveyed over 900 Women's and Gender Studies graduates (1995–2010) from around the globe about their experiences as students and their career paths. In the survey, we have graduates from Georgia State University to the University of Ghana. This is currently the *largest global data set* about contemporary Women's and Gender Studies graduates! Over 125 institutions are represented in this survey. We also conducted interviews with a small sample of men and women

## WHAT WE AIM TO GIVE YOU IN THIS BOOK

- We encourage you to be proactive in thinking about your education. We encourage you to consider how your undergraduate education prepares you for life after college, beyond how to write a resume and apply for a job.
- We help you make connections between the rich, intellectual tradition that Women's and Gender Studies offers you as a student and why that might be of value to you.
- We help you apply the critical thinking skills that you are developing in your Women's and Gender Studies classes to your academic and professional career.
- We affirm your desire to translate what you do in the classroom to a lifestyle of praxis, theory, and learning after you graduate.
- We affirm your desire to make a living doing what you believe in and love.
- We bring together information and up-to-date research in one easy-to-read guide.

who responded to our survey. For this edition, we also reached out to WGST graduates who did not take part in our survey.

The book you hold in your hands begins by acknowledging the opportunities and challenges that face the typical Women's and Gender Studies student. We address why choosing to focus on Women's and Gender Studies in an academic environment is a unique experience. We also provide a contemporary framework for students to understand themselves as a type of "change agent."

This framework allows you to think in a new way about the benefits of pursuing work in Women's and Gender Studies and what you have to offer employers once you graduate. We prepare students with skills for the "emotional management" that many will face in pursuit of their training.[2] This book will provide you with the skills and tools to navigate any resistance that you may face while pursuing your coursework or career goals. From the scenarios presented in the beginning of this section, if you face any similar circumstances to those experienced by Kendra, Delia, Shane, and Miguel, after reading this book, you should have more resources in your toolkit for responding to tough questions and situations. Another goal of this book is to enhance your ability to integrate what you learn in your Women's and Gender Studies classes into your life (before and) after you graduate. Thus, we take a holistic approach to the Women's and Gender Studies student.

We have witnessed many students (and professors) struggle with some of the challenges that we identify in this book. We hope this book will help people explore the many work and career options available for Women's and Gender Studies graduates and realize their potential. Given the transformative potential of Women's and Gender Studies at the undergraduate level, we would like to see students find more encouragement and support for this interdisciplinary field of study.

Ultimately, we believe this book will also be useful to parents, college advisors, career counselors, and fellow faculty colleagues. But most of all, this book is for you—the college student.

## Who We Are

We come to this book as scholars, teachers, workers, life coaches, and leadership trainers. As a team, we bring strong and unique skills to writing the pages that follow. We have a long, combined history of learning, teaching, and mentoring in Women's Studies at various institutions as graduate students and professors. We also have disciplinary ties to other academic fields (Michele is a political scientist by training with a Ph.D. from the University of Michigan, and Cheryl is a sociologist with a Ph.D. from the University of Nevada, Las Vegas). Our collaboration on this book is the result of a long-standing professional relationship and friendship. Not only did we have the privilege of co-teaching a course together, but we have been able to encourage and support each other in a variety of roles, ranging from mentor and colleague to friend. We believe that a Women's and Gender Studies degree not only provides the intellectual tools to succeed in life, but is also an area of study that fosters an environment of community, leadership, and empowerment. You will learn more about us as you move through the book, but below we share snapshot profiles.

## Michele

I attended Bard College, a small, private liberal arts college that in the late 1980s, did not have a well-publicized Women's Studies major, minor, or concentration. Early on, I began taking cross-listed classes that had either "women" or "feminist" in the course description (e.g. "Women and Contemporary Anthropology" and "Feminist Political Theory"). My mother was a civil rights advocate and influenced me enormously to believe that women can and should be equal stakeholders in the world. I was a dual major in Creative Writing and Political Studies. I was deeply influenced by feminist literary theory and contemporary women authors. On my own, I practically inhaled the works of other women writers that I read, including Toni Cade Bambara, Alice Walker, Isabel Allende, and Ursula Le Guin. Maybe you, too, through your Women's and Gender Studies classes, have found incredible authors whose works you cannot put down.

Through Political Studies, I was exposed to feminist political theory and feminist legal theory. Although formal Women's Studies classes were not regularly offered, there were several faculty members willing to commit themselves to teaching about women's lives. What I could not get in the classroom, I tried to fill in on my own. I read *Ms.*, *off our backs*, *On the Issues*, and other feminist magazines and journals. Maybe you are reading magazines such as *Bitch*, *Bust*, or *Ms.* I took full advantage of the amazing feminist speakers who came to campus, including bell hooks, Amber Hollibaugh, and Jo Freeman.

The tools and theory-building skills I acquired in my classes prepared me to write a senior project (required of all Bard students)[9] on rape law reform of the late 1970s and 1980s, relying heavily on the work of legal scholar Catherine MacKinnon. Although I did not specifically tell any of my professors that I had almost been sexually assaulted when I was 16, I think I was drawn to the topic because of personal experience. I found it intellectually stimulating to study feminists who were interested in rape law reform. I came to understand both the opportunities and the barriers they faced as they confronted laws that differentially positioned women and men in relation to sexual assault. I can still remember how outraged I felt when I discovered that many state laws condoned "marital rape."

The laws of the 1960s and 1970s claimed the sexist view that wives had no right to refuse a husband's sexual advances, and therefore no legal recourse after being sexually assaulted (or battered). For me, being able to read theoretical works by feminist legal scholars and political theorists and discuss the thorny issues of rape and sexual assault from both personal and academic vantage points distinguished my classes focusing on feminism and women's advancement from others.

One of the reasons I went to graduate school right after college was because I felt a deep urgency to bring new voices and new ways of knowing into the academy, especially those from historically "marginalized communities" (e.g. women of color from impoverished backgrounds). I was eager to continue studying how feminist theory challenged typical assumptions about everyday social patterns that seemed "natural." I had already begun to apply some concepts that stemmed from my classes in feminist theory through my activism on campus on a variety of issues (e.g. reproductive rights). In my graduate school applications, I quoted Audre Lorde, the self-defined black, lesbian feminist warrior poet and author who inspired me throughout my studies. She said, "In our world, divide and conquer must become define and empower" (Lorde 1984: 112). Those words resonated deeply with me because I felt that coalition-building and self-definition were the building blocks of feminist theory and could be applied to many situations.

I chose to attend the University of Michigan because of the dynamic work on gender and sexuality taking place there. They had an established

Women's Studies program that offered a graduate certificate in the field of Women's Studies. I deepened my knowledge base in gender and criminology and in scholarship by women of color, and I learned how to ask new questions about women's lives.

I never thought that much of my academic career would focus on women and HIV/AIDS. As an undergraduate, I researched feminist legal reform in the area of rape and sexual assault. In graduate school, I found my way into feminist criminology courses offered in the department of sociology. I became fascinated with female lawbreakers and how the criminal justice system responds to women. This led me to conduct ethnographic research in Detroit with women who were actively using crack cocaine and engaging in street-level sex work. At the time, there were very few cultural or academic spaces that critically examined how women (especially women of color) were coping with the rapid deterioration of urban environments. Over a four-year period, I met women who had been in the "life" and were now HIV-positive and creating and conducting grassroots activism on behalf of themselves and other stigmatized women. I conducted in-depth interviews with 16 women who were transforming the political landscape through their community activism. Their political participation challenged many assumptions political scientists typically make about women's activism.

By the time I finished my graduate training, I felt compelled to study marginalized women with HIV/AIDS who had become politically active and to talk with a wide variety of scholars across disciplinary lines. After the dissertation, this work resulted in my book, *Workable Sisterhood: The Political Journey of Stigmatized Women with HIV/AIDS*. Although my doctorate is in Political Science, I actively choose to define myself as an interdisciplinary scholar. This choice reflects my training and deep commitments to creating interdisciplinary conversations in which women's lives are researched with increasing complexity and rigor—a legacy reflecting my core interest in Women's Studies.

As a faculty member in Women's and Gender Studies at the University of North Carolina (UNC) at Chapel Hill, I teach students from a wide variety of backgrounds. As a former Director of Undergraduate Studies in my department, I counseled students on course selection, internship opportunities, and career options. I enjoy helping students tackle what at first feels like the daunting question, "What do I do with this degree?"

I definitely consider myself an "ambassador" for Women's Studies. And, as I often meet people who have no idea what a "Women's Studies professor" is or what makes Women's Studies unique, or how vital and needed our voices are in the academy, I have to practice some of the very same skills that are presented in this book—so I view these encounters as useful opportunities to frame a message about the value of Women's Studies research and training that feels inviting and perhaps connects to issues women and men might struggle with or have heard about in the news: pay equity, the number and visibility of female elected officials, ongoing high rates of sexual assault, violence and assault against the LGBT community, representations of women athletes, and the number of women globally living with HIV/AIDS.

### FOR YOUR LIBRARY

Rudolph P. Byrd, Johnnetta Betsch Cole, and Beverly Guy-Sheftall (Eds.) (2009). *I Am Your Sister: Collected and Unpublished Writings of Audre Lorde.* Oxford: Oxford University Press.

Rory Dicker and Alison Piepmeier (Eds.) (2003). *Catching a Wave: Reclaiming Feminism for the 21st Century.* Northeastern, MA: Northeastern University Press.

Amber Hollibaugh (2000). *My Dangerous Desires: A Queer Girl Dreaming Herself Home.* Durham, NC: Duke University Press.

bell hooks (1984). *Feminist Theory from Margin to Center.* Boston, MA: South End Press.

bell hooks (2000). *Feminism is for Everybody: Passionate Politics.* Boston, MA: South End Press.

Audre Lorde (1982). *Zami: A New Spelling of My Name.* Trumansburg, NY: Crossing Press.

Audre Lorde (1984). *Sister Outsider.* Trumansburg, NY: Crossing Press.

Courtney E. Martin and J. Courtney Sullivan (Eds.) (2010). *Click: When We Knew We Were Feminists.* Berkeley, CA: Seal Press.

### *Cheryl*

I attended Bowling Green State University (BGSU), a mid-sized public university in northwestern Ohio, in the mid-1980s. When I entered college, I really had no idea what I wanted to declare as a major. I was "undecided" my first two years and then chose Interpersonal and Public Communications as my major. Eventually, I discovered Popular Culture. I was excited (and a little scared) to declare a major in a subject that many considered nontraditional and limited in future career opportunities. Yet, I was encouraged by the professor of my Popular Music course to choose this area for my degree, and I have never regretted the decision. During my first year, as I was fulfilling my core requirements, I happened upon a Women's Studies course. This course challenged me and made me question my world as I had known it, growing up in Beavercreek, Ohio—a middle-class suburb of Dayton. Eventually, I found myself taking more courses in Women's Studies and discovered that I could minor in it fairly easily with the number of credits I had accrued in this area during my five years at BGSU (they were cross-listed with my other core and major requirements).

It was also during my time at BGSU that I became an activist. The late 1980s and early 1990s was a period in which the pro-choice/pro-life debates about abortion had burst into the public arena.[4] Operation Life (a pro-life grassroots organization) was staging rescues at abortion clinics. While researching the history of abortion in Bowling Green, I had the opportunity to interview the founder of the Center for Life—a feminist abortion clinic in Toledo, Ohio—and take a tour of the establishment. This encounter was significant, in that it enabled me to assist and support a friend who wanted to terminate her pregnancy. It also motivated me to put my pro-choice beliefs into practice by not only standing in solidarity with the clinic when the Center was targeted for a rescue, but also by taking part in two pro-choice marches on Washington, DC.

My initial goal to continue my reproductive health activism after college was fulfilled when I had the fortune to volunteer and eventually become employed with Planned Parenthood of Miami Valley as an HIV educator and counselor in the early 1990s. Not only was I educated about contraceptives and sexually transmitted infections (especially HIV and AIDS), but I was able to interact with and hear the everyday lived experiences of women and men who were trying to negotiate issues of sexuality, power, family, gender roles, economics, social class, race/ethnicity, and stigma. In addition, Planned Parenthood emphasizes education and knowledge, and my job there fostered my interest in further learning. My work involved comprehensive sexual education presentations in local community, public-school classrooms on sexually transmitted diseases (STDs) and birth control.

While I loved my position as an HIV educator and counselor, I found that I was limited in my ability to assist clients who were survivors of sexual assault. Agency and public health funding can only do so much, and I began questioning larger issues about the connection between reproductive health and public resources. My concerns eventually led me to pursue further education. Beginning at the University of Toledo, I pursued graduate work in Sociology and completed my journey at the University of Nevada, Las Vegas (UNLV). I was influenced by my experience working at Planned Parenthood, and my graduate work largely addressed issues of gender, sexuality, and stigma.

My dissertation, "Vectors, Polluters, and Murderers: HIV Testing toward Prostitutes and the State of Nevada," was a qualitative case study examining the role of the state in regulating gender and sexuality. The overall aim of my study was to investigate how public policy is influenced by existing attitudes and beliefs about the association of disease with prostitution. Through textual analysis of legislative and legal records, interviews with policymakers, and observations of legal and criminal justice procedures, I analyzed the process by which policymakers integrate and disseminate sources of information for decision-making purposes. This research is important not only in raising questions about the state in relation to gender and sexuality, but also because it focuses these questions locally on the state of Nevada.

While completing my dissertation, I gained valuable work experience through teaching introductory level and upper division Women's Studies courses and serving as the Graduate and Professional Student Association president. I have taught in several Women's Studies departments over the past several years, both at four-year state institutions and community colleges. Currently, I am re-exploring issues of reproductive and public health at the Southern Nevada Health District, where I am employed as a disease investigator with the Office of HIV/AIDS/STDs. I feel that my previous research on HIV testing of prostitutes in the state of Nevada, my experience with a local HIV prevention Community Planning Group (CPG-SoN), and my background in women's reproductive and sexual health have brought me full circle.

## Women's and Gender Studies Students Change Their Communities While Still in School

Our shared undergraduate histories of an interest in Women's and Gender Studies and exploring co-curricular opportunities and activist interests—on and off campus—is mirrored by the graduates in our research. Our study finds that a whopping 72 percent of all graduates in Women's and Gender Studies were active in campus organizations, local organizations, national organizations, and global organizations, or *created* new organizations while pursuing their undergraduate degree. In many of their organizations, graduates often noted that they took on leadership positions.

Several of the organizations that students created were self-described "feminist clubs" that created space for like-minded women and men to come together. They also created feminist-inspired literary publications. Students participated in student chapters of national organizations (such as NOW, the National Organization for Women) or participated directly through the local or state chapters of these organizations. The organizations themselves span a wide variety of topics, though many of them are focused on women, gender, and sexuality issues. Graduates were also active in honor societies, forums, and organizations that promoted cross-cultural dialogue, student newspapers and magazines, radio and television programs, arts programs, sororities and fraternities, small feminist-oriented clubs, women's leadership programs, religious organizations, intramural sports, and programs mentoring at-risk youth. And, if some students interned or took advantage of a service learning opportunity, they often joined that organization as a member. It was also not uncommon for students to list that they were active in organizations that spanned campus, local, state, national, and international concerns.

This very high rate of participation suggests to us that there is an incredible drive for many students to connect the theory they learn in the Women's and Gender Studies classroom to the world. They begin the path of being a change agent early on and then strengthen their civic engagement skills. We will explore this link between theory and action in Women's and Gender Studies training further in Chapters 1 and 2. Moreover, the valuable experience that undergraduates receive by participating in community and campus groups can create strengths and skills that can be used later on in employment situations.

Below are representative examples of the types of international, national, state, local, and campus organizations that graduates were members of and actively participated in:

- Actiongirls (feminist activist group) and CJAM Radio (feminist talk show) (University of Windsor, Canada)
- American Association of University Women (AAUW)
- American Civil Liberties Union (ACLU)
- Amnesty International
- Arizona State Women's Coalition
- Bangladesh Association for Young Researchers (University of Dhaka, Bangladesh)
- Bedford/Sackville Literacy Network (Canada)
- Campus Anti-Sexism Society (Instituto Universitário de Lisboa, Portugal)
- Campus Coalition Against Trafficking (Montclair State University)
- Canadian Federation of University Women
- Caribbean Student Alliance (University of Delaware)
- Center for Women and Transgender People; American Indian Counsel and Sexual Assault Support Team (Oberlin College)
- Charleston Women's Collective
- College Partnership for Kids
- College Republicans
- Critical Resistance (a national organization dedicated to opposing the expansion of the prison-industrial complex)
- Feminist Students United (University of North Carolina at Chapel Hill)
- Gay and Lesbians of Notre Dame (Saint Mary's College)
- Golden Key Society
- Habitat for Humanity
- Halifax Women's Network
- Hillel
- Liberal Party of Canada
- Macalester College Peace and Justice Committee (Macalester College)
- March of Dimes

- Men Against Sexual Violence (MASV)
- Michigan Italian-American Association, Do Random Acts of Kindness (University of Michigan)
- Michigan Women's Justice and Clemency Project
- National Association for the Advancement of Colored People (NAACP)
- National Society of Collegiate Scholars
- OUTloud (LGBT organization) (Hollins University)
- Pomona College Women's Union (Pomona College)
- Queer Insurgency (University of Southern Maine)
- Queer Issues Committee (Minnesota State, Morris)
- Radical Cheerleaders and Inside-Out Writing Project (a crafts/ writing workshop space for incarcerated women) (University of California, Santa Cruz)
- ReelOut Queer Film Festival (Queen's University, Kingston, Ontario, Canada)
- Religious Coalition for Reproductive Choice (University of Washington)
- Single Parents on Campus (University of British Columbia,Vancouver, Canada)
- Student Association of Vegan and Vegetarian Youth (University of Rochester)
- Student Global AIDS Campaign and Advocacy for Adult Male Survivors of Sexual Assault (University of Michigan, Ann Arbor)
- Swarthmore Asian Organization (Swarthmore College)
- Take Back the Night
- The Finnish Association for Women's Studies
- Toni Cade Bambara Collective (Spelman College)
- Tufts Student Sexual Assault Response Assistance (SSARA) (Tufts University)
- United Nations Development Fund for Women (UNIFEM)
- Vagina Monologues—V-Day Project
- Voices for Planned Parenthood (VOX)
- Women for Choice
- Women's Health Collective (University of Massachusetts, Amherst)

- Working Advocates to End Racism (University of California, Santa Cruz)
- Young Democrats of America

## Structure of the Book

*Transforming Scholarship* focuses on the action steps you will need to take along each stretch of your journey as a Women's and Gender Studies student and graduate. In each chapter, you will find important information, resources and self-discovery exercises to support your active participation in taking ownership of your academic career.

Chapter 1 introduces the history of the birth of Women's and Gender Studies as an interdisciplinary area of study. It orients you to the intellectual landscape that you are exploring in your academic setting. We explore the meaning and value of Women's and Gender Studies in academic life in this chapter: you will find out why you are part of a unique and distinguished learning community that contributes ideas, skills and talents to the global marketplace and public life. You will also learn some demographic information about Women's and Gender Studies professors and students.

Chapter 2 focuses on information about the multiple learning components and options available for many students and how to decide between internship, honors thesis, or study abroad options. Chapter 2 will allow you to assess what options you have available to you in your academic context and how you may want to choose among those options or supplement them.

Making the most of your Women's Studies training by becoming an advocate and partner in your education is the core theme of Chapters 3 and 4. Chapter 3 provides you with some tools to think about how to communicate with others, why you chose Women's Studies in the first place, and what you think the benefits are. We want to equip you with the ability to communicate well with others—good communication skills are a necessity for any college student, but they are strategically important for students in Women's and Gender Studies. Although you are most likely to find affirmation about Women's and Gender Studies from professors and peers, you may find that others (such as friends, parents, co-workers, the general public) may need more information from you about what Women's and Gender Studies is all about before they express any enthusiasm.

Chapter 4 asks you to think about your inner strengths and the external skills and knowledge your Women's and Gender Studies training has provided you with. We encourage you to spend time assessing the work that you have done in Women's and Gender Studies during the course of your academic career. We build on and extend the work of pioneering researchers Barbara Luebke and Mary Ellen Reilly, who conducted research on early Women's Studies graduates (Luebke and Reilly 1995). They posit that Women's Studies majors develop a unique set of skills, including: empowerment, self-confidence, critical thinking, community building, and understanding differences and intersections among racism, homophobia, sexism, classism, ableism, anti-Semitism, and other types of oppression. We update and extend this critical work and provide a new set of lenses to help students evaluate themselves on these and other inner strengths and external skills. To explore your possible inner strengths and external skills, we ask you to try out a few exercises at the end of the chapter.

Chapters 5–7 concentrate on the theme of using your Women's and Gender Studies education to transform your world. These chapters will prepare you for the process of transitioning from academe to your professional life.

Chapter 5 provides critical information about women and men in the world using what they learn in Women's and Gender Studies. We highlight many employment sectors where one could use a WGST degree. We also draw from interviews with employers, directors, and chairs of Women's and Gender Studies programs, as well as students, to help capture the diversity of career options for students.

In Chapter 6, we present and develop the idea of Women's and Gender Studies students as *change agents*. Briefly, a change agent is an undergraduate who has strong experiential learning capabilities and a commitment to public engagement beyond the borders of the academic classroom. A change agent may be someone who organizes a collective action, begins their own feminist organization, or even works within an existing system and organization and radicalizes it in their own way. The size of the change is not as important as the motivation and vision behind it.

Through our research, we have identified three categories of change agents and how they relate to career pathways in Women's Studies:

*sustainers*, *evolvers*, and *synthesizers*. You can use these terms initially to identify yourself and investigate options for further skills development in pursuing your dream career or whatever your next step may be. You will enjoy learning about the diversity and variety of occupations available to you, and this should help put to rest the idea that Women's and Gender Studies students do not have marketable skills. You will hear the stories of seven graduates who have been change agents in their own right and are professionally successful. You will learn of successful graduates who are often invited back to their educational institutions for "career day." You will hear of their triumphs and challenges in the process of finding one's way in the professional world. While seven graduates are profiled in depth, these profiles are augmented by a variety of data gained through research using online surveys and interviews.

Finally, Chapter 7 provides strategies for ways to make a graceful and seamless transition from college to the professional world. One of the hardest experiences that students have shared with us over the years regarding their post-graduation transition is that they sometimes find themselves as the only "feminist" or person committed to gender equity in their office, graduate program, or new circle of friends. We help you explore the expectations that you may have as you move into new situations (such as work, graduate school, or travel) after graduation. Invariably, graduating Women's and Gender Studies students feel the tension of leaving the ethos and praxis of Women's Studies, the secure college environment, and the inevitable adult contradictions of living in an unpredictable world that is fraught with inequality. We also tackle some issues and concerns that may be on the horizon for graduates, including how to build and sustain feminist communities. We suggest that building feminist-friendly allies and networks can be seen as an extension of some of the skill-building you developed as an undergraduate. We highlight some resources and organizations that will help you during this critical time.

We have included several features in this book that will help you move through the material more easily. The sidebars contain facts or short examples related to our comments or definitions of terms used along the way. They may also contain quotes from our survey or our interviewees. We identify our interviewees using first name, the year graduated, and the institution attended. We leave our survey responses anonymous.[5]

For both interviewees and anonymous responses, we use a general designation of "WMST" to indicate their program or department. Most chapters features one or more Points of View (POVs) and Spotlights. Points of View are written by scholars to delve into an issue. Spotlights feature an extended discussion on a theme or topic. Spotlights allow student voices to emerge to show how they have lived the goals and principles that underlie Women's and Gender Studies throughout their undergraduate careers and beyond. You will also see "For Your Library"— these sections will suggest books, articles, and other materials for you. We have also included a detailed description of the research methods we used in gathering the stories and experiences of Women's and Gender Studies graduates in the Appendix.

This book is an important step on your academic path to deepening your commitment in Women's and Gender Studies and pursuing your degree and your career. We are excited about the many possibilities that you will discover along the way. We also hope that this book will inspire you to mentor others who may express an interest in WGST. We know how daunting it can be to think about all the challenges that await you as part of your journey—from finishing coursework to finding employment as a Women's and Gender Studies graduate. But you are not alone, nor set adrift in uncharted waters. Throughout this book, think of both of us as your de facto "wo-mentors", here to guide you on your journey and help you to realize what strengths you have developed as part of your degree, how those talents can best be marketed and utilized in the workforce, and how you can continue your Women's Studies education and activism outside of the classroom and into the community.

## CASE IN POINT: ONE STUDENT, ONE COURSE

Dr. Robert Pleasants shares his experience about the difference that just one class in Women's and Gender Studies made in his life. He is the Interpersonal Violence Coordinator at the University of North Carolina at Chapel Hill.

I took my one and only Women's Studies course my last semester at the University of North Carolina at Chapel Hill. I'd like to say I enrolled because I was passionate about social justice and eager to learn feminism, but those weren't exactly my motivations. In truth, a good friend and on-and-mostly-off-again girlfriend was a Women's Studies major, so I enrolled hoping to better understand and maybe impress her as well. To my surprise, the experience far surpassed my self-serving expectations.

Maybe you had a similar experience in your first Women's Studies course: the novelty of a course that encouraged reflection and personalization of knowledge; the realization that a professor might actually care what you and other students do outside of the classroom; those moments of striking clarity that simultaneously enlighten you and turn your world upside down. Instead of being a class that simply helped me understand women, the course provided a theory and a language that made sense of the inequalities I always saw but did not really fully understand. It also helped me understand myself and the world around me, encouraging me to think about the relationship between the two.

So imagine my frustration at the end of the semester: I felt inspired in a way I had never experienced in my four years of college, I wanted more, and . . . I was graduating. As things turned out, my plan to understand and impress my ex worked, and so I gained a new partner who shared my interest. Together, we continued to seek new knowledge of feminism, continuing conversations with friends about gender issues, seeking feminist media and books, and holding each other accountable. Simultaneously, we asked ourselves what we could actually *do* with this new knowledge. So we volunteered, first as community educators teaching middle- and high-school kids about relationships, harassment, and sexual assault. Then, when my partner started law school, we began volunteering together as crisis line volunteers at an agency for survivors of relationship abuse, and also meeting great new feminist friends. When I started graduate school in the field of Education, I began working part-time at the agency. Because my dissertation was on men learning feminism, I once again took classes in Women's Studies and read even more. I was also fortunate enough to teach a class on Gender and Violence, working with amazing feminist undergraduates. Two of them realized the university did not have any staff members solely devoted to violence prevention, so in collaboration with two other graduate students and me, they painstakingly amassed research and support across campus, successfully lobbying for a new position on campus.

A year after finishing my Ph.D., I realized the job we created was the perfect fit for me. I applied for the job and got it, and since then I've been lucky enough to get paid to spend my time fulfilling my passions for teaching and feminism. Needless to say, I'm glad I decided to take that one class.

# Notes

1.  Some of the related fields include Africana Women's Studies; Ethnic and Women's Studies; Feminist Gender Studies; Feminist, Gender, and Sexuality Studies; Feminist Studies; Gender Studies; Gender and Sexuality Studies; Gender and Women's Studies; Multicultural and Gender Studies; Study of Women and Gender; Women and Ethnic Studies; Women and Gender Studies; and Women, Gender, and Sexuality Studies (Kimmich 2009). Throughout the book, we use "Women's and Gender Studies" as an inclusive term where possible and to note the historical development of this interdisciplinary field. We also address the evolution of Women's and Gender Studies in Chapter 1.

2.  Emotion management and emotion labor are sociological concepts largely developed by Arlie Hochschild (1979, 1983). Drawing upon Irving Goffman's concept of "impression management," Hochschild explored how emotions may be manipulated or invoked to either suit the situation at hand or to intentionally change one's own perspective. Emotion labor is often expected based on one's positionality (i.e. gender, age, sexuality, race/ethnicity, and parent status). For more information, see Goffman (1959) and Hochschild (1979, 1983). You may find yourself having to manage and respond to other people's perceptions of you because of your interest in Women's and Gender Studies. You may find that people make assumptions about your sexual identity and political beliefs. We discuss these issues in depth in Chapter 3.

3.  A senior project at Bard is the equivalent of an honors thesis at other institutions.

4.  The abortion wars of the late 1980s and early 1990s were a time of public activism on a national, state, and local level in the US over the continued legality of abortion. In 1973, the U.S. Supreme Court affirmed women's access to legal abortion in *Roe v. Wade*. Ever since that decision, pro-life (or anti-choice) activists have mobilized in order to challenge this verdict. Organizations such as Operation Life helped stage protests ranging from blockades of abortion and reproductive health clinics to large-scale demonstrations in Washington. Conversely, pro-choice (or anti-life) activists responded to threats against clinics (and practitioners) in their own right. For an excellent analysis, see Mason (2002).

5.  We note the few occasions when we use a pseudonym to protect the confidentiality of an interviewee.

# 1
## CLAIMING AN EDUCATION
### YOUR INHERITANCE AS A STUDENT
### OF WOMEN'S AND GENDER STUDIES

In one of your WGST classes you have probably read the well-known and anthologized essay by poet, essayist, and feminist Adrienne Rich that discusses "claiming an education." In this inspiring essay, Rich highlights the importance of being an active participant in the process of becoming educated. This piece stirred an entire generation of students, both women and men, to apply themselves to their interests, to take ownership of their education, to question what they were taught and how it was relevant to them. Our overall aim in this book is to give you the tools to thrive in Women's and Gender Studies. One way to do that is to understand Women's and Gender Studies' unique history and to be able locate yourself within it. Most students have some knowledge of the early history of Women's Studies, but this cursory understanding often eludes you when someone pointedly asks, "What is Women's Studies? Isn't Women's Studies just a response to oppression?" Questions about the goals and roots of Women's Studies can often be surprising to students. The foundation about WGST that we provide here will enhance your current understanding of the politics and debates surrounding the role of WGST in higher education and its public perception. In Chapter 3, we focus on helping you to find creative ways to respond to those skeptics and naysayers.

This chapter highlights the history of Women's and Gender Studies, providing some background about why the field is interdisciplinary in nature. We look at how Women's Studies evolved into Women's and Gender Studies. We take you behind the scenes to help you understand that what happens in a Women's and Gender Studies classroom is an outgrowth of activism, debate, and rich intellectual tradition. We also provide a contemporary picture of Women's and Gender Studies—who your professors are, and who is likely to sit next to you in the classroom (or share a virtual classroom). You will also hear from graduates about what they have considered valuable in their training.

This chapter will provide you with conceptual and practical tools as you walk the path of "claiming your education" in Women's and Gender Studies.

## QUIZ: HOW MUCH DO YOU KNOW ABOUT THE HISTORY OF WOMEN'S AND GENDER STUDIES?

How much do you know about the birth of Women's and Gender Studies? See how many of the following questions you can answer.

1. What was the first Women's Studies program in the United States?
2. True or false: Most professors in the 1970s who taught Women's Studies did not get paid for their classes.
3. What is feminist pedagogy?
4. Why does Women's and Gender Studies value research, theory, and praxis?
5. What is the National Women's Studies Association?
6. Where were the first Women's Studies courses offered in the United States?
7. What is the relationship between the civil rights movement, the women's rights movement, and student activism for the discipline of Women's Studies in the US?
8. How many countries around the world offer WGST degrees?
9. True or false: Community colleges play a vital role in training students in WGST.
10. What topics might you have covered in one of the first Women's Studies classes on women's health?

**ADRIENNE RICH, FROM "CLAIMING AN EDUCATION"**

I have said that the contract on the student's part involves that you demand to be taken seriously so that you can also go on taking yourself seriously. This means seeking out criticism, recognizing that the most affirming thing anyone can do for you is demand that you push yourself further, show you the range of what you can do. It means rejecting attitudes of "take-it-easy," "why-be-so-serious," "why-worry-you'll-probably-get-married-anyway." It means assuming your share of responsibility for what happens in the classroom, because that affects the quality of your daily life here. It means that the student sees herself engaged *with* her teachers in active, ongoing struggle for a real education.

(Rich 1979: 27)

You will discover the answers as you keep reading! But they are also at the end of the chapter (page 73).

## "Back in the Day": The Birth of Women's Studies

Today you stand as some of the latest in a long line of students who paved the way for Women's and Gender Studies on campuses across the US and now the world. Women's Studies has its roots and origins in the social movements of the 1960s and 1970s, specifically the civil rights and women's rights movements. Women's Studies courses, and other interdisciplinary studies (e.g. American Studies), were born largely due to student activism and demand. This was a time when more women in the United States were attending colleges and universities than ever before!

While many students attending college during the late 1960s and early 1970s were "traditional" in age and pre-college education, many others were nontraditional (e.g. veterans, married or divorced women, those of different socio-economic strata, racial/ethnic backgrounds, and sexual orientations). This generation of new students (and new professors) created a unique culture in higher education that challenged the status quo as we describe below. Feminist activism spilled onto college campuses, forcing new questions about academic study. The earliest integrated Women's Studies programs at major universities were founded around 1970, although there were a few courses in Women's Studies (and/or courses on "women" or "feminism") that were offered at some colleges and universities before this time. While acknowledging the importance of individual and group-level change in the classroom, the first Women's Studies educators knew they had to change the very structure and curriculum of higher education. At many of the newly coeducational colleges and universities of the 1970s, Women's Studies developed as part of the process of incorporating and integrating women into their campus communities. Often the first Women's Studies professors taught new courses unpaid out of their absolute commitment to this academic endeavor!

While there were programs in existence that assisted women in going back to school (such as displaced homemaker programs), they did not challenge the status quo of the institution per se. Women who were either entering or returning to higher education in the 1960s and 1970s were questioning larger social structures (such as the state, family, military) in relation to their own lives, and education was one of the arenas where palpable change could be achieved. A great example of the tone of this era (which still resonates today) is the Older Women's League (OWL) manifesto, "Why OWL?" Written in 1970, it captures the sentiment of women who fought to challenge traditional gender roles that often left women as widows or divorced, unprepared for the workplace, and discriminated against when they were able to obtain employment. OWL also took up the sexist ways in which society viewed women as

---

**EXCERPT FROM "WHY OWL?"**

In general, the Women's Liberation Movement is a young movement. Statistics on age are not available but observation indicates the average age of women participating in the movement to be around 25. Older women in the movement are exceedingly rare. OWL (women 30 and above), unlike the younger women's liberation groups, was consciously created by women who:

1. Felt different from the main body of the movement because of age, life experiences, family commitments and goal orientations.
2. Felt that we had experienced long years of personal oppression and participated in the events of life (child birth, child rearing, marriage, divorce, homemaking and careers) that many of the younger groups theorized about.

they aged. They fought for job training, employment services, better childcare options, and a housewives' bill of rights.[1]

### Creating Change and the Importance of Research, Theory, and Praxis

Early Women's Studies faculty were innovative pioneers in creating this new academic endeavor. They wrote their own textbooks, compiled and shared reading lists, developed new curricula, organized conferences, and established academic journals. Their courses provided the first opportunity for women's lives and experiences to be studied seriously in higher education from a gender-inclusive perspective. Previously most scholarship was male dominated. The advances made by these innovators were in concert with the skills and knowledge they had gained as members of civil rights, liberal, and radical women's groups and organizations. The early twin goals of Women's Studies as an academic enterprise were: (1) to document and redress the exclusion of women's experiences from the traditional male-defined curriculum; and (2) to pose interdisciplinary questions and analyses across the social sciences, arts, humanities, and sciences. Early on, scholars realized that no single discipline could answer or address women's experiences. Therefore, a commitment to multiple approaches and perspectives from a variety of disciplinary communities in addressing women's lives took root. Faculty emphasized acknowledging and studying women's lives through women's own diverse experiences. Early founders believed that Women's Studies needed to stay connected and relevant to the everyday issues that women faced, and to work on challenging the myriad of persisting inequalities.

From the beginning of the institutionalization of Women's Studies in the academy, the concept of integrating research, theory, and praxis became central. This "triad" (the concept of research, theory, and praxis as being equally valued) is a unique feature of Women's Studies in higher education, and you will hear it mentioned as you progress through coursework. We will explore this concept more in this section, but in Chapter 2 you will have an opportunity to see how the triad is reflected in your training thus far.

### Research

In the academy, one of the primary ways that knowledge is advanced and legitimated is through the publication of scholarly articles and books based on original research. In the early phases of the movement, Women's Studies faculty contributed to the academic knowledge base that had been primarily androcentric, or male-centered, in nature. Scholars during the 1970s and 1980s spent much of their time documenting the ways women's experiences were left out of various types of research projects and priorities, and one aspect of this inquiry was to question the stereotypes about women that were pervasive in research (Hesse-Biber and Leavy 2007). These stereotypes were prevalent in science and other seemingly "neutral" forms of empirical research. Hesse-Biber and Leavy discuss a well-known example by anthropologist Emily Martin, who pioneered a critique of gendered bias in the sciences:

> She examined textbooks that dealt with human reproduction and found that these texts tended to construct a story where romance and gendered stereotypes about the egg and sperm were created, re-created, and enforced. She found that typically the egg was spoken about with the terms that depicted its passivity, where it "is transported," is "swept," or even "drifts." The sperms, in contrast, were typically spoken about in active, aggressive, and energetic terms, such as "velocity" and "propelling," where they can "burrow through the egg coat" and "penetrate" it.
>
> (p. 17)

> Martin shows that so-called truthful and objective medical textbooks were infused with nonobjective stereotypes, shaping both the medical and cultural understanding of natural events ... She argues that medical textbooks were depicting gender stereotypes through scientific language that had little basis in reality.
>
> (p. 37)

Researchers began to ask new questions when women were included in the center of analysis. This meant rejecting the idea that women could simply be "stirred" into disciplines without a serious rethinking of research and theoretical approaches. Scholars looked everywhere for answers in the social sciences and humanities. They examined culture, systems of representation, the analysis of literary texts, creative expression, and the ways in which institutions are shaped by and reflect ideas about gender and society.

## WHAT'S IN A NAME?—WOMEN'S STUDIES, GENDER STUDIES, OR SOMETHING ELSE?

You may be in an academic unit that does not use the moniker "Women's Studies." Programs and departments are in an intense period of redefining Women's Studies, Gender Studies, and Sexuality Studies. You may be studying these tensions in some of your classes. In this book, we use the term "Women's and Gender Studies" inclusively, noting both the historical formation of "Women's Studies" and its transformation over time.

The act of naming is powerful. Not only does it have an impact on how we think of ourselves, but also on how others perceive us. In the 1990s, discussions about the use of "Women's" versus "Gender" Studies began to emerge in electronic listserv forums such as WMST-L (an online community of Women's and Gender Studies scholars). Those who advocate for retaining "Women's Studies" point out the historical roots of the discipline as a response to the lack of scholarship and curriculum regarding women. In other words, "Women's Studies" was the academic response to the women's rights movement. Women's Studies put *women* at the center of analysis. Some people are worried that "Gender Studies" will depoliticize both feminist scholarship and contribute to women's subordination. The use of gender as a category is not a "neutral" concept, but in fact has the potential to re-establish privilege to those group members who society constructs as normative—men of a certain heritage or class. Similar arguments have been made regarding the terms "Gay" versus "Sexuality" Studies, as well as African American/Native American/Chicano versus Ethnic Studies. Another concern of "Women's Studies" advocates is that this name change has been encouraged by institutional actors outside of the discipline for financial and economic reasons (e.g. enrollment numbers, resource sharing) rather than as a response to changing theoretical and political identities.

Conversely, those who support "Gender Studies" see the name change as reflecting the shift away from binary identity politics in which a single category (women) can represent the complexity of experiences of individuals and groups who experience gender differently based on their race, ethnicity, sexuality, age, ability, or social class. Some see Gender Studies as inclusive and less likely to make essentialist assumptions about "all women". As the very concept of women has been questioned by post-modern and post-structuralist theory, as well as by the transgender and intersex community, many question the term "Women's Studies" as being too reductionist, limiting, exclusive, and normative.

A recent development in naming has been the combination of Women's Studies and Gender Studies in the single name, Women's and Gender Studies. For many advocates, not only does this acknowledge the historical roots of the discipline, but it also attempts to incorporate critiques in order to describe the field's current theoretical canon accurately. For some, this is yet another example of accommodation or an "add and stir" approach in which prevailing structural issues are not challenged. For others, Women's and Gender Studies has a history of acknowledging limitations and responding to them. As we see it, the fact that Women's/Gender/Feminist/Sexuality Studies exists and continues to explore the very names by which we identify shows the continued application of theory into practice, as well as an intimate engagement with politics that reaffirms the very roots of our existence as an academic and intellectual endeavor.

For more information, see http://userpages.umbc.edu/~korenman/wmst/womvsgen. html#TopOfPage.

Researchers also used multiple methods to explore new questions about women and gender, including: experiments, oral histories, historical analysis, surveys, textual analysis, ethnographies, and other qualitative data gathering.

*Theory*

Theory, the second piece to the conceptual triad, is an important component in Women's Studies. It is grounded in experience, critical reflection, and interaction with the larger world. In many disciplines, ideas, concepts, frameworks, and perspectives that had been defined as normal, universal, and centrally important were revealed to focus on a small number of people—usually upper middle-class, heterosexual, able-bodied white men. The development of theory as a vital tool with which to challenge oppression and domination has become central in Women's Studies. Early Women's Studies scholars sought new theoretical concepts to explore the features of women's lives that had yet to be fully understood (e.g. sexual violence, prostitution, motherhood). Scholars in Philosophy and Political Science took up central concepts of citizenship, political participation, and democratic rights, and rethought them by looking at women's experiences. Scholars in Theology began questioning the interpretation of foundational works of organized religion, and questioned the very language that is used in religion and faith-based communities to marginalize women (see Christ 1992; Daly 1993).

We think it is important to stress that many Women's Studies scholars were also making changes in their own disciplines, and creating

groups within their professional organizations that would make scholarship on women a priority. For example, in Sociology, the foremothers
of Sociologists for Women in Society (SWS, an organization within
Sociology dedicated to supporting and promoting gender scholars and
research through conferences and their own publication) were making
changes within Sociology, as well as in Women's Studies. Thus, Women's
Studies emerged in concert with changes happening in established
disciplines by the very women (and men) who were also shaping it.

*Praxis*

Finally, we turn to the concept of praxis. Praxis is about the integration
of learning with social justice. As a term, it means that seeking knowledge
for knowledge's sake will not change structures of domination and
oppression in women's lives.[2] Praxis is about applying one's knowledge
to challenge oppressive systems and unequal traditions. It is related to the
well-known phrase "the personal is political" espoused by many advocates
of the second-wave women's movement. Over time, for those in Women's
Studies, it has meant training students to think and learn about inequalities
beyond the borders of the classroom. This integrated triad of concepts
helps to distinguish Women's Studies' intellectual goals from other disciplines. Women's Studies as an academic endeavor seeks to weight all three
of these concepts equally in teaching, research, and engagement outside
of the academy. This emphasis speaks to the way in which the field is
informed by and engaged in activism and advocacy that in turn shape the
creation of new knowledge.

*NWSA—Professional Outcome of an Academic Movement*

Every academic discipline has its own professional organization, and
the field of WGST is no different. The National Women's Studies
Association (NWSA) was formed in 1977, and signaled an important
moment for Women's Studies. NWSA's emergence as a key player in
the academic landscape, with the members to prove it, suggested to the
larger academic community that there was enough interest in teaching
and research among people who considered themselves committed to
Women's Studies to form an official association. NWSA continues to be
the premier organization for scholars and students of Women's Studies.
It holds an annual conference with over 1,600 attendees, in past years

## STUDENTS AND THE NWSA CONFERENCE

The annual conference of the NWSA encourages undergraduate and graduate representation through participation in roundtables, poster sessions, and paper presentations. Between 2006 and 2009, between 30 percent and 46 percent of the NWSA membership was students (undergraduates and graduates), and between 41 percent and 46 percent of the conference registrants were students. These are significant numbers. You may find yourself working with a professor and being asked to present your work there. Or you can take the initiative and find out about presenting your own work there. If your institution is a member of NWSA, they receive three student memberships for free. If you are interested in attending, this could lower the cost. NWSA also has regional representatives across the country. Some of the regions also host conferences that students can attend, as well as present at. (Data gathered by NWSA staff.)

including K-12 teachers, college professors, undergraduate students, graduate students, higher education administrators (such as deans, etc.), and women's center directors.

Women's Studies practitioners also find support through a variety of professional organizations, ranging from those tied to their "home discipline" to caucuses, sections, or organizations that promote the advancement of women, women in academia, workplace issues, and research and scholarship on women and gender, such as the Association for Feminist Anthropology, the Association for Women in Computing (AWC), the Association for Women Geologists (AWG), the Association for Women in Science (AWIS), the International Association for Feminist Economics (IAFFE), the Modern Language Association's (MLA) Division on Women's Studies in Language and Literature, the Western Association of Women Historians (WAWH), Sociologists for Women in Society (SWS), Society for Women in Philosophy (SWIP), Society of Women Engineers (SWE), and the Women's Classical Caucus (WCC).

There are also organizations that were formed in the nineteenth century to support female co-eds and utilize the resources of women who had achieved a college degree. The AAUW is an exemplary organization devoted to researching issues that affect women in academia (as well as providing generous support for scholars through fellowships).[3]

## Transformation of the Classroom

Another part of your inheritance is the Women's and Gender Studies classroom.

You have probably heard of, or read about, the social unrest of the late twentieth century. During the 1960s and 1970s, student activists in the US protested not only the war and government policy, but also the very knowledge that was being taught and produced in establishments of higher learning or post-secondary educational institutions. Students and faculty alike were experimenting with the structure and style of teaching, ranging from consciousness-raising sessions in the classroom, changing the physical structure of the classroom itself (such as seating, moving the classroom from inside to outdoors), and emphasizing student participation rather than the passive learning model of the "banking concept of education" (see Friere 2001). People experimented with class design to provide a better format for engaging students. This time of transition had a profound effect on the development of the Women's Studies classroom and teaching practices. You might have noticed that you are often seated in a circle that creates a space where everyone faces everyone. It might seem strange to you that a simple change such as this—seating students in a circle where they can see and hear one another—was unique and transformative. But it was! This new arrangement allowed for a greater accountability for each student, the possibility for rapport to form more deeply between students and faculty, and a more level playing field in which the distance between professor "knowers" and student "learners" was decreased. This arrangement also served as a type of "container" when strong emotions were expressed.

Faculty members in the 1960s and 1970s drew upon a new teaching style that was more participatory and personal, which later became known as "feminist pedagogy."[4] They helped to develop the concept of "student-centered learning." The new courses offered faculty and students the opportunity to conduct in-depth scholarly work on subjects that had previously not been a part of the college curriculum, or were at the margins of more traditional disciplines, such as domestic violence, women's roles in historical periods, and women's literature. By listening to and valuing the experiences of students, topics that may have been largely ignored rose to prominence, as they reflected the everyday concerns and interests of students. Rather than being the objects of study (such as wife and

## THE WOMEN'S AND GENDER STUDIES CLASSROOM: STUDENT REFLECTIONS

I think the fact that I felt included and accepted in a classroom discussion about my own gender was important. This way people feel more open to discuss things in a "round-robin" forum. What better of a time to talk about issues affecting women, than with *other* women, in a *women*-friendly environment! *That* is why I loved this as my minor!

(Libby, 2007, North Dakota State University)

Being immersed in Women's and Gender Studies classes has heightened my ability to critically reflect upon myself, others, and the world around me. While I have always valued time to reflect, these courses have enhanced the quality and depth of my reflections in many areas of my life, from dynamics at family gatherings and uses of gendered language, to service involvement in the community and a different perspective on history. My degree has shown me how I can pursue my passions for incarcerated women's rights, affordable, accessible reproductive healthcare, creating nonjudgmental, inviting spaces for immigrant communities, and women's empowerment during the pregnancy and birthing processes in direct and indirect ways, and encourages me to connect and devote myself to these interests as my life and career progress.

(Kimmie, 2011, University of North Carolina at Chapel Hill)

mother in nuclear family structures, as challenged by Betty Friedan in *The Feminine Mystique*, deviant career woman, and/or over-sexualized prostitute or woman of color), Women's Studies was able to do more than just "add women" superficially to traditional curricula. Women's Studies courses allowed students to choose what subjects to study, to question how subjects would be studied, to challenge ideas of objectivity and power within research, and to create knowledge that would support the changes occurring on local, state, and national levels due to feminist organizing (including rape laws, domestic violence, women's health advocacy, women entering nontraditional occupations, wages for housework).

### Time Travel: What You Might Have Learned in an Early Women's Studies Class

We are transporting you back in time to an early Women's Studies class to explore the overlapping connections students made in the classroom and in their lives during the 1970s, one phase of the second-wave women's movement. The fight for women's healthcare provides a useful example. Let us imagine that you took a class on "Women and Health: History, Tensions, and New Beginnings" offered for the first time in 1977. At the time this course was taught, you probably not only had access to a variety of birth control options, but abortion has been legal for four years. Discussion was emerging about environmental hazards and health from early pioneers such as Rachel Carson's *Silent Spring*. Also in 1974, First Lady Betty Ford went public about her fight with breast cancer. If you were enrolled in this early Women's Studies course, you might have found yourself investigating and discussing why there were so few women doctors in practice. In the 1970s, fewer than 10 percent of all doctors were women. You and your classmates would have focused on the many ways that women faced widespread discrimination both as consumers and providers of healthcare (Baxandall and Gordon 2001). You might have heard from your classmates powerful anecdotes about feeling ignored, infantilized, dismissed, or ridiculed in an everyday encounter with a male physician. You would have spent time reading new feminist scholarship that critically examined the ways that childbirth had become an increasingly medicalized procedure that benefited the schedule of physicians and hospital staff, but left many women feeling alienated from their bodies. You might have been amazed to read historical accounts of the role of midwifery in the US and Britain during the sixteenth and seventeenth centuries. Feeling motivated from discussions in class, you might have joined or even created a "women's health group." These informal groups sprang up around the country and "provided direct services, promoted health education, and agitated to change the mainstream health movement" (Baxandall and Gordon 2001: 117). Your professor might have stressed how important it was to gather narratives from women's lived experiences and bring them into the classroom. So, one of your options for a short assignment might have been to interview a woman in your family who was older than you about her experiences accessing and receiving medical treatment.

Toward the end of the semester, one of your longer assignments may have asked you to research and reflect on the ways that current treatment of minority women in the healthcare system were connected to a history of U.S. imperialism. In order to do this, you would have to draw on concepts of marginality, the interplay of racism and sexism, and economic discrimination that you had learned from other Women's Studies classes.

The professor would have suggested scholarly articles and books from the established fields of Economics, History, and Sociology, and perhaps new scholarship emerging in Ethnic Studies and African American Studies. Your professor might have also directed you to feminist periodicals, including *Ms.*, but also to smaller magazines and journals that proliferated during the 1970s. In completing and reading for this assignment, you would have seen that there were gaps in the way most disciplines treated the subject of minority women and health. Indeed, Women's Studies, though an interdisciplinary analysis, was trying to create new knowledge about women and health, not just by closing the gaps, but by creating new areas of inquiry and novel ways of defining the problems. You would have put into practice the interdisciplinary process of creating an original way of gathering data, incorporating new voices, and generating knowledge that tries to highlight the "why and how" that women experience unequal treatment in the area of health. Toward the end of the semester, your professor might have suggested that for women's needs and concerns to be fully addressed in the healthcare system, it would not be enough just to create more women doctors (the "add and stir approach"), but it would also require a rethinking of the roles of health, well-being, and the healthcare system.

Finally, if you had read the newly published *Our Bodies, Ourselves* for class—devoted to explicit discussion and photos of sexual and reproductive issues and stressing that women were experts on their bodies—you might have rushed out and purchased this book for your female friends and relatives. This class could have even triggered a re-evaluation of your emerging goals for employment and spurred an interest in becoming a doula, doctor, midwife, or nurse!

We hope this brief example gives you a sense of the energy and enthusiasm that was generated in those early Women's Studies classes, and how students often found ways to connect their experiences directly to the social movement happening outside the classroom.

### FOR YOUR LIBRARY

Rosalyn Baxandall and Linda Gordon (Eds.) (2001). *Dear Sisters: Dispatches from the Women's Liberation Movements*. New York: Basic Books.

Boston Women's Health Collective (2005). *Our Bodies, Ourselves: A New Edition for a New Era*, 4th ed. New York: Touchstone Press.

Sandra Morgen (2002). *Into Our Own Hands: The Women's Health Movement in the United States, 1969–1990*. New Brunswick, NJ, Rutgers University Press.

*Programs, Departments, Research Centers, Curricula: What Does it Mean for You?*

As stated in the introduction, Women's Studies programs and departments have proliferated across U.S. higher education and globally. As with many interdisciplinary fields, academic programs such as Women's and Gender Studies can have a variety of organizational features. Understanding about how your program or department is organized empowers you to pursue the options and choices that may be available to you.

There are typically two models of Women's and Gender Studies programs and departments and how they are organized. In the first model, there are self-governing academic departments with faculty. The second model pertains to small and mid-sized academic programs where faculty are shared across departments and programs. The organization of Women's and Gender Studies into programs and departments tends to reflect a particular U.S. perspective. Across the globe, Women's and Gender Studies at the undergraduate level might be organized as well into "programmes" or research centers.

In the first model, the department is self-contained and has autonomy in how (and who) it hires and tenures, how it develops and delivers curricula, and how resources are allocated to faculty and students. The second model usually includes a program with shared faculty lines. This means that there is usually a director of the program, but he or she is housed in another department (e.g. anthropology). The director coordinates other faculty members who have shared lines across the university to teach and do service for the Women's Studies program. In this model, faculty "homes" are (usually) within the traditional disciplines, where department chairs have the authority to choose the amount of support they give their faculty in teaching Women's Studies courses. Women's and Gender Studies has developed over the past three decades through these different models, and there is no model that is inherently better than another—all are institutionally specific. Each model has different implications for students, but, more importantly, both of these models have been successful in the establishment of training Women's and Gender Studies students.

At the end of the chapter, we suggest some ways to find out how Women's and Gender Studies is organized in your institution.

In discussing how Women's and Gender Studies fits into higher education, we would be remiss if we did not acknowledge the important role that community colleges play in higher education in the training of students, especially women students. A recent American Association of University Women report on women and community college experience argues that community colleges play an integral role in providing access to women, especially during the economic recession. They note that in 2010, women made up 57 percent of the students" at community colleges. Now, more than "4 million women attend the nation's two-year public colleges, which is more than the number of undergraduate women attending either public or private four-year colleges and universities" (American Association of University Women 2013). And Women's and Gender Studies classes are flourishing within community colleges (Roy 2009). Faculty members in community colleges make a significant commitment when teaching Women's and Gender Studies because they already have high teaching responsibilities and usually do not have an appointment in a program or department (Roy 2009). Many professors at community colleges, however, are committed to helping students both fulfill their potential and "overcome daunting obstacles to meet their goals" (Roy 2009: 62). They are also excited about meeting the growing demand for Women's and Gender Studies classes at the community college level. DeAnna Beachely's story below exemplifies the growth at the community college level. She is a faculty member at the College of Southern Nevada and chair of the Women's Studies program:

> I have been teaching Women's History since 1993, and Women's Studies classes since 2005, at the College of Southern Nevada (CSN), located in Las Vegas, Nevada. In my first year of teaching, my department chair asked me to teach a Women's History class that had not been taught in over 10 years. I said yes, and after about 10 months of preparation, I taught the class. It was an eye-opening and empowering experience for me on a personal and professional level.
>
> In 2004, after several years of planning, CSN created a Women's Studies degree program. There were a core group of six or so women faculty members from History, Sociology, and Philosophy who crafted our founding statements and planned

curriculum for a two-year degree program. We have no separate department and no full-time faculty member devoted solely to teaching Women's Studies. We do have one joint appointment in Women's Studies and Communication. We rely heavily on full-time faculty members who teach one or two classes for us a semester (I teach one Women's Studies class per semester). We have an amazing group of dedicated part-time faculty who reach the largest number of students and inspire some of them to become Women's Studies majors or minors. I teach a History of the American Women's Movement class, which offers me the opportunity to reach our majors and those who are interested in finding out more about the women's movement.

It was a couple of years between the argumentation, planning, and, finally, the implementation of the Women's Studies program at CSN. When I had raised the idea of creating a Women's Studies program with a former administrator, sometime in the late 1990s, the scoffing response I received was, "there are no Women's Studies programs at community colleges," to which I immediately countered that there definitely were, and proceeded to name several community colleges that I knew did have a Women's Studies program. Fortunately, that administrator was gone by the time we proposed the creation of the Women's Studies program at CSN.

It has been almost 10 years since the program began at CSN. We are still a relatively small program in terms of our majors (10 declared), but we have had graduates from our program for eight years. A large number of students have been exposed to Women's Studies by taking a class that serves as a diversity requirement, WMST 113: Race, Class, and Gender. We have added new classes to our curriculum, including The Economics of Discrimination, and are looking for ways to be able to hire either a full-time person (my wish), or another joint appointment. The college is in the early stages of implementing a faculty-advising program, to enable students to get advice from faculty in the field. I am in the process of receiving that training, so that I can help our majors and minors. Many of our majors plan to further their education with a BA in Women's Studies. Long-term plans include working in healthcare, rape crisis centers, women's shelters, and to offer legal assistance for low-income women.

Our students range in age from the traditional college-aged student, to the returning student, to the nontraditional student. It is wonderful to see so many young people engaged in the discipline and excited about their future path. It is also heartening to see returning students or nontraditional students, who have real-life experience that has motivated them to devote their lives to women's issues.

## Understanding the Legacy

Activist and political roots are part of Women's Studies history, which it shares with Chicano Studies, American Studies, Peace and Justice Studies, Native American Studies, Environmental Studies, and African and African American Studies. Not surprisingly, these interdisciplinary fields are sometimes attacked as less scholarly because of their political origins. Traditional disciplines, without seemingly overt activist beginnings, by comparison, look neutral and unbiased. I (Michele) was surprised to find when I did my dissertation field research, the discipline of Political Science (often exclusively focused on quantitative analysis) emerged as a field through Philosophy and Civics. One hundred years ago, a person studying the field of Politics was just as likely to read literature and study languages as he (or she) was to learn statistics. Political Science, as a discipline, went through major shifts post-World War II, and then again in the early 1980s. The truth is that the boundaries of what a discipline encompasses are ones of constant change and development. Knowledge and what is perceived as important in the make-up of a discipline shifts and changes. In 100 years, we can assume that Women's Studies will be configured very differently than it is now. We will return to this point about Women's and Gender Studies origins, and the ways in which it is sometimes viewed by others, in Chapter 3.

Congratulations! You have just breezed through a brief sketch of the legacy that you have inherited as a WGST student. As you can see, Women's Studies, as a distinct academic interdisciplinary field, would not have been possible without the social movements that preceded its founding. Moreover, given its origins in social movements, Women's Studies was, from its beginnings, activist in orientation. Professors and students saw Women's Studies as committed to transforming women's roles in the world, and not simply understanding such stratified roles. Its goal was not "disinterested" academic inquiry; rather, Women's Studies focused on ending gender oppression and challenging traditional paradigms. Indeed, the relationship of Women's Studies to the women's movement was crucial in establishing and developing the field. The women's movement, in particular, helped pressure colleges and universities to establish Women's Studies programs and helped establish the study of women and gender as a worthy endeavor.

Practitioners of Women's and Gender Studies have also worked as allies in supporting the growth of student services on college campuses and universities, including centers of diversity and multicultural affairs, LGBTQ offices, and women's centers, thus affecting the overall quality of contemporary student life.

## POINT OF VIEW

### INTEGRATING TRANSFEMINIST PERSPECTIVES INTO WOMEN'S AND GENDER STUDIES CURRICULUM

#### Dr. Mel Michelle Lewis, Goucher College

Women's and Gender Studies is a constantly evolving field. Dr. Mel Michelle Lewis explores how she has shifted her teaching and research over the past several years in response to shifts in the field.

My pedagogical project is both personal and political. As a black queer cisgender feminist lesbian femme, my approach to Women, Gender, and Sexuality Studies (WGS) curriculum centers intersectional identities and experiences and acknowledges the body as text in the classroom. I have taught WGS at the undergraduate level for nine years, first as a graduate student at a large state university and as an adjunct instructor at a state honors college. I am now a junior faculty member at a small liberal arts institution, my alma mater, charged with the task of developing new courses that reflect my program's recent shift from "Women's Studies" to "Women, Gender, and Sexuality Studies." Integrating transfeminist perspectives into my WGS curriculum has highlighted multiple theoretical intersections and lived experiences that frequently remain marginalized in Women's and Gender Studies inquiries.

Transforming the scholarship requires us as feminist pedagogues to engage gender variance and transition, as we explore social constructions and frameworks that are dependent upon disciplined gendered bodies. Anne Enke notes, "both feminist and transgender studies acknowledge the mutual imbrications of gender and class formations, dis/abilities, racializations, political economies, incarcerations, nation-alisms, migrations and dislocations, and so forth."[5] Although the relationship between transgender studies and WGS has been fraught with questions regarding borders, boundaries, and belongings, I have found that WGS students are able to make clear connections between systems of oppression, and easily integrate transfeminist perspectives into their class discussions and research projects. Students acknowledge the ways in which early Women's Studies inquires made gender visible, and trace this genealogy through feminist, queer, and trans* scholarship.

As a feminist black queer studies scholar, I also call students' attention to the commonalities between the political projects of Black Queer Studies and transfeminist perspectives. Mae G. Henderson and E. Patrick Johnson describe the project of Black Queer Studies as "fundamentally a liberatory one—in the sense that it is grounded in the assertion of individual rights balanced by communal accountability in the interest of ensuring social justice."[6] In much the same way, I contend that a liberatory approach to WGS must grapple with black queer and transfeminist perspectives, among many others. We must recognize not only the complexity of personal identifications, but also the ways in which systemic forms of sexism, racism, heterosexism, homophobia, transphobia, and other systems of domination are all contingent upon one another for meaning and operation.

One of my classroom lessons begins with an exploration of feminist responses to gender-based violence, such as street harassment and rape, including Slut Walk, Hollaback!, Take Back the Night, and Men Can Stop Rape. We then identify the correlations and systemic connections between high rates of street harassment and murder of trans* and gender variant women of color. The resulting transfeminist perspective then expands to include racial profiling and "stand your ground" laws as they relate to masculine people of color, immigrant communities, and other marginalized groups.

Another lesson asks students to make connections between sexual and reproductive health debates from a feminist perspective, and trans* healthcare issues that also support agency, education, and access. From a transfeminist perspective, students recognize that the rhetoric in opposition to agency, education, and access is related. A classroom discussion examined policies that restrict access to birth control, and mandate ultrasounds, parental consent, and spousal notification for pregnancy termination procedures. The critique then extended to include the gatekeeping practices of mental health providers, surgeons, and parents that restrict access to gender confirmation prescriptions and procedures. Students asserted that in both instances, "someone else knows what you should do with your body better than you do," and reflected on the "third party permission slip" aspect of both scenarios. The revelation that feminist and trans* activism and scholarship in support of agency, education, and access also have a lot in common is a formative experience for many students.

Throughout each course, I also highlight a black feminist standpoint; we apply the concepts of intersectionality and the matrix of domination, while integrating a transfeminist perspective. Patricia Hill Collins writes, "Intersectional paradigms remind us that oppression cannot be reduced to one fundamental type, and that oppressions work together in producing injustice." She contrasts the matrix of domination with an intersectional approach, highlighting its organizational nature. "Regardless of the particular intersections involved, structural, disciplinary, hegemonic, and interpersonal domains of power reappear across quite different forms of oppression."[7] I encourage my students to think through the ways in which oppressions work together to produce individual injustices, and how oppressions are simultaneously organizing social systems of power and dominance. This transfeminist exploration leads us to recognize that we cannot continue to assert that there is only so much identity to go around within the demarcated boundaries of each group, or that there is only so much justice available regarding the activist and academic act of privileging pursuits and voices. With this intersectional lens in place, students often quote and put into practice inspirational ideas that insist all forms of injustice are linked, and call for solidarity and multi-issue approaches.

Although I allow room for engaging fixed (yet always unstable) identity categories in the classroom, noting that I have an affinity for my own named identifiers. As an "Other," I feel it is unjust to police the porous boundaries of gender, race, sexuality, or any other social formation. Transfeminist perspectives offer WGS critical theoretical tools for teaching and learning about the gendered body, as well as relationships between gender identity, expression, and larger social constructions of power and privilege.

Transfeminisms provide a framework for integrated analysis that pushes students to think about gender in broader personal and political terms. My students who have had these transfeminist conversations seem to be less interested in the borders and boundaries of identity. Instead, a transfeminist perspective inspires a more complex vision of gender social justice work. I believe this vision is at the center of new WGS curriculum and the future of feminist praxis.

## FOR YOUR LIBRARY

We encourage you to do further reading about the history, debates, and development of Women's and Gender Studies. You will feel more informed when you talk to your professors (always a plus!) and various publics, and it will help you understand the larger patterns that have shaped the knowledge that you are learning.

Jane Aaron and Sylvia Walby (Eds.) (1991). *Out of the Margins: Women's Studies in the Nineties.* Bristol, PA: Falmer Press.

Marilyn Jacoby Boxer and Catherine R. Stimpson (2001). *When Women Ask the Questions: Creating Women's Studies in America.* Baltimore, MD: Johns Hopkins University Press.

Ann Braithwaite, Susan Heald, Susanne Luhmann, and Sharon Rosenberg (Eds.) (2005). *Troubling Women's Studies: Pasts, Presents, and Possibilities*. Toronto: Sumach Press.

Florence Howe (Ed.) (2000). *The Politics of Women's Studies: Testimony from the Thirty Founding Mothers*. New York: The Feminist Press.

Ellen Messer-Davidow (2002). *Disciplining Feminism: From Social Activism to Academic Discourse*. Durham, NC: Duke University Press.

Joan Wallach Scott (Ed.) (2008). *Women's Studies on the Edge*. Durham, NC: Duke University Press.

Robyn Weigman (Ed.) (2002). *Women's Studies on its Own: A Next Wave Reader in Institutional Change*. Durham, NC: Duke University Press.

## You and the Contemporary Moment: Professors, Students, and the Classroom

In this section, we turn to what is going on for you as an advanced student of Women's and Gender Studies.

### Your Women's and Gender Studies Professor

If we were to rely solely on media images of a category called "Women's and Gender Studies professors," it would be slim pickings. In the past 50 years, it was unusual to even see a woman *portrayed* as a college professor. Typically, stereotyped images of college professors included rumpled, white, older befuddled men (i.e. the absent-minded professor) who pontificated to a classroom (often of other men), or lecherous, leather-patch-and-tweed white men who used their position and influence to seduce naive co-eds (have you ever seen *Animal House*?). If female students of Women's Studies were represented at all in the movies, they were portrayed as ethnic print-wearing, Birkenstock-shoed, vegetarian, cheerless, angry, man-hating women in films such as *PCU* (1994). These characters were one-dimensional misrepresentations of women who often "only needed a man" in order to become happy.

Recently, however, media representations have begun to challenge these stereotypes of students and professors. In films such as *Nutty Professor II: The Klumps* (2000) and *Something's Gotta Give* (2003), Janet Jackson and Frances McDormand are portrayed as smart, witty women who challenge the main male character's ideas about love and life. In fact, at the end of the previous decade, HBO (a major cable network in the US) made news by initiating conversations about developing a comedy series entitled *Women's Studies*, which would follow the day-to-day life issues experienced by a Women's Studies professor (Andreeva 2009).

Witty, complicated, and even problematic depictions of feminism and Women's Studies now populate airwaves, including the horror film *Women's Studies* (2010), the satire *The Dictator* (2012), the comedy *Girls* (2011), and the online series *Vag Magazine* (2010–) and *Portlandia* (2011–). With the rise of increasing numbers of female filmmakers working across various digital media, we believe that we will continue to see more diverse and complicated depictions of both second- and third-wave feminism(s) and Women's and Gender Studies students and professors.

Women's and Gender Studies professors come from a diversity of intellectual backgrounds and training. Historically, people who were known as Women's Studies professors were activists and academics from other fields who were interested in women's lives. Many of the faculty members we trained with in college, for example, might have claimed the title of feminist or Women's Studies academic, but were not formally trained in Women's Studies. They typically advocated and fought to have Women's Studies on their campuses, supported the advancement of female faculty, and took on equity issues. But their main intellectual work continued to be in their home discipline and department. In their disciplines, they put questions about gender front and center and published research in discipline-specific journals. Many women and men who pioneered Women's and Gender Studies are considered baby boomers (i.e. people who were born between 1945 and 1964). Soon, this group will be retiring from the discipline, and those of us who will inherit their legacy are women and men who have advanced degrees (such as MAs and Ph.D.s) or graduate certificates in Women's and Gender Studies.

The next wave of Women's Studies professors are women (like us) and men who have trained in some formal way at either the under-graduate or graduate level in Women's Studies. Your Women's Studies professor most likely possesses a Ph.D. (Doctor of Philosophy), a JD (Juris Doctorate, or law degree), or another advanced professional degree (e.g. MPH, a master's in Public Health; MSW, a master's in Social Work, etc.). It is also common to find scholars who have trained in one of the traditional disciplines, including Anthropology, English, History, Political

Science, or Sociology, and who also possess a graduate certificate or master's degree specifically in Women's Studies. Scholars who have pursued Ph.D.s in Women's and Gender Studies at one of the over twenty doctoral-granting programs are also increasing. According to a recent report by the National Science Foundation (NSF), "Doctoral Recipients from U.S. Universities. According to a recent report by the National Science Foundation (NSF), "Doctoral Recipients from U.S. Universities: 2012 Digest," in 2012, approximately 115 Ph.D.s were awarded in the Social Sciences category of "area/ethnic/cultural/gender studies." Of these, 38 were male and 77 were female. This number is quite impressive when you compare the number of degrees awarded under this category in 1998 (14) (www.nsf.gov/statistics/nsf10309/pdf/tab47.pdf). Unfortunately, this information may be misleading because of the lack of a specific reference to Women's and Gender Studies, as well as the number of Ph.D. candidates who receive Women's and Gender Studies degrees, but may be part of a joint program within another discipline or some other institutional issue. Current trends indicate that the number of faculty who teach in Women's and Gender Studies who hold a Ph.D. in Women's and Gender Studies will continue to increase as demand for Women's and Gender Studies curricula continues to grow in higher education.

## POINT OF VIEW

### RECENT WOMEN'S STUDIES Ph.D. SPEAKS

#### Dr. Adriane Brown, Augsburg College

Dr. Adriane Brown exemplifies the next generation of Women's and Gender Studies professors. She holds a BA in Women's Studies and an MA and Ph.D. in Women's Studies from Ohio State. She is Assistant Professor and Director of Women's Studies and Director of the Women's Resource Center at Augsburg College.

I'm in my second year of a full-time faculty appointment in Women's Studies, but I've been teaching Women's Studies classes since I was a master's student. Based on my experience teaching at several comprehensive public universities, a Big 10 university, and a small liberal arts college, I'd say that teaching Women's Studies presents a handful of challenges and a tremendous amount of rewards. There's always that one student who's unhappy about being in a Women's Studies course and resists the material, and my job as an instructor is to figure out how to give that student the best possible experience in my class. Also, many students come in with an assumption that we're in a post-sexist, post-racist era, and I have to strike a balance between acknowledging how far we've come and providing students with evidence of how far we still need to go. These can be some of the most rewarding students to teach, because during the class, they often experience that feminist "click" on some issue that's important to them. And then there are the students who come into the class already hungry for Women's Studies. These are students who speak in every class, who come to my office and talk about their activist work and their feminist frustrations—for those students, my job is to provide additional challenges and guidance. The balance of these groups of students is what makes my job both challenging and fulfilling.

I was part of one of the earliest cohorts of Women's Studies Ph.D. students at the Ohio State University (the first cohort graduated in the mid-2000s), though the department itself has been around for decades. My cohort included both master's and Ph.D. students, but three of us were specifically working toward Ph.D.s. Really, I can't say enough good things about my program—I had a fantastic advisor and always felt supported in my intellectual pursuits. The Women's, Gender, and Sexuality Studies department (as it's now called) at OSU is one of the most institutionally stable I've seen, so I was lucky to never experience any of the anxiety about dissolution that many students in interdisciplinary programs feel. Being on the job market, on the other hand, was an incredibly stressful journey. I only applied to tenure-track positions because I didn't want to repeatedly move my family around, but in retrospect, that severely limited my prospects. I got one campus interview my first year but no offers, so I ended up doing adjunct work for my first post-Ph.D. year while I braved the job market yet again. On my second attempt, I got an offer from Augsburg College, a small liberal arts college in Minneapolis—which, in a completely improbable coincidence, is my favorite city in the entire country. For me, getting a faculty job was like winning the lottery—it felt both that exciting and that unlikely, given that there were several jobs for which I was one of 400 candidates.

As a member of the first generation of Women's Studies faculty who holds a Ph.D. in Women's and Gender Studies, I often find myself reflecting on the ways that my three Women's Studies degrees have shaped me as a scholar and teacher. One of the main reasons I pursued Women's Studies was the interdisciplinarity of the field. While all but one of my academic mentors have had degrees in traditional disciplines, I was able to benefit from their collective experiences in fields such as Geography, Sociology, English, Media Studies, and History to forge my own intellectual path. My research (which examines girls' gendered, racial, and sexual subjectivities in digital media) is decidedly interdisciplinary, incorporating visual and textual analysis, in-person and instant-messenger interviews, ethnography, and autoethnography, and I don't think I would have been afforded that kind of freedom in a traditional discipline. My particular Ph.D. program at Ohio State also had (and still has) an incredibly strong grounding in feminist theory—I took approximately five or six different feminist theory courses— and those theoretical foundations have imbued my research and teaching in really rich and diverse ways.

The thing I'm still struggling most with is balancing my academic life—which includes teaching two classes a semester, advising majors, supervising independent studies and student research projects, directing the Women's Studies program, and directing the Women's Resource Center—with my personal life. This kind of model is fairly typical at small liberal arts colleges, where there are fewer faculty to go around than at large institutions, and where we're expected to engage in a lot of service and individual work with students. In addition to my full-time faculty position, I also coach high school debate, which takes up a couple of nights a week and most weekends from September through January. And finally, I have an incredibly understanding partner and a five-year-old son who like to see me occasionally. For me, engaging in a diverse set of personal and professional commitments is an essential part of feminist praxis—my research on girlhood and my work with high school debaters are mutually influential. I think that feminist academics, in particular, want to feel connected to activist pursuits outside of the academy. Those commitments aren't often evaluated in tenure review processes, though, and our activist lives pile onto full-time faculty commitments, which can easily become overwhelming.

Clearly, I keep busy, and I dealt with a lot of stress and anxiety in my first year at Augsburg College. I started out this year—my second year—with three New (Academic) Year's resolutions aimed at reducing my stress level. First, I'm keeping my work e-mail inbox empty. A full inbox is an immediate stress trigger for me, and I sometimes failed to respond to e-mails last year when they fell down in the queue. I now respond to e-mails during specific windows and immediately delete them or file them away. Second, I'm reserving Fridays as off-campus work days. My campus office is located inside the Women's Resource Center, and I found last year that my on-campus work days were filled with both scheduled meetings and unscheduled student drop-ins, so I wasn't able to progress on my research in the way that I'd hoped. Reserving one day a week for focused, meeting-free writing time is really critical, especially for early career academics. Finally, I've resolved to take better care of my body. I read Layli Maparyan's *The Womanist Idea* recently, and I was really compelled by her argument that self-care can be envisioned as a womanist/feminist methodological practice. I engaged in a lot of stress eating last year and paid for a gym membership that I rarely used, but this year I've scheduled time three days a week to work out. I'm being realistic about the kind of exercise I dislike—running—and the kind I enjoy—swimming, hiking, and yoga—so that I'm more likely to actually complete a workout, and I'm making sure that I eat nutrient-dense foods to keep my energy up. It's early in the year, but if I can keep up with these strategies, I think that my research–administration–teaching–mentoring balance will improve, and that this balance will also enable me to be a more present partner and parent.

Women's and Gender Studies, as an interdisciplinary field, has paid attention to issues of underrepresentation of groups, and is committed to promoting a diverse faculty, particularly promoting the visibility and advancement of women of color. So how are we doing in the US? A recent National Women's Studies Association (NWSA) report, "Mapping Women's and Gender Studies," which partnered with the Ford Foundation and the National Opinion Research Center, found that 30.4 percent of Women's Studies faculty are faculty of color, compared with 19 percent of faculty nationally in other disciplines (National Women's Studies Association 2007).[8] This is a good trend for Women's and Gender Studies, but it still requires institutional commitment and effort to maintain and/or improve these numbers. There are, however, fewer data available to critically assess how Women's and Gender Studies, as a field, is faring in hiring individuals from other marginalized groups, including lesbians and other members from the LGBT community, physically challenged individuals, or men.

### Women's and Gender Studies Students—Who Are They?

Who's that sitting next to me?

There are lots of reasons why students come to Women's and Gender Studies. Think, for example, about your own learning path. What made you switch from, say, a Business major to Women's and Gender Studies? What identities do you have as a Women's and Gender Studies student and why? Although there is no existing comprehensive international database about Women's and Gender Studies students, we wanted to touch on who might be in the classroom with you (or who has been in the classroom with you). You may have been exposed to some of the ideas discussed in your Women's Studies class through one of your parents' involvement in women's and gender equality movements, your own experience with activism, or from classes in middle or high school. We are seeing more and more students who have had some positive contact

## THE GROWTH OF THE WOMEN'S AND GENDER STUDIES PH.D.

Over the past three decades, doctoral programs in Women's and Gender Studies have been evolving. There are currently 22 doctoral programs in Women's and Gender Studies. Some are dual-degree programs—for example, the University of Michigan offers a dual degree in Women's Studies and Psychology. The continued growth of these programs suggests a community of scholars and students engaged in ongoing questions that matter.

- Arizona State University (AZ): Gender Studies
- California Institute of Integral Studies (CA): Women's Spirituality
- Claremont Graduate University (CA): Women's Studies in Religion
- Clark Atlanta University (GA): Africana Women's Studies
- Emory University (GA): Women's Studies
- Indiana University, Bloomington (IN): Gender Studies
- Ohio State University (OH): Women's Studies
- Pennsylvania State University, University Park (PA): Women Studies
- Rutgers University, New Brunswick (NJ): Women's Studies
- State University of New York-Stony Brook, Buffalo (NY): Women's and Gender Studies
- Texas Woman's University, Denton (TX): Women's Studies
- University of Arizona (AZ): Women's Studies
- University of California, Los Angeles (CA): Gender Studies
- University of California, Santa Barbara (CA): Feminist Studies
- University of Iowa (IA): Women's Studies
- University of Kansas (KS): Women, Gender, and Sexuality Studies
- University of Kentucky (KY): Gender and Women's Studies
- University of Maryland, College Park (MD): Women's Studies (with five areas of study)
- University of Michigan, Ann Arbor (MI): four joint Ph.D. programs (Women's Studies and English, History, Psychology or Sociology)
- University of Minnesota, St. Paul/Twin Cities (MN): Feminist Studies
- University of Washington (WA): Interdisciplinary Gender, Women, and Sexuality Studies (and other chosen discipline)

For more detailed information, see the NWSA "Guide to Women's and Gender Studies" web page (www.nwsa.org/research/theguide/phd.php).

with Women's and Gender Studies prior to taking our courses. Some students enter Women's Studies already familiar with the key perspectives of the field. We think this trend is the fruition of the hard work of activists, educators, and many in the nonprofit sector who are committed to gender equity and the promotion of Women's Studies. Still, for many students, finding Women's Studies is an unanticipated discovery and an area of study with which they had not previously been familiar (unlike English, History, Education, Business, Communication, etc.).

The graduates in our survey comprise a good picture of Women's and Gender Studies students.

### Your Women's and Gender Studies Classroom: Data from Graduates

During the course of your undergraduate studies in WGST, you may have become close with the other students in your classes. You may have shared some intimate information about your experiences growing up, your thoughts and beliefs about controversial topics, and your hopes and fears about your life after graduation. Yet, what are some of the overall characteristics of Women's and Gender Studies graduates?

Women's and Gender Studies majors and minors at the undergraduate level are predominantly composed of female students,[9] although not all students identify as either "women" or "men." As gender and transgender politics have become more visible on college campuses, the gendered composition of our students has reflected this. Ideally, biological determinism should not play a role in who can major in Women's Studies, but as evidenced in the works of feminist scholars such as Emi Koyama (2003), debates still erupt in feminist academic and activist communities about whether men can be feminists and the role of transmen and transwomen in "female-centered" spaces.

Yet, the preponderance of females in Women's Studies should not be surprising, given the history of the field. Women's and Gender Studies offers the opportunity to study issues of power and gender dynamics in a way that supports many young women's learning trajectories. However, in the past several years, the male participation has risen, and we think that several factors are responsible for this. Due to the women's movement, more men have been raised in egalitarian households over the past three decades, and are generally interested in women's lives. Some male students come to view classes in Women's Studies as an extension of their interests shaped by family dynamics. Women, men, and transgendered students take Women's and Gender Studies courses and enjoy them enormously, and see that they can study in this interdisciplinary field. Additionally, male, female, and intersex students often take an Introduction to Women's Studies course as part of fulfilling general educational requirements and decide that they wish to take more. They may also find classes on masculinity and gender that are of interest. Many learn how the construction of gender cannot be seen in isolation, and therefore the study of masculinity is important for men, as well as for women, to understand the construction of gender for their own lives, and those of their peers.

According to our study, the overwhelming majority of Women's and Gender Studies students identify as biologically "female" (95 percent), followed by "male" (4 percent), with the rest identifying as "intersex" or "other." Even though many of our respondents did identify with traditional classifications of sex in the survey, the nature and placement of the question was raised as an issue by several participants:

> I'm a trans man, and I know you want me to say "female," but really, this question is worded awfully. And it sucks that the sex I was assigned at birth is regarded as more important than how I identify (which I assume you consider it to be, based on this being the second question in the survey).

Contemporary Women's and Gender Studies scholars have sought to question and challenge binary sex classifications; therefore, it is not surprising that some respondents do not identify with ascribed or "traditional" sex or gender categories.

The majority of the graduates who answered our survey were born in the United States (82 percent), with about 9 percent born in Canada. Other graduates hail from a variety of countries, including Germany, South Korea, Brazil, Australia, Kenya, Russia, Scandinavia, Japan, and China. After graduating with their degree in Women's and Gender Studies, the majority of those surveyed now live in the United States (83 percent), with about 2 percent residing in either the UK or Canada. Other places your fellow classmates may reside after graduation include Germany, Scandinavia, the Netherlands, South Korea, Spain, Italy, Trinidad and Tobago, or Ghana.

As for race and ethnic identities, the majority of Women's and Gender Studies graduates marked "white" (82 percent). About 5 percent of the graduates marked "black/African American," 3 percent identified as Hispanic/Latino, 4 percent claimed an Asian or Pacific Islander heritage, 1.5 percent claimed a Native American or Alaska Native ancestry, and less than 1 percent claimed a Middle Eastern identity. About 6 percent of those surveyed claimed a multiracial/multiethnic heritage, along with a few respondents who identified as Roma and Jewish. Survey respondents were given the opportunity to claim as many ethnic identities as they felt appropriate, as well as describing their racial/ethnic heritage in the "other" category. However, the classification system used also reflects the traditional "big five" categories commonly used in the United States by survey researchers and government entities. As the majority of Women's and Gender Studies graduates either were born or raised in the United States, these racial/ethnic categories may be familiar; yet, as recent debates over the census—and as raised in Women's and Gender Studies classrooms—have shown, these classifications do not capture the complex heritage of our graduates in the United States or Canada, nor in the world.

In addition to the mix of students in the Women's and Gender Studies classroom in terms of biological sex, racial/ethnic classifications, and countries of origin, the age of graduates varies as well. The majority of those in our survey (who all graduated between 1995 and 2010) were 23–26 years of age (31 percent) at the time of their graduation. Another 29 percent were 27–31 years of age, with 18 percent being 32–36 years of age at graduation. By comparison, the most prevalent range in which our graduates started their Women's and Gender Studies degree program is 18–22 years of age (84 percent). Therefore, more "traditional" aged undergraduate students are actively choosing Women's and Gender Studies as part of their degree selection process.[10]

While there has been a lot of debate about the institution of marriage, not only in the Women's and Gender Studies classroom, but also in the realm of politics, law, and media, as well as in families in the United States and abroad, only 29 percent of the graduates surveyed identified as "married." Another 2.1 percent identified as being in a formal, legal domestic partnership. The majority of those surveyed identified as either being "single, never married" (42 percent), being in an "informal" domestic arrangement and/or "living together" (19 percent). Only about 10 percent of those surveyed identified as either being divorced or in a dissolved civil union. As legal marriage or formal legal domestic partnerships are not uniformly available to everyone who participated in our survey, the "single, never married" majority may reflect this issue. Yet, many of those surveyed described their relationship status in other ways. It seems we currently lack a good term for those who are in long-term, long-distance relationships.

As the number of Women's and Gender Studies departments and programs have increased since its inception, we found that the majority of graduates surveyed were majors (61 percent), with minors comprising almost one-quarter (24 percent) of the sample. About 7.2 percent of the respondents indicated that they had a concentration in Women's and Gender Studies. We also acknowledge that internationally, a major or minor may not have an equivalent.

Many Women's and Gender Studies programs emphasize a global or multicultural perspective, and this is reflected in the fact that one-third of our respondents participated in an international studies or study-abroad experience. Of those who participated in undergraduate study abroad, 36.7 percent had some Women's and Gender Studies courses as part of their overseas curriculum.

While about one-third of Women's and Gender Studies graduates experienced an international studies program, 45 percent of graduates completed an internship during the course of the undergraduate experience. Of those who completed an internship, 58.5 percent received college credit for their internship.

After completing a degree in Women's and Gender Studies, there are a variety of ways that graduates stay in contact with their colleagues from their classes and degree programs. E-mail (58.8 percent) and social networking sites, particularly Facebook (53 percent), were the primary methods of communication. Yet, a fairly high number of graduates have face-to-face meetings (39.2 percent). Unfortunately, 27.4 percent of those surveyed have not stayed in contact with anyone since they graduated with their degree.

Many of our graduates had a variety of experiences in terms of getting prepared for their professional lives and careers. The majority of those who responded to the survey (40.1 percent) utilized campus career services. Another source of information on careers for our graduates was guest speakers (38.6 percent). About one-quarter of those surveyed (25.6 percent) received information from seminars. "Books/pamphlets"

### SPOTLIGHT: MATT EZZELL

Matt is an activist and professor, and was a Women's Studies major who graduated in 1995 from University of North Carolina at Chapel Hill. Women's Studies was not entirely foreign to him because he had a sister who graduated with a Women's Studies minor, and when he was in high school his mother went back for an MA in Literature, specializing in contemporary African American women's novels· "I saw how rewarding it was for them. I thought I'd take a class . . . to see what it was about." He also was interested in understanding his sister's lifelong struggle with eating disorders, which began as a young girl. By high school, Matt had an awareness that the way he and his sister were treated was different, based on their gender identities. This was a formative experience for him as a young man: "I really highlighted the modeling industry as the problem. I saw women who looked like my sister . . . I knew there was something wrong with the media and modeling industry. That was the start . . . the seed."

Soon after arriving at college, he took a Sociology class cross-listed with Women's Studies, "Introduction to Sex and Gender in Society":

> I went in thinking, this class is going to help me learn more about my sister's experience and it's going to help me be a better brother to her and help me make sense [and] understand what she is going through. And I definitely got pieces of that . . . But what I did not anticipate is that I learned more about myself as a man in this culture than I did about women. And that was transformative. It gave me a more informed critical lens to see the social world, it gave me more language to make sense of my experiences as a man and my sister. I never identified with the norms of dominant masculinity and did not know what to do with that. I tried to fit in and was uncomfortable with doing that. I grew up in a small town in North Carolina where football was king, and I did not play football and I had no desire to, and that was not easy and that marked me as different within the community of boys in that town, and finding Women's Studies was something that gave me [an understanding of] the social construction of gender, [which] was transformative. It showed me what it could mean to be a feminist and identify as a feminist.

We will return to Matt's story throughout this book.

and "websites" each accounted for 15.5 percent of our samples as a source of information about careers and professions. Sadly, 32.2 percent of our respondents indicated that their department or program did not offer career services. It seems that Women's and Gender Studies undergraduate departments and programs need to assess how they prepare students for life after their degree and develop resources to assist them in this endeavor.

After completing an undergraduate degree in Women's and Gender Studies, a notably high 57 percent of those who responded to the survey completed some graduate or professional degree courses.

During the past two decades, many Women's and Gender Studies departments and programs have been instrumental in supporting the development of Queer and Sexuality Studies (or allies of new inter-disciplinary perspectives). Many biologically identified or transgendered men find Women's and Gender Studies to be compatible with their sexual identities and interests. For example, many men participate in campus organizations and events directed by LGBT centers and/or women's centers. On many campuses, these entities have long-standing coopera-tive working relationships in which students gain internship or volunteer experience while simultaneously receiving credit in their Women's Studies units.

Ultimately, the Women's and Gender Studies classroom is a global classroom. In our experience, we have seen that our classes have become increasingly diverse in terms of social class, nationality, ethnicity, and sexual orientation. Over the course of your academic career, you are likely to be taking classes with students who have been shaped by a variety of experiences and social contexts.

### A New Kind of Student

The work that you have committed to in Women's and Gender Studies has a rich intellectual and social history. For the past four decades, the university has been producing a new type of student in higher education. We believe Women's and Gender Studies students are emerging as a type of educational pioneer (Luebke and Reilly 1995; Boxer and Stimpson 2001). What do we mean by this? Women's Studies' early twin goals of reaching across the disciplines to answer questions about gender and challenging the status of women were innovative in higher education.

Since that time, Women's and Gender Studies has developed classroom practices and pedagogical styles that have been adopted by many other disciplines. It has broadened the traditional liberal arts education to encompass a specific focus on inequality, power, and advocacy that continues to be distinctive. The student–professor relationship has also been rethought—moving from an expert–student relationship to a relationship of co-collaborators. Women's and Gender Studies has pushed for curricula transformation, and that translates into students who have been trained to learn multiple perspectives and to demonstrate the application of knowledge in pursuit of a more equitable society. It encourages students to evaluate their goals and values, as well as synthesize knowledge. The emphasis on synthesizing knowledge and applying it in new contexts is exciting to students, and encourages them to become involved in issues they care deeply about. A number of Women's and Gender Studies graduates discuss this as one of the primary components of their training that they value highly. As Celeste, a double major in Psychology and Women's Studies, explains:

> I find that Women's Studies training broadens your thinking—you start to see opportunities to improve the institutions/groups/etc. you are a part of; you begin to incorporate programs, etc. that are inspired by lessons you learn in Women's Studies.
>
> For example, in my sorority, KD [Kappa Delta], we have a Girl Scout troop that we do various activities with and, at the same time, we have been donating to the Dove Foundation in support of their campaign for "real beauty." After a class about the social construction of women's bodies and learning a great deal about eating disorders and distorted body images among young girls, I spoke with our leaders, and we began to have "workshops" with our Girl Scout troop during which we discussed "beauty" (kinds of beauty, what it means to a be a "beautiful person," etc.). My knowledge gained from this Women's Studies class, as well as the passion it excited in me surrounding this issue, sparked a cross-pollination of awareness in activism that hopefully encouraged healthy lifestyles and positive body images among young, active girls, who will soon be (or are already) "at risk" for succumbing to the many pressures regarding appearance that are faced by girls today.
>
> (Celeste, 2010, University of North Carolina at Chapel Hill)

Our research and framing about the unique role of Women's and Gender Studies students in higher education is complemented by discussions of how Women's and Gender Studies students view themselves. Narratives and vignettes can be found in the scholarly articles, magazines, online discussions, and several introductory textbooks in Women's Studies that have emerged over the past two decades.[11] One Women's Studies graduate, reflecting on applying her Women's Studies training now as an obstetrician and gynecologist, says that de-masking "unspoken assumptions" was an important lesson that she now uses in her work environment:

> Being realistic and intelligent about power relationships and inequities is another lesson of Women's Studies. Being a student of Women's Studies did not influence my career choice, [but] it helped shape my values, how I see the world, and what I see as my role in it as an African American woman. I value women as full members of society in whatever roles they choose. However, I recognize the world as gendered and unequal. I feel that I have a responsibility to change that status quo wherever possible . . . These values are neither objective nor neutral. But the fallacy of objectivity is another lesson of Women's Studies.
>
> (Thompson 2002: 634)

Another Women's Studies graduate has found that the training to examine how assumptions about gender shape the world has been useful after college: "I left the Women's Studies program at SUNY [State University of New York] New Paltz with energy and enthusiasm to go out into the world and make a difference in the lives of women." She joined the Peace Corps and discusses how her Women's Studies training led her to think critically about the challenges of working with women and children on health literacy, given many of the structural dimensions of their lives:

> My Women's Studies education gave me an understanding of the problems that women living in the Third World face. It also gave me insights into how grassroots level initiatives work. It was with these things in mind that I was able to reach as well as be taught by the women of The Gambia. I learned in Women's Studies the importance of listening and learning from women of different cultures. I knew that what I needed to do was to join the women in their work.
>
> (Rivera 2006: 634)

Her Women's Studies education allowed her to consider working in a participatory way with the women, to begin to understand the complexity of their lives as both distinctive and similar to her own. It also allowed her to re-evaluate what she thought about "women's work" and how underappreciated it was. Her training, she says, "enhanced my appreciation for the work women do and enabled me to bring to the world of women's work insights and ideas that will somewhat ease women's burdens" (Rivera 2006: 635).

A core theme of what you are hearing through these accounts is the role of what is often defined in higher education as "civic" engagement. Women's and Gender Studies students come from a long tradition of supporting students to understand and contribute to the social world. But how do we think more critically about the relationship between civic engagement and Women's and Gender Studies? To examine this concept further, we talked with Dr. Catherine M. Orr, Associate Professor and Chair of the Department of Women's Studies at Beloit College. She and several Women's and Gender Studies colleagues from around the country have been working on how to document the role of civic engagement in Women's Studies:

> Whether it's running a mentoring group for girls at a local junior high school, taking a leadership role on a collaborative media project to promote a neighborhood community center, or staffing a rape crisis center hotline, Women's Studies students bring a unique set of perspectives to their civic engagement work.

But, first, what is civic engagement?

Civic engagement is a catch-all term that describes learning that happens outside of the college or university classroom that benefits both the student (by expanding his or her abilities to apply knowledge across multiple contexts) and the community beyond the campus (by providing volunteer labor and cultivating the next generation of community-minded individuals). And whether it is called "service learning," "experiential education," "community-based learning," or "mentored internships" in non-profit organizations, civic engagement has become central to the mission of most U.S. colleges and universities. In fact, over 90 percent of students, administrators, faculty, and student affairs professionals agree that "preparing students to contribute to the community should be an essential goal of a college education" (Schneider 2009: ix).

What is different about civic engagement in Women's Studies? Women's Studies situates civic engagement in a unique curricular context. With the discipline's historical roots in activist movements, its social justice mandate, and its reflective approach to its own knowledge production, Women's Studies offers students a distinctive method for learning how to grapple with the tensions between theory and practice in civic engagement contexts. By encouraging critical reflection on, say, the values of "the community" or "the good citizen," a Women's Studies approach to civic engagement demands that students *analyze the historical and cultural foundations that create the need for their service in the first place*, as well as *interrogate their own motivations* to "help others."

For example, Tobi Walker, former program director of projects at Rutgers' Center for American Women and Politics, notes that in her service learning courses, she tells students that "community can be a problematic concept . . . [in that it] necessarily excludes, defining some individuals as 'inside' and some as 'outside'" (Walker 2000: 28). In this manner, Walker is asking her students to rethink the very concept of community as an inherent "good."

Analyzing the foundations of what so often goes unquestioned is at the heart of civic engagement in Women's Studies. Following this principle, a Women's Studies professor might ask her student, who is doing a service-learning project at a community center in a poor neighborhood, "How is the need for a community center in this particular neighborhood a product of prior exclusions? And how does knowing about the historical and cultural legacies of this particular community inform how you do your work there?"

In addition to bringing analytical concepts to bear on what the student encounters in any community-based context, civic engagement in Women's Studies requires some amount of personal reflection, in which the student is asked to consider how his or her own historical and cultural location (e.g. gender expression, racialized identity, regional bias, class interests, sexual orientation, professional experience, level of education, age, etc.) has an impact on what he or she is able to learn from and do for others in any given context. Without such self-awareness on the part of students, differences of race, culture, class, etc. can too often disrupt their best efforts to "do good." In this way, Women's Studies teaches students entering communities that are not their own that: (1) they are products of historical and cultural forces; (2) these forces form both their sense of selves and differences among individuals but are neither neutral nor simply chosen; and (3) the students themselves are responsible for attempting to negotiate as best they can the impacts of these differences in that community-based context.

Ultimately, the goal of a Women's Studies approach to civic engagement is to prepare students to make their classroom learning relevant, worthwhile, and, in the best cases, truly transformational for themselves and others.

### Women's and Gender Studies Today: Contributing to and Fulfilling the Academic Mission

Women's and Gender Studies, through its focus on what voices have been excluded from knowledge, has consistently posed valuable questions to higher education. These courses also tend to meet other university-wide requirements that colleges and universities collectively consider to be important. In fact, the expectations that universities and colleges have for their students are often reflected in the front pages of your college curriculum under the description of the core curriculum courses you must satisfy in order to graduate. While the specific courses offered at your particular institution may be unique, the curriculum for your college and university has largely been influenced by a growing interest of educators and state officials alike to produce a well-rounded student who has been exposed to a variety of perspectives. These concerns get codified into standards that are encouraged by accrediting boards, state legislatures, state and university systems, and boards of regents and trustees. Women's and Gender Studies has played an important role in shaping what a civically engaged, globally competent student looks like with liberal arts training.

WGST majors and minors receive instruction and coursework that satisfies both global and diversity requirements for outside review boards, and institutional demands as well.

### The Global Presence of Women's and Gender Studies

Women's and Gender Studies is flourishing in many places around the world. In the above section, we drew heavily on how majors, minors, etc. are organized in the U.S. system. When we look outside the US, we see some differences in how "undergraduates" are trained globally. In many parts of the world (such as the UK), undergraduate education is post-secondary education up to the level of a master's degree. Below, we provide a snapshot of both established programs and programs that have emerged more recently.

- The Institute for Women's Studies in the Arab World (IWSAW) at the Lebanese American University offers six courses that address the topic of Women's and Gender Studies: "Introduction to Gender Studies," "Representations of Women in the Arts and the Media," "Women and Economic Power," "Women in the Arab World: Sociological Perspectives," "Psychology of Women: A Feminist Perspective," and "Issues and Debates in Feminist Theory." They are in the process of preparing a graduate program (MA) in Gender Studies (see http://iwsaw.lau.edu.lb).
- The Center for Gender Studies at the University of Basel, Switzerland, offers a bachelor's, master's and Ph.D. program in Gender Studies. The Center for Gender Studies was founded in 2001 and is chaired by Professor Dr. Andrea Maihofer. Prior to 2001, generally, Gender Studies was not widely institutionalized in Switzerland. Since then, the Center has become an independent unit in the Department of Social Sciences and Philosophy in the Humanities. In 2005, the Gender Studies bachelor's, master's and Ph.D. programs were successfully evaluated by international experts commissioned by the University of Basel. Alumni often send their publications (published doctoral dissertations or research results) to electronic newsletters or platforms (e.g. www.gendercampus.ch) in order to announce their findings to a wide audience. There are former students in government jobs as diversity and/or equity managers and others who informally put their gender expertise to use in their specific job situations—in the Federal Department of Public Health, for example. The Center offers the possibility of a graduate degree in Gender Studies (in cooperation with other Swiss universities; see Center for Gender Studies University of Basel (Switzerland) 2014). The Ph.D. program at the University of Basel consists of about 14 members. Many postgraduates find work in the public sector, administration, or communication,

or find employment as gender equality experts at larger companies. The master's degree in Gender Studies (always in combination with another major) provides a broad spectrum of possibilities after graduation.

- The University of Auckland's Women's Studies program has been reorganized into a more streamlined Gender Studies program. It is run under the auspices of the Anthropology Department and consists mostly of Social Sciences courses with a few Litera ture courses available on a less-regular basis. It became available for a major, minor, BA honors (this is a graduate degree in New Zealand), MA, and Ph.D. in 2011. The undergraduate programme consists of eight courses (see University of Auckland 2014).

- Women's and Gender Studies is offered through the Institute for Gender and Development Studies at the University of the West Indies, St. Augustine Unit. This is an autonomous multidiscip-linary and interdisciplinary unit located in the Office of the Vice-Chancellor of the University. Currently, a minor in Gender Studies or a minor in Gender and Development are offered. Many of the students enroll in the graduate program and pursue a postgrad-uate diploma in Gender—or do a master's or a Ph.D., or go to law school. Others find work in the nonprofit sector, work in local and regional nongovernmental organizations (NGOs), work for international organizations such as the UN, UNDP, IDRC, UNIFEM, and UNICEF, or enter into public service, getting employment in government ministries that deal with gender and gender affairs (see http://sta.uwi.edu/igds).

As these examples show, Women's and Gender Studies programs, departments, majors, and concentrations vary considerably around the world. Gabriele Griffin, editor of *Doing Women's Studies: Employment Opportunities, Personal Impacts, and Social Consequences* (2005), has been instrumental in illuminating Women's and Gender Studies programs and graduates in the European Union context. Not only is Griffin able to describe the nuances of Women's and Gender Studies graduates and programs in the UK, but the impact of U.S. Women's and Gender Studies' trends abroad.

## POINT OF VIEW

## WOMEN'S STUDIES IN THE UK—THE POSTGRADUATE EXPERIENCE IN THE 2000s

Gabriele Griffin, University of York, UK

Women's Studies has transformed scholarship in the UK as much as in the US. But there are significant differences: in the UK, in 2013, in contrast to the US, there are very few learning routes, programs or centers (there are no departments) with the title Women's—or, indeed, Gender—Studies. This discipline flourished in the 1980s and 1990s, but then experienced a steep decline in terms of actual named programs.[12] Simultaneously, women's and gender research has expanded massively, and there is a vast related inter/national infrastructure in terms of journals, conferences, publications, and websites. Feminist work has become firmly embedded in most Social Sciences and Humanities disciplines, and in this sense it represents a success story. But otherwise, feminism and Women's and Gender Studies are much less overtly present than they used to be in the neoliberal university as it is currently articulated, not least because strongly ideologically invested academic agendas, and the feminist one falls under that category, are out of favor in our market-driven economies.

One interesting way—not so much discussed in the U.S. context—in which this has impacted on British academe where higher education itself has become an international commodity is that Women's and Gender Studies centers or institutes, such as the one at the University of York where I work, attract female (and occasionally male) students from around the world, including from countries such as Jordan, Malaysia, Russia, Ghana, Thailand, Hong Kong, Taiwan, China, Korea, India, Pakistan, Bangladesh . . . Many of these countries have major modernization and change projects, and a gender agenda is part of the requirement of international funders such as the World Bank, the United Nations, etc., not least to encourage female participation in the paid labour market. Hence, students from such countries are often supported by their governments or other funders to take Women's Studies postgraduate degrees. Such students are often in their 30s and 40s, they already have a career in their home countries either in a university or in a government body, and they come to UK centers to learn about gender theory and to conduct research on issues relevant to their countries, frequently in relation to domestic violence, women's education, women's employment, sexuality, or issues of poverty and development. In these preoccupations, they can be quite removed from the concerns around identity, queer studies, body politics, fat studies, etc., which, much more commonly, fuel "native" students' interests. Such international students may also come with strongly held beliefs, including religious ones, about women and femininity. For instance, at the end of a session on the nature/nurture debate, one student rejected, out of hand, the notion of socialization, maintaining, "It's God, isn't it?" Often, these International students are married and have (left behind in their home country) children, neither of which is common among the "native" students. Indeed, being or getting married may be the condition on which they are "allowed" by their families to pursue higher education. The encounter with Western academic demands and standards, ways of conducting research, and expecting debate may be quite new to these students, and certainly transforms their outlook on life. Some want to stay and move into academe in the UK, but such jobs are very difficult to come by, for any students, in the current recessionary decade, and given visa restrictions. Others are required to return home and work in the university or government context that sponsored them. This can be difficult, as academic cultures are radically different across countries, and (re)adjusting to, for example, strongly hierarchized patriarchal cultures where women have little say is difficult.

"Home" students also face difficulties, as there are very few academic jobs around, and such jobs continue to be the most desired. Since the late 1990s, it has become more common in the Humanities, too, to have projects requiring postdoctoral researchers, and many current Women's Studies students who want to remain in academe have at least one period as a junior researcher on a project. This enables them to beef up their publications and academic experiences record, and from there they tend to find academic jobs.

After reading Griffin's analysis of Women's and Gender Studies in the UK, you may want to consider how similar this perspective may be for you depending on your cultural background, as well as give you areas to consider if you want to pursue graduate education in Women's and Gender studies in the UK.

## Graduates Speak to You

So far in this chapter, you have learned some of the historical context that contributed to the development of Women's and Gender Studies in higher education, time-traveled back to an early Women's Studies class, and discovered the role that Women's and Gender Studies has played in shaping a new kind of student. You are committed to Women's and Gender Studies but may be wondering, "How will this training help and support my interests overall?" You might feel daunted or overwhelmed at the possible ways to apply your interest in WGST. You may not be receiving positive support for your choice. We thought this might be a good time for you to hear how graduates from our survey reflect on their choices. If you ever face doubts or feel challenged, you are not alone! In our survey, we asked graduates: "What advice would (or do) you tell other students or friends considering a course of study or degree in Gender and/or Women's Studies?" While we received many emphatic responses that said "Do it!" and "Go for it!" below we highlight some of our longer and more detailed answers:

> It's a fantastic interdisciplinary degree that gives you the communication skills employers need. You'll use these skills the rest of your life. Put it together with a foreign language, internships and study abroad and you can't be beat. Do what you love. Follow your bliss ... A Women's Studies degree is a fabulous, well-rounded liberal arts course of study, and I would do it again in a heartbeat.
>
> (2003, WMST major, Hollins University)

> Please study Women's and Gender Studies because it applies to the threads of our making as humans. I do not for one minute regret doing a minor in Women's and Gender Studies; it changed my perspective on the world for the better. Women's and Gender Studies impacts every part of our lives and expands one's views and intelligence regarding such areas as the workforce, education, domesticity, violence, poverty, and love. Women's and Gender Studies is not only about human rights for females, but also about how humans interact with one another in every sense. It teaches the history of nations and can help you to better understand how, for instance, racism, sexism, and heterosexism affect our everyday lives.
>
> (2009, WMST minor, St. Norbert College)

> Major in what you believe in. Job markets are always changing. You will have many jobs. And if you study something you are passionate about, the chances are at least some of those jobs you will have will be deeply fulfilling.
>
> (2003, Gender Studies major, University of Southern California)

> I would encourage more men to participate because Gender Studies isn't just about women, nor should it be only the focus of women. If some men knew that feminism was really just about equality, then I think we'd have a happier world.
>
> (2005, Gender Studies major, University of Notre Dame)

I wouldn't hesitate to recommend it. It has certainly added a dimension to my life that I wouldn't have anticipated. I didn't get into this until I was in my 40s. I can't imagine how my life would have been different if I had been able to do this degree right out of high school.

(1996, WMST major, University of British Columbia)

Women's health is a fascinating, empowering area to be in, and nursing is a profession with great potential for intellectual growth, career advancement, and flexibility. I would not have arrived at women's health nursing if I had not studied Women's Studies first.

(2005, WMST and French, double major,
Dickinson College)

I have talked to a few undergraduate students who worry about the employability of Women's Studies graduates (or whose parents worry about this). I tell people that from my own experience and perspective, employers (and grad school admissions committees) in many arenas are less interested in what someone's undergrad major was, and more interested in skills like critical thinking, writing, communicating with people of diverse backgrounds and perspectives, etc. Women's Studies courses provide a lot of opportunities to develop these kinds of skills, and can prepare students for a range of future career paths.

(2003, Gender and WMST double major,
Oberlin College)

I found it personally interesting, but I also knew I was going to law school after I completed my undergraduate degree. Thus, for me, it was a good forum for learning critical analysis, researching, and writing, as well as developing an understanding of multiple perspectives of an issue or topic. No doubt there are more opportunities to do interesting work or further studies in this space now than there were 15 years ago.

From a more personal perspective, my mother was Chinese, and came from an arranged marriage in which my grandmother was an object and who could only speak when spoken to. My father was from a very traditional patriarchal Scandinavian house- hold who favored sons over daughters. It was eye-opening for me to realize I could do and be so much more than what I had grown up to believe. I loved challenging traditional ideas, rules, and norms! The Women's Studies curriculum was great for me—it was in my undergraduate studies that I began what has been a lifelong journey of self-discovery, trying to understand who I am, what I have been told is me, what and who society expects me to be, and what and who I'd like to be going forward. I would probably have undergone a similar journey of exploration in any case, but a Women's Studies degree gave me the space and frame of reference in which to structure my thinking in more meaningful ways.

In addition to changing the way I view myself as a woman, it has changed the way I view other women in all walks of life. I do a lot of international travel for my work, with a focus on environmental and social issues in emerging markets I am particularly sensitive to the role of women in their communities and thinking about how women are a vastly underserved segment of the population in terms of access to capital and banking. They are also the most likely segment of the population, along with children, to be negatively impacted by the development of major projects or by poor health and safety standards of employers in their local communities. Further, they are less likely to be able to be heard in the absence of appropriate grievance mechanisms. I am always thinking about how we can include these types of considerations at the top levels of business decision-making in banking institutions that finance the companies and projects in these communities, or provide the financial products to serve and provide access to capital to the individuals in these communities.

I would further add that by challenging traditional notions of what it means to be a woman, and what we understand about sexuality, my Women's Studies courses opened my mind to alternative approaches to gender roles and sexuality. This has made me generally a more open and accepting person over the years. Coming from a small, very close-minded, conservative, provincial town in Michigan, this was an important step for me in recognizing, being more sympathetic to, and accepting "nontraditional" lifestyles. I am so much richer for opening my world to different people with different views, value systems, and lifestyles. I take this into my personal and professional life and, given the international nature of my work and extensive travel I have done on a personal level, I have found that I am intellectually interested in and curious about people everywhere and what makes them who they are—nature/nurture, cultural norms and influences, geography, race, creed, origins, sexuality, etc. This makes me a better person, a better professional, a better advocate.

(1995, WMST major, University of Michigan)

We think that the last respondent captures a frame of mind the Women's and Gender Studies education strives for—supporting students to live their lives fully, take on meaningful employment, and speak up on issues that they care about. The benefits of Women's Studies continuing to thrive in higher education include creating students who are ready for deep civic engagement and a vibrant community of scholars that contribute cutting-edge knowledge to the most pressing societal problems.

## ANSWERS FOR QUIZ: HOW MUCH DO YOU KNOW ABOUT THE HISTORY OF WOMEN'S STUDIES?

1. San Diego State University.
2. True. Most professors in the 1970s who taught Women's Studies did not get paid for their classes.
3. Feminist pedagogy is a set of theoretical assumptions about how to interact with students, and encourages a participatory and personal approach to how knowledge is produced in the classroom.
4. Women's and Gender Studies, as a field, believes that research, theory, and practice are interconnected and important for developing new knowledge, both inside and outside the academy.
5. The National Women's Studies Association is the professional organization of scholars and practitioners who teach and research in the field of Women's and Gender Studies.
6. San Diego State University.
7. Many early Women's Studies professors were involved in social protest movements of the 1960s and 1970s. Also, more female students began attending colleges and universities during the 1970s and brought social justice questions to the classroom.
8. Over 50 countries have colleges and universities that offer Women's and Gender Studies degrees.
9. True. Community colleges play a vital role in training students in Women's and Gender Studies.
10. Topics in one of the first Women's Studies classes on women's health might have included: women's experience of discrimination in the medical system, the history of midwives in the sixteenth and seventeenth centuries, and the lack of female doctors.

## POINT OF VIEW CONTRIBUTORS FOR CHAPTER 1

**Dr. Mel Michelle Lewis** is an assistant professor of Women, Gender, and Sexuality Studies and affiliate faculty in Africana Studies at Goucher College. Her research focuses on the intersections of race, gender, and sexuality, specifically addressing black queer feminist thought, identity and performance, and feminist critical pedagogies.

**Adriane Brown** is Assistant Professor and Director of Women's Studies and Director of the Women's Resource Center at Augsburg College. She is proud to note that all three of her degrees are in Women's Studies, and fully believes in the value of the interdisciplinary, intersectional modes of inquiry that characterize Women's Studies as a field. Her research interests lie at the intersections of girlhood studies, media studies, subjectivity theory, and life narrative theory.

**Gabriele Griffin** is a Professor at the University of York in the Centre for Women's Studies, UK. Her main research interests are in women's contemporary cultural production, women's theatre, diaspora studies, narrative and identity, and research methods in the arts and humanities.

 ## YOUR TURN: EXERCISES

### FINDING OUT MORE ABOUT YOUR LEARNING COMMUNITY

If you are a recent major or minor, we suggest that you take the time to become more familiar with the history of your program or department. Don't be shy! Go now and investigate your Women's and Gender Studies program if you have not done so already. Find out if there is an undergraduate advisor in the program. Usually, there is an assigned faculty member who has the responsibility of orienting students to the program. Arrange to speak with that person, visit the department or program's website, and gather the available literature on your program. You can even request to meet with the chair or director of the program. Students are often hesitant to do this, but directors and chairs truly enjoy talking with students about their curricula and how they can serve your interests. You can also talk with a professor whose class you are taking.

If you are not a recent major or minor, you want seek to deepen your rapport with a particular professor by asking them to share with you a little about their journey to teaching Women's and Gender Studies. There are many different routes to becoming a professor, and hearing several different stories can deepen your understanding and appreciation for your professors. Here are some starting questions for one-on-one conversations with professors. Begin by asking them about their own academic experiences: "What did you major in as an undergraduate?" "What did you study as a graduate student?" "What is your research about?" "How does it connect to women's lives, gender, or sexuality?" "How did you come to teach in Women's and Gender Studies?" "What professional conferences do you typically attend to present your research?" "What professional conferences do you attend?" "Do you attend the National Women's Studies Association conference? If so, what do you find useful about attending?" "Does the department offer credit or other support to undergraduate students to attend academic conferences?" "How does the program or department's curriculum fit within the college or university's mission and general education requirements?"

Make it a practice to try to meet with all your professors at least once during the semester. Attending your professor's assigned office hours can go a long way in building rapport. Chatting with your professor about the program and your interests allows the professor to get to know you, too. This is a good practice for students to take up. After all, in the spirit of Adrienne Rich's (1979) powerful words, Women's and Gender Studies students should not just get an education, but claim one. You may find that a semester or year later, you would like to ask your professor for a letter of recommendation for a job application or for graduate school. It would be best to do so after having established a relationship. That professor will remember you and be able to craft a more personal and effective letter in support of you.

If you were fascinated by the section, "Back In the Day," undertake a fun research project by exploring the kinds of courses that were taught (along with any existing syllabi), when your department or program was first founded. What similarities and differences can you can see in the types of courses offered between then and now?

## Notes

1. See Kolmar and Bartkowski (2010).
2. Praxis has its roots in ancient philosophy and the writings of Aristotle. Later it was associated with nineteenth-century Marxist thought, as well as with twentieth-century neo-Marxist writers such as Georg Lukács and Paulo Freire.
3. Here is a sampling of organizations in professional disciplines that promote gender equity:
   Feminist Philosophers: http://feministphilosophers.wordpress.com
   Western Association of Women Historians: www.wawh.org
   Association of Women in Psychology: www.awpsych.org
   Organization of Women Architects: www.owa-usa.org
   Women in Science and Engineering (various websites): http://cs-www.cs.yale.edu/homes/tap/sci-women-groups.html
4. The term "pedagogy" refers to theories about teaching and learning; "feminist pedagogy" has been the preferred term in Women's Studies.
5. See Enke (2012: 1).
6. See Henderson and Johnson (2005: 6).
7. See Collins (2007: 18).

8. This figure is based on a National Center for Education Statistics (NCES) report published in 2003 on post-secondary faculty at degree-granting institutions (see National Women's Studies Association 2007).
9. The use of the word "female" is intentional here.
10. Unfortunately, we did not inquire on the survey as to whether students declared their major/minor/concentration prior to attending college or university, after their first Women's and Gender Studies course, or during their matriculation process.
11. See the work of Australian Women's Studies researcher MaryAnn Dever (2004), *Ms.* magazine's ongoing collecting of responses by Women's and Gender Studies graduates to the question "What has women's studies meant to your life? And what are you currently doing with your women's studies degree?" (available at www. msmagazine. com), Luebke and Reilly (1995), and vignettes from various Women's Studies students presented in Kesselman, McNair, and Schniedewind (2008).
12. See Griffin (2009) and Hemmings (2011).

# 2
# DEVELOPING THE CORE OF
# YOUR ACADEMIC CAREER
## COURSEWORK, INTERNSHIPS,
## STUDY ABROAD, AND MORE

How are you claiming your education? How can you make the most of your education through courses and other possibilities that may be open to you?

In this chapter, we take it as a given that you are already a declared major, minor, or concentrator, and have some practical knowledge of what is required of you.

What this chapter offers is a guidepost to begin to reflect on and assess how your training is serving you, and what possibilities and opportunities to deepen your training exist that you have not thought about. We discuss the metaphorical heart of Women's and Gender Studies: electives, internships, praxis projects, and co-curricular opportunities. We also get you in gear to ask thoughtful questions of what you are learning. We introduce you to the core pathways that Women's and Gender Studies graduates often pursue post-graduation—sustainer, synthesizer, and evolver—based on our research, and invite you to muse about what features of a particular pathway you might currently be on.

Let us say you have taken the required introduction to a Women's and Gender Studies class, an elective, and a feminist theory class. What is next? How do you make choices to focus on areas of interest?

We have seen some students follow a teacher they like and take every course possible. That provides both a rapport and a deep pool of knowledge in one or more subjects. However, we also want you to be intentional and craft a plan for your academic career that connects with your overall interests.

## Core Courses and Cross-Listed Courses from Across the University

As you learned in the last chapter, one reason why Women's and Gender Studies has developed an interdisciplinary model is that during its formation, scholars saw that all the disciplines presented either biased knowledge about women or that women were missing from the discipline altogether. No single disciplinary perspective could correct this neglect. Thus, Women's and Gender Studies argues that the sum of knowledge is greater than its parts. You will usually have a broad array of electives to choose from. In many undergraduate programs, you will find courses on globalization and women, women and health, gender and communication, leadership and women, feminist research methods, and gender in science. Depending on your institution, you may see cross-listed courses on women and business, and women and public health. Increasingly, classes in Sexuality Studies are also offered and administered in Women's and Gender Studies programs and departments.[1]

The nature of interdisciplinary study allows you to deepen your perspective in, for example, gender and politics by taking cross-listed classes in public policy, political science, and communication. Taking elective courses also allows for comparative perspectives, such as: "What are the driving questions that political science raises about women and gender versus those raised in anthropology?

By the middle of your academic career, you want to ask yourself the questions: "What am I building toward?" "How do the courses I have taken fit in with my overall interests?" "What is missing or what types of learning opportunities have I not yet explored?" If you are a double major in Women's and Gender Studies and another discipline: "Where do these areas meet and create intellectual synergy for me?"

## The Internship or Practicum Experience

Theory is intimately entwined and elevated with practice. This philosophy has shaped Women's and Gender Studies, and helped move students out of the classroom and into the world. Women's and Gender Studies is also committed to reducing hierarchy and power asymmetries, and to raising awareness about organizations (and organizational forms) that have helped foster and maintain social change. Thus, it is important for students to experience activism firsthand by working with activists/ mentors/potential employers. Students can then compare and contrast their on-the-job experiences with those they may have studied in class. Ultimately, Women's and Gender Studies fosters learning opportunities that support students in their explorations of how to bridge theory and practice.

An internship provides you with valuable work experience in a given field. Internships usually have a faculty mentor or coordinator to act as a liaison between the organization providing the internship and you, the student. You are typically awarded university credits for the semester you work as an intern. When asked about their most valuable school experiences, aside from being in the classroom, many students describe an internship that helped them put into practice what they were learning in class. Maria, a former student of Michele's, agrees: "I can honestly say that interning was one of the most rewarding experiences I have had at Carolina." Maria interned for a lawyer who specialized in divorce, custody, and domestic violence cases. She learned how to do formal tasks such as preparing and filing Certificates of Service, the etiquette of a courtroom, and legal terminology. One of the most valuable lessons for Maria was an assignment that was given to her. The main lawyer (and another Women's Studies intern) had discovered the lack of compiled information available to victims of sexual assault or rape on the UNC campus. Throughout the semester, Maria and the other interns worked on compiling a brochure to help students on campus know their options and how to proceed if ever assaulted. They worked with the Dean of Students office, Campus Counseling and Wellness Services, the Carolina Women's Center, and referenced the Honor Code. She felt that it was an important contribution to gather the plethora of resources into one brochure:

> Hopefully, with the distribution of this brochure around campus, our efforts will help one person take the action that is right for him or her.
>
> (Maria, 2009, University of North Carolina
> at Chapel Hill)

Employers typically look for candidates who have conducted an internship in their professional field of interest. Internships are also a great opportunity for students to find out what they might *not* want to do. Each of us has had conversations with students who came to Women's and Gender Studies after finishing coursework, or even graduating in another field, only to find that what they once thought was their dream career was, in reality, a nightmare. For example, students who thought their gift was counseling discovered that they had a talent for grant-writing and data analysis. Others were able to channel their fears of public speaking into a persona that shone during public presentations.

Internships are a main way that many in our survey found direction to take the next step.

In the following Spotlight, Saswati Sakar discusses her experience with an internship, and how it provided her both tangible skills and a pathway to exploring more of her interests.

## SPOTLIGHT: SASWATI SAKAR

For me, social justice work evolved through an ongoing trajectory—where every step along the route further crystalized my commitment to feminist work. I grew up in Kolkata—a city in Eastern India—with strong sociopolitical ambience. I grew up questioning, analyzing, debating—which in so many ways prepared me for my graduate degree in Philosophy. However, it wasn't until my graduate years in Kolkata that I got introduced to Women's and Gender Studies. We were the first batch of students who were introduced to a master's class called "Feminist Studies." Learning about the feminist concepts and theories, the importance of dismantling binaries was exciting. I was convinced that I wanted to pursue my second graduate degree in the field. At the time, Women's and Gender Studies—as a branch of social science/humanities—was yet to make its way to a formal graduate level coursework in our state, and there were few near me that I could access. Hence, I decided to relocate to the US to pursue my master's degree in Women's Studies. I found myself going to Minnesota—a state with a rich history of advocacy around violence against women, home to a graduate program at Minnesota State University, Mankato that "grew out of the feminist movements of the 1960s and 1970s." What an exciting transition! The two years of my graduate coursework at Minnesota State University, Mankato helped me formulate a strong theoretical foundation, and critical pedagogical framework for social change work. It gave me the tools to look at social justice work from a global, anti-oppression framework. I wanted to learn more about its practical application, but how? That is where the role of internship was so helpful to me. Internships help you figure out what kinds of skills you have, what exactly you are good at, and where you want to go next

I was able to obtain an internship at the Feminist Press in NYC, an innovative feminist publishing house that gave me direction. My internship at the Feminist Press exposed me to an enormous volume of global literature that looked at women's experience of violence through a politically nuanced framework. I deepened my critical thinking skills and also learned some hands-on skills of project management. Inspired by that experience, I decided for my master's thesis to look at the post-menopausal lived experiences of South Asian women from Kolkata, and how social perceptions and stigma further reinforces the gender binary and patriarchal stereotypes. The process of thesis-writing started with an epiphany where I realized the discomfort I felt in discussing female bodily processes. The thesis was a journey for me that crystallized my passion to work on gender-based violence and challenge the existing stereotypes, myths, and misinformation that further perpetrate violence against women. Instead of pursuing more graduate work, I decided I wanted to work with my own community—the South Asian immigrant community—which led me into my position at Manavi, a South Asian community-based violence against women organization. In my role as a Technical Assistance and Training Manager at Manavi, I managed the development and delivery of trainings nationwide, oversaw two federally funded technical assistance programs, administered Manavi's research initiatives, led a transnational policy advocacy coalition on women's rights issues, and served on the Faculty of Advocacy Learning Center—a national advocacy training project conducted in partnership with Praxis International and Office of Violence Against Women (DOJ). Through my work at Manavi, I realized the complexity of the stigma associated with sexual violence, and how the larger community continues to remain silent.

All through these years, I felt thankful to the ways my degree in Women's Studies helped me analyze and understand this work differently, by underscoring the value of conscious-raising, constructive criticism, and dialoguing within the global anti-oppression/social-justice framework.

## Praxis or Activism Project

Another element of some Women's and Gender Studies programs is a praxis or activism project. As discussed earlier, praxis is the concept of putting theory into action. Over the course of your degree, certain topics or research questions may continually resonate with you and make you want to spring into action! Praxis, activism, or collective action projects allow students in either an independent study or formalized class structure to pursue original research, or to initiate activism on their campus or in the community.

Depending upon the goal of the class, you often have a choice of working independently or as a group on a project. For example, some classes might encourage independent research as a way for students to develop the ability to be self-directed. Other departments recognize that group praxis or collective action projects are characteristic of most organizational structures. Sometimes, decision-making structures are traditionally organized and others seemingly have no organizational form. These courses allow you to set the parameters of your project, as well as determine the rules of group interaction and of feminist principles of consensus. These projects also demand that you complete the project to the best of your ability over the course of the semester and present your accomplishments for evaluation by your peers and professors.

## Capstone Course or Honors Thesis

Capstone courses—or honors theses—vary greatly from campus to campus, but you can be sure of one thing: they are designed for you to really explore a subject that fascinates you. At some institutions, a capstone course is a senior seminar that focuses exclusively on a particular theme. On other campuses, the course is used to connect students' learning experiences with projects that are outside the classroom. The honors thesis, or senior capstone project, usually allows a third- or fourth-year student a focused amount of time on one project of interest. Some departments or programs may incorporate a feminist methods or methodology course in addition to, or as part of, the capstone course. For example, students may be asked to perform original research as part of a capstone course that addresses how feminist research approaches differ from other disciplinary perspectives. A senior capstone project may be completed alone or in collaboration with other students in your cohort or class.

Honors theses are usually researched and written by one student. If you were interested in pursuing an honors thesis, you would probably need to apply toward the end of your junior year. A high grade point average and a research class are usually the standard requirements. This is a great option for students interested in research or extended creative activity, and who want to work intensely with a faculty member, typically over the course of a year. You will form a committee, usually comprising your faculty advisor and main person responsible for helping you with the project, and one or two other faculty members.

At the end of the yearlong researching and writing process, you meet with your committee to officially defend the central arguments you have made in the honors thesis. Two or more faculty members serve on the committee and ask you questions for an assigned time period. The purpose of the defense or oral presentation at the end of the process is to allow you the opportunity to present your work and critically discuss the research process. This can sometimes be an emotional and powerful experience—conveying to others the passion you have for the subject you chose to study so intensely.

In sum, an honors thesis provides you with an excellent opportunity to work on research, writing, and presentation skills. It also may provide you with opportunities for publishing and/or presentation at an academic conference. You may also use a chapter of an honors thesis for a writing sample for graduate school. If you are a junior and think you might want to start an honors thesis project, do not hesitate to talk with your mentor or a faculty member about the requirements.

## Study Abroad

An old adage states that travel is one of the best teachers. We live in an interconnected, global world that relies on informed global citizens. Study abroad (also known as education abroad)—another type of applied learning possibility—is increasingly becoming an accessible and affordable option for many students. More students are traveling abroad for a semester or longer than in previous decades. We think studying abroad deserves important consideration from anyone interested in Women's and Gender Studies. Over one-third of graduates we surveyed said that their study-abroad experience was connected to work in Women's and Gender Studies.

Your college, university, and/or program may offer the option of studying abroad. Given its institutional arrangement, it may have partnered with another organization or university to provide you with a direct experience in that country. The more common way for a student to pursue this option is by visiting the study-abroad office (or equivalent) on campus. This office should be able to direct you to gender-specific programs of study at other universities. According to Caryn Lindsay, Director of International Programs of Elizabeth and Wynn Kearney International Center at Minnesota State University, Mankato, if you are considering education abroad, you should begin planning your experience early in your college or university career. Besides applying for financial aid and other scholarships, it is important to speak with your academic advisor regarding college credit and how your international courses will satisfy degree requirements. Often, study-abroad program courses satisfy general education requirements. Therefore, your upper division and specific degree requirements will be achieved at the university or college from which you will graduate. Organizations your study-abroad office may refer you to in your search for international educational opportunities include the Council on International Education (CIEE, www.ciee.org) and the American Institute for Foreign Study (AIFS, www.aifs.com). Both of these organizations offer programs that have specific courses in Women's and Gender Studies and LGBT Studies. For example, some of the courses listed for study abroad in fall 2010 and spring 2011 in Stellenbosch, South Africa, include:

- Global Health 214/314 (3) HIV and AIDS: A South African Perspective;
- English 344/444 (2) Queer Studies: An Introduction;
- English 314/414 (2) Women Writers Interrogating Empire;
- courses in political science regarding transition and conflict; and
- courses in conservation ecology.

All the courses are taught in English, yet students can also pursue language studies in courses ranging from French, German, and Spanish to Mandarin and Xhosa. Besides courses, the Study Abroad Program at Stellenbosch University also offers service learning opportunities, as well as a certificate.

Your study-abroad office will be able to direct you to an incredible array of options for traveling. Additionally, you may want to talk with a financial aid officer to find if various kinds of financial aid are applicable to potential study-abroad opportunities. At the end of the chapter, we offer some programs that may help with financial assistance to study abroad.

Besides study-abroad opportunities offered by international organizations, some departments offer courses developed by their faculty (usually during winter break, spring break, or summer) on a specific international topic and/or experience. Often, this course may relate to your professor's current area of research, or an area in which he or she is considered an expert. The benefit of studying abroad can include credit for your experience, which counts as part of your official coursework, familiarity with the professor who is teaching the class, and colleagues with whom you can share your experiences when you come back home. Students may spend their semesters abroad studying comparative feminist movements in places such as the Netherlands, India, or South Africa, for example.

Dr. Jennifer Fish, Associate Professor and chair in the Department of Women's Studies at Old Dominion University, in her Point of View, discusses her unique experience taking students abroad in a variety of different contexts, and what she and students gained.

## POINT OF VIEW

### TRANSFORMING STUDY ABROAD THROUGH WOMEN'S AND GENDER STUDIES

#### Dr. Jennifer Fish, Old Dominion University

Activism defines the theoretical foundations of Women's Studies. As students "live feminist theory" in applied work, they strengthen their disciplinary knowledge while contributing to social change through a range of access points—from legal advocacy, to feminist entrepreneurship, to direct service experiences. To align with the discipline, feminist-centered international study immersion courses reach beyond the classroom and immediate community to place students at the intersections of nation, language, ethnicity, ability, sexuality, class, caste, race, physical ability, and gender. Feminist-centered study-abroad courses often challenge predominant trends in the field of international education. With capitalist forces in higher education, we see noted patterns that promote the "export" of privileged, predominantly Western students to various parts of the world for intensive short-term exposure experiences. The contact with "other cultures" in these courses promises increased "marketability" for students as they transition from university life into the global world of work. Study-abroad courses, in most cases, benefit those with more privilege. At the same time, they often limit contact to a particular form of international exposure. In many ways, these global immersions reproduce asymmetries of power by polarizing the experiences of the global exchange "tourist" and the exotic "other" under study. Given these predominant trends, a feminist interrogation and reorientation of study abroad provides transformative moments that capture the theory-praxis connections at the heart of the discipline.

The tools of teaching, theory, and praxis central to Women's Studies provide a framework for the creation of international immersion courses that approach cross-cultural education from a position of feminist solidarity. By centering on sustained relationships and a co-commitment to social justice in study-abroad courses, students learn to appreciate the feminist value placed on difference, interrogate the meanings of standpoint, and build global solidarity with individuals and organizations. In this sense, Women's Studies is uniquely positioned to create distinct international learning experiences by drawing upon the central tenets of the field—through activism, an emphasis on relationships as central to the co-creation of knowledge and an integration of the study immersion experience from the range of disciplines woven within the discipline.

These feminist foundations have informed my own work in leading study-abroad courses to South Africa for nearly a decade. Drawing from my training in feminist methods, I designed a course that centered on the opportunity to build and sustain reciprocal relationships with civil society organizations and women leaders throughout the country. By placing students from U.S. universities in contexts where they worked alongside a range of local experts and activists, central themes of race, class, and gender justice emerged in ways that are only possible through global immersion. For example, in one of South Africa's most under-resourced communities, students work alongside the Grandmothers Against Poverty and AIDS organization to look at the role of elder women in responding to the care deficit. As they work with the Simelela crisis center, race, class, gender, sexuality, and age differences inform every dimension of their contact with survivors of sexual violence. And as they spend a "day in the life" of a South African domestic worker, the lingering impact of the apartheid era crystallizes the central theoretical consideration of the role of individual and collective activism in the context of prevailing social structures. This landscape of social change in South Africa's transition from apartheid to a democratic, human-rights ideology of governance allows students to delve into such core theoretical issues, as they engage on an applied level with the continued pursuit of social equality and justice. In every dimension possible, students are asked to "give back" as they learn from the organizations and the national context where activism has played a central role in social reconciliation, national dialogue, development, and the pursuit of justice. This process of working in partnership with South African communities over the course of a long-standing global exchange program captures the scholar-activist framework central to Women's Studies, as both a discipline and a social movement for rights.

By working in a feminist orientation to study abroad, students center their experience on relationships in the field setting. The personal and organizational connections students develop in the field contribute to a much larger and longer-term reciprocal partnership between activists and academics. Organizations benefit from the skills and contributions of student researchers, while the experiences students acquire in their direct contact with women "on the ground" provide vital lived experience data that inform larger community-based research projects. Through their direct contact in South African organizations, students have taken part in more extensive scholarly projects, including books, journal articles, and creative exhibitions. In these ways, feminist-oriented study-abroad courses inform institutional knowledge on the central distinctions between volunteerism and community-based research as a vibrant form of knowledge production.

In line with Women's Studies, the sustained, relationship-centered design of such global immersions express the larger ideological commitment to global solidarity that remain central to the field. As the South African expression of *ubuntu* conveys, "I am because we are." These contained immersive micro-instances of transnational contact express this value, which captures the underlying and historical foundations of feminism in ideology and practice, while building wider networks of global solidarity.

## What Does Connected Learning Mean to You?

Often, qualitative and quantitative research in Women's and Gender Studies suggests that students learn how to grapple with "I" voice, and connecting theory and research and practice (see Lovejoy 1998; Luebke and Reilly 1995).

A student new to Women's and Gender Studies must often adjust to the emphasis on the integration of reading, research, and personal experience. There is an assumption in Women's and Gender Studies analysis that the "I"—or the self—is a resource, witness, and aide to developing theory. Reading and reflecting on your own personal narratives (either through documentaries, personal essays, or fiction) and synthesizing that with data-driven research may feel like a stretch—it is! Women's and Gender Studies classrooms regularly probe material that creates emotion, tension, and conflict. Discussing difficult topics in a critical, sensitive, and confident way can be one of the biggest adjustments that a student can make. Some students may find this work uncomfortable or too revealing, others may find it refreshing:

> WMST classrooms are very open and safe, which is liberating in terms of speaking up and encouraging debate. Sometimes, this feeling increased when it was a class of all women, but I don't

think people held themselves back too much even if there were male students. For me, these classes were tangible proof of how feminism can change the way you feel by changing the environment. This feeling is only an appetizer, however, because the goal is for the whole world and everyone in it to feel as accepted as I did in my WMST classes.

(Carla, 2008, University of North Carolina
at Chapel Hill)

We asked our interviewees to reflect on what makes the Women's and Gender Studies classroom unique for student learning. Matt Ezzell, whom you met in Chapter 1, echoes many other students' experiences:

[My Women's Studies class was a] different type of experience within academe than I had ever been exposed to just in terms of how class was structured. Students facilitated every day in class with the graduate teaching assistant. We [students] would meet outside of class and we would talk about what we wanted to do and then we would do presentations and facilitate. It was just different ... I didn't know education could be like that. It wasn't the model in every Women's Studies class that I had, but most of my classes in Women's Studies had an active and collaborative learning component to them, even if it wasn't the dominant form.

Eva Marie, a Women's Studies major, builds on Matt's comment and names the guiding principles of feminist pedagogy (which are often in operation in many Women's and Gender Studies classes), discussed in Chapter 1:

What I found unique about a Women's Studies classroom was the feminist pedagogy. I did not know what the concept meant, at first. But as I gained access to the definition, it made sense to me. It [was] a way of teaching that exposed the instructor and the student to new information. The teacher, along with the student, continues to learn through class sessions. The new information that the professor acquired through the previous sessions may have an influence in changing the curriculum for the next semester. In my experience in Women's and Gender Studies classes, they are not lecture classes. Professors learned from students as well. The environment that is created through feminist pedagogy helps students gain confidence in expressing their opinion.

The different experiences that are shared through concepts of the course can bring students together [and] may carry [over] into a common bond outside the classroom.

(Eva Marie, 2010, Minnesota State University, Mankato)

Conversely, it would be a mistake to think that all Women's Studies classes always stress personal experience or self-analysis as the only tools for students to use. Women's and Gender Studies is an academic enterprise that not only adheres to, but also accepts, certain conventions regarding truth claims, whether ascertained through hypothesis testing and the conventions of the scientific method, critiquing truth claims through philosophical conventions, weighing evidence and arguments through legal processes, or engaging in textual analysis. Women's and Gender Studies faculty are trained in a variety of disciplinary perspectives, and we hold students to the same standards that are applied both internally and externally to Women's Studies scholars.

There is a variety of tools and skills that professors employ in the classroom, ranging from traditional methods of evaluation and assessment (such as exams and quizzes), to journals, group projects, and papers. Given the interdisciplinary nature of your learning, you may be asked to attend research colloquia held in Women's and Gender Studies that invite guest speakers. Or you may be asked to attend seminars or special talks about research on gender and sexuality that your program co-sponsors with other departments. You may then be asked to summarize the main points from these talks and figure out how they translate into the work you are undertaking in the classroom.

## WHAT'S COMPELLING ABOUT YOUR WOMEN'S AND GENDER STUDIES CLASSES?

As you move through your classes in Women's and Gender Studies, it may be helpful for you to reflect on the qualities about the class that you find compelling. Is it the way the instructor engages students? Is it the quality of the assignments that you are being asked to complete? Are you being asked to locate your own lived experiences as part of the learning process?

## Connecting Core Interests to Employment

Although later in the book we devote two chapters to specific issues of employment, we think it important for you to begin thinking about what kinds of skills you have. As you are preparing for your academic career, it is never too early to talk with a career services counselor. We asked Dr. Katherine Brooks for some advice. Dr. Brooks is a counselor who specializes in career counseling and coaching, particularly for liberal arts students and alumni. She is currently the Executive Director of the Office of Personal and Career Development at Wake Forest University. Her book *You Majored in What? Mapping Your Path from Chaos to Career* provides practical and conceptual tools to liberal arts students to better succeed in the workplace.

> *Michele and Cheryl*:  In *You Majored in What?*, you make a case that students must think differently in how to approach and plan for the relationship between major and career. Can you say how this applies to Women's and Gender Studies as a more recent kind of specialization that typically doesn't have a linear path?
>
> *Dr. Brooks*:  Studying Women's and Gender Studies is a perfect example of a nonlinear major when it comes to careers. There are some careers that might directly benefit from Women's and Gender Studies: teaching in the field of Gender Studies or a closely related field, managing a nonprofit organization dealing with issues germane to Women's and Gender Studies, research (medical or other) related to gender issues, etc.
>
> But for the most part, what becomes important for students pursuing this major is the ability to articulate its value to an employer. Most employers will either not be familiar with the major, or might have a superficial or even negative perception of it. As a result, the student needs to be prepared to explain the knowledge and skills they obtained through the major, rather than focus on the specific courses. It will be important for the student to understand what qualities are needed for the job they would like to do, and find ways to connect those qualities to their major. For example, if the position they are seeking requires writing skills or cultural sensitivity, the student will want to explain how those skills are acquired through their major.

*Michele and Cheryl*:    Are there trends that you're seeing in the kinds of positions students with liberal arts degrees are currently obtaining?

*Dr. Brooks*:    Since the recession began in 2008, there has arguably been a relentless pressure on college students to "succeed" in the job search—which usually translates to finding a high-paying job. Yahoo! and other online news outlets constantly produce lists of the "10 Best Careers," which are almost always defined by the salary. And those positions are usually in three fields: high-tech/engineering, healthcare, and finance. Liberal arts students can, and do, go into these fields—often after obtaining a graduate degree. But salaries are only one element of a meaningful career—other factors become important as well, such as an opportunity to make a difference, to apply your skills/talents, and to pursue something that interests you.

Liberal arts students who are interested in business careers tend to investigate opportunities in fields such as consulting, finance, pharmaceutical sales, marketing, and fashion merchandising. Those who are drawn to the arts often look into careers in advertising, publishing, public relations, and media. Those who seek social careers look at opportunities in education (including Teach for America), social services, nonprofit management, museum work, and other related fields.

*Michele and Cheryl*:    We've found from our research that career service counselors often assume that Women's and Gender Studies students want to work in the nonprofit sector and therefore minimize other possibilities. How should students prepare to make the most of their visit with career services?

*Dr. Brooks*:    This goes back to the stereotyped view of a major. It would be like someone assuming that a Religion major wants to become a minister or an English major wants to teach English. They might—but they also might not.

Before meeting with a career counselor, the student should think about the careers that have interested them over the years. I have an exercise in my book called "Possible Lives," where I have students map out careers they have considered in the past or wish they could pursue and then look for the threads connecting them, or the themes that show up. Sometimes, they learn that they are interested in careers that involve travel, for example, so that becomes a starting point for a discussion. A career with a theme of "travel" can cross the boundaries of business, government, or nonprofit work—or even be the start of an entrepreneurial venture. So thinking in terms of themes, talents, and interests can help the student get out of the major "box" someone might put them in.

What students don't want to do is just show up and expect the career counselor to know what they should do. Students must take an active approach—tell the counselor the fields that interest them and ask how to find connections to those fields. Or, if they don't know, find out what assessments or other activities might be available to them to learn more about their career interests. The most important thing is to take an active role in pursuing your career—don't expect anyone else to do it for you.

*Michele and Cheryl*:   Are there key things that students should be doing by the end of their junior year to prepare them for applying for positions before they graduate?

*Dr. Brooks*:   Yes, they can set the stage for a successful job search by:

1. Creating a strong social media profile. This means setting up a LinkedIn account with a professional picture and strong profile, creating a Twitter or Pinterest site that focuses on their areas of professional interests, cleaning up any online problems (removing bad pictures, etc.), and making sure they have tightened up the security on their Facebook account.
2. Taking leadership roles in an organization or two, acquiring an internship or other experience in a career field of interest (it's OK if they change their mind—experience is always good). Seeking out experiences they can create stories about for employers.
3. Creating a strong resume and cover letter, and improving their writing skills so they craft strong e-mail messages to potential employers.
4. Networking with alumni to learn more about career fields they are interested in.
5. Taking classes (credit or non-credit; online or in the classroom) that provide them with specific skills needed for their field of interest. For instance, if they are thinking nonprofit manage-

ment, they might want to learn basic budget management, or the skills of fundraising. If they are thinking about a career in business, they might want to learn to use Excel or database management systems. If they are interested in a graphics or design-related career, they might want to know the Adobe Creative Suite.

This is a good time for us to discuss the rubric of sustainer, evolver and synthesizer. These are the three patterns of career pathways that we found in our research with WGST graduates. In Chapter 6 you'll see this typology again with representative examples. For now, we'd like you to look at the following categories and consider how they might apply to you. Make a note of your insights and refer back to them in Chapter 6.

1. *Sustainers*: You may be on the path to being a sustainer if you:
   • consider yourself an activist;
   • are interested in pursuing topics specifically related to gender issues (i.e. intimate partner violence, women's health); or
   • think of yourself as a great networker.
   To consider further: Sustainers tend to draw on their activist networks as they seek new employment

2. *Evolvers*: You may be on the path to being an evolver if you:
   • have a high tolerance for risk-taking;
   • feel you that you are good at many things and could be happy doing several different kinds of jobs; or
   • like to think about how to combine WGST with other interests (personal or professional) that at first glance seem unrelated.
   To consider further: Evolvers like to pursue multiple interests, which means they are often developing new skills.

3. *Synthesizers*: You may be on the path to being a synthesizer if you:
   • have high energy and passion for trying new things;
   • have a history of activism and/or volunteerism; or
   • have an interest in entrepreneurial activities.
   To consider further: Synthesizers tend to want some of their work to directly relate to gender, but they are also content to find ways to support gender equity through avenues of volunteering or activism.

### Co-curricular Opportunities

Undergraduate student culture varies widely across campuses. We encourage you to investigate what other forums exist where you can talk about issues of interest to you as a Women's and Gender Studies student. Rapport and friendship happen pretty naturally through courses as students bond through shared learning experiences. Your Women's and Gender Studies program or department may offer informal and formal opportunities for students to meet each other and learn about research opportunities, fellowships, awards, and other important happenings (e.g. a major's night, an end-of-year celebration). Your program or department may also host an annual lecture or speaker series highlighting scholarship in Women's and Gender Studies or a topical speaker on issues of interest. Inquire about ways that your academic unit keeps students informed (e.g. a Facebook page). Taking advantage of these opportunities will afford you the ability to expand your network. What you do on campus can also enhance what you are learning in the classroom. Applying what you know in a real-world context allows you to develop skills that can be transferred to future places of employment.

If you have not already, you may want to investigate other groups on campus that work on women's and gender issues. You will probably find a number of active organizations that focus on women's issues and sponsor well-known events such as "Take Back the Night" (sexual and partner violence event) or "The Vagina Monologues." If you do not find something that interests you, create your own group! Fashion it to fit your own interests and goals, and share the passion you have with others (see the sidebar about Project Dinah overleaf).

Additionally, find out if your campus has a women's center. There are many women's centers on college campuses across the country. Women's centers serve the needs of faculty, staff, and students through a variety of programs. Each of us has worked with students who interned or worked for women's centers who gained valuable experience planning events and organizing and leading groups.

Campus life offers a variety of options for pushing outside of one's comfort zone. We encourage you to investigate student groups and communities that you normally wouldn't. Kim Anichowski explores her experience in a sorority and how she had to unlearn certain stereotypes.

## SPOTLIGHT: KIM ANICHOWSKI

When I was a sophomore in college I got the idea to join a sorority. My friends immediately thought I would become a stereotypical drunk, ditzy and a shell of what I used to be. Having gone through that experience and come out the other side at graduation, made me realize there is a similar link between what sorority girls and feminists go through. While there are many stereotypes and misconceptions about both feminists and sorority members, we share a common commitment to social justice, gender rights and societal issues.

Unfortunately, for many Women and Gender Studies students and sorority members, the commonalities between feminism (and Women and Gender Studies departments/ majors/minors) and Greek life (specifically sororities) are often neglected or fostered, even though both of these institutionalized entities encourage self growth and determination, sisterhood/collective consciousness, and activism.  At no point in my college sorority "education" was feminism ever discussed (whether good or bad). Now that I have graduated I have realized there was little or no dialogue between women in sororities and Gender Studies majors/minors. In fact I cannot recall anyone in my sorority with a Liberal Arts major that focused on Women and Gender Studies or who took a Women's Studies class. That dialogue didn't exist. And I don't think it was out of spite or distaste for one another. There was a massive lack of under-standing between the two groups. People seem to forget that both groups are striving for the same things, equality at home and in the work place, academic and extracurricular leadership on and off campus.

Being a part of a sorority for me was important because of the ideal of "sisterhood" or a place where members can accept and explore all aspects of our gender identity without judgment or ridicule. Within the sorority, we are all bonded by our shared experiences. As I went through the pledging process, we talked about what we wanted out of life, how to pursue personal and intellectual growth. All of these things transferred to life after college. We are still bonded by that sisterhood. It has created an expansive social and professional network that can be utilized well after college is over. My sorority in particular has an online blog where you can post job openings or your resume for other sisters to see. It is unbelievably supportive to know there are people out there to pass along a good word or your resume so you can pursue that personal and professional growth that was cultivated over four years. I have sisters in medical school who are becoming obstetricians/gynecologists and focusing on reproductive rights. I have sisters in law school who volunteer at the American Civil Liberties Union (ACLU) trying to do whatever they can. I even have sisters in Washington DC working for senator writing policy that affects everyone.

I won't deny that the stereotypes about sororities still exist and that more dialogue needs to occur. Some people see sororities and feminism as contradictory. How can someone fight for community rights and hold fundraisers, while throwing parties on the weekend? Having the insight to know these disparities exist is the first step to fixing them and the first step to being able to shed light on all the great endeavors sororities make towards working for equality and the community. The first step in the process is to challenge prevailing stereotypes and work on opportunities to foster dialogue and common grounds for collaboration. Perhaps in the future, the divide between feminism, Women and Gender Studies and sororities will be a remnant of the past.

Moya Bailey is a Spelman College alumna, national activist, and blogger, and earned her doctorate in Women's Studies at Emory University. She highlights how she developed her interest in Women's Studies and how her activism on misogyny in the hip-hop world began as a discussion in her Women's Studies classroom. Her story is a compelling example of theory and practice coming together as a catalyst for change:

> I identified as a feminist in high school, which was a bit different from my peers. And I had an Advanced Placement (AP) psychology professor who identified as a feminist [in high school] and we talked about lots of issues. I tried to organize pro-feminist actions. When I got to Spelman, I already had that leaning. And it was difficult at first because I was in the sciences and also in Psychology.

It was a difficult transition for Moya in the Psychology department. She felt that the department was not interested in the kinds of questions and experiences she wanted to raise. In what she deemed as a negative and conservative environment in Psychology, she felt as though she was being "pushed out." During her first year on Spelman's campus, she quickly became active on campus:

> It was actually through activism and student networks that I got involved in Women's Studies. All my friends [in the] second semester of my first year were connected to activist organizations on campus and all the organizations were connected to the women's resource center and were tied to the Women's Studies department. And finally a professor asked me, "Why aren't you

## STARTING PROJECT DINAH

Project Dinah, a women's safety and empowerment initiative at the University of North Carolina at Chapel Hill, has gained campus-wide press and attention in recent years. Its mission is to end all sexual violence on campus and in the community through education and advocacy. Women's Studies majors and minors at UNC often find Project Dinah an important organization to be actively involved in, because it puts into practice the academic knowledge about sexual violence that they learn in the classroom.

Project Dinah has grown to include many members, and now offers a variety of programs, but it was founded in 2005 by a small group of passionate first-year students who were moved to activism after discovering the prevalence of sexual assault on college campuses—such as *one in four women* will be victims of assault or attempted assault as part of their college experience. Receiving seed money in 2004 helped this group of students to distribute safety whistles and resource cards on campus. Project Dinah later became an independent and officially recognized student organization.

Since its inception, Project Dinah has organized the annual "Take Back the Night" march and rally. In 2009, Project Dinah incorporated a SpeakOut with "Take Back the Night," during which volunteers read anonymous testimonials of survivors. UNC students and community members were invited to post their stories online at www.speakoutunc.blogspot.com.

Another event that is designed to promote healthy communication between sexual partners is "I Love Female Orgasm"—Project Dinah's most well-known program. This event has attracted more than 500 students in each of the past two years. Other sponsored programs have included free self-defense classes and a benefit concert for the Orange County Rape Crisis Center, as well as a variety of initiatives co-sponsored with the Carolina Women's Center.

a Women's Studies major? You're doing all this organizing with the feminist groups on campus. You can be Premed and a Women's Studies major." "Oh," I said, "I hadn't realized that."

Moya quickly changed her major from Psychology and Premed to Premed and Women's Studies: "I was really happy and content in Women's Studies." It was a pivotal point in her academic career:

When I got into my Women's Studies classes, I finally got the language that I needed to articulate what was happening in my world. So, growing up in an all-white environment as the only black girl, there were a lot of dynamics that were happening in many of my classes that I didn't have language for. So, getting into Women's Studies classes, I found out, "Oh, that's racism," "Oh, I have internalized some of these racist things and internalized sexism." Having that language was really affirming to me because I could see it's not me, it's the system. That was liberatory for me.

Moya came to national attention as a junior in college when she helped to organize against Nelly, a popular rapper, which sparked a national discussion on the role of misogyny in hip-hop, rap lyrics, and videos. Below, she discusses how this activism organically emerged from her Women's Studies class:

> Nelly was supposed to do a bone marrow registration drive and the Student Government (SGA) president told me that he was coming. His controversial video "Tip Drill"[2] was airing around that time, too. I said, "He's going to come to campus?" The SGA president brought this issue up in a Women's Studies classroom, and there was a discussion among the class and professor [Beverly Guy-Sheftall] about what we should do. Should something be done? At the time, I was president of the feminist group on campus.

Given Nelly's popularity and support, at first Moya was not sure if anything would get the attention of students: "I was like, 'No one is going to come if we do anything . . . No one is going to come.'" Her class debated various actions they could take. "[At first] we thought we should write a letter. We finally settled on trying to invite him to have a conversation about sexism and misogynist images in his music when he came to campus." They thought a dialogue would be the most constructive approach rather than trying to organize a protest of his coming.

Around the same time that Moya and her classmates were strategizing about how to raise awareness about misogyny in Nelly's and other rap videos, some of Nelly's public relations people had come to campus to check out location and safety. They saw flyers that Moya's feminist student group had made. They had named Nelly the "Misogynist of the Month" because of the "Tip Drill" video. There were flyers of this "Misogynist of the Month" posted around campus. Although there was not a scheduled protest or demonstration, Nelly's people believed that there would be during Nelly's visit.

Moya and her group had decided against a protest, because at that point there were a small number of people who were interested in having a critical dialogue on the day that Nelly arrived. "Nelly's team decided to pull out and then went to press saying that they didn't want a protest at Spelman, and it erupted into this huge thing." Nelly's team also put pressure on the SGA president to guarantee that there was not going to be a protest if Nelly did come. "And the SGA president said we can't guarantee the students won't do anything," and so the SGA stood up for this small group of students.

> And then it didn't end up happening. So, all of this erupted from an event that didn't even actually take place. We decided to show the video on the day [that Nelly was supposed to arrive] so people could see what we were upset about and [we] had signs up. Because [the] press had gotten wind of the story, [and] they still came to this non-event. It was huge, all the press came up . . .
>
> It was really something that happened in a classroom with a few students—it was not the majority of campus, and so in the public frame it was "Spelman Says No to Nelly," but a lot of students were upset with us because they wanted to meet him and they wanted him to come. What was so powerful to me [was] that just a few vocal students were able to scare Nelly into not coming and being accountable for the music he makes.

This critique of how hip-hop and rap videos position women, especially African-American women and women of color, created a ripple effect that Moya could not have anticipated—it opened up a national dialogue and launched her and others into critical and public conversations. Some outcomes included that *Essence* magazine started a yearlong "Take Back the Community" campaign, and the television channel BET developed specials on "Hip-Hop in America" and had ongoing discussions about artistic responsibility.

Moya believes in the power of a few committed people to take action against inequality: "I'm just amazed at the ripple effect of something so small." Moya's experience is an important reminder of "the power of a vocal few—it doesn't take a lot of people to make something happen." She was able to challenge status-quo thinking about the portrayal of women (especially African-American women) in contemporary videos.

**POINT OF VIEW**

## CLAIM YOUR REPRODUCTIVE JUSTICE EDUCATION

### Carol Mason, University Of Kentucky

In 1977, the American poet Adrienne Rich delivered a speech titled "Claiming an Education" to a group of women at Douglas College. She encouraged students not to expect to passively receive an education, but to actively claim it by being responsible to their selves. She told them, "Responsibility to yourself means refusing to let others do your thinking, talking, and naming for you; it means learning to respect and use your own brains and instincts; hence, grappling with hard work." In the current climate of extraordinary efforts to curb reproductive and sexual rights, many GWS students are claiming their reproductive justice education.

If you are passionate about rectifying the injustices perpetuated by efforts to judge, regulate, and punish sexual and reproductive lives, there is a wide range of opportunities for study, activism, professional development, and community solidarity. The reproductive justice movement is alive on campuses and off. You can be a part of reproductive justice (RJ) if you feel strongly about any of these issues:

- double standards that judge promiscuity differently for men and women;
- racialized sex stereotypes that denigrate people of color;
- racist and heterosexist ideas about what makes a family or constitutes parenthood;
- surveillance of immigrants and their "anchor babies";
- attempts to outlaw abortion and birth control;
- neocolonial exploitation of surrogates who gestate and give birth to babies meant to be reared by others;
- hypocrisy of those who participate in the commodification, abuse, and deprivation of children while also working to deny people the right to opt out of bringing children into a society that exploits them;
- adoption regulations that deny LGBTQ parents, perpetuate white supremacist ideas about which babies are desirable, or exploit birth mothers;
- medically unnecessary, state-mandated procedures and policies, such as ultrasound or parental notification, as a requirement for abortion;
- denial of health insurance coverage for transgendered people who give birth, take hormones, or have sex-reassignment surgery;
- health insurance coverage for pills that enhance erections but not for birth control pills;
- court-ordered caesarean births, sterilization, or long-acting reversible contraception;

- denial of treatment but endorsement of prison for pregnant women who use drugs; and
- resource extraction and toxic dumping resulting in birth defects and disease in poor communities and communities of color.

What can you do to transform your passion into action, research, and collective goodwill? Here is how to claim your RJ education and build the RJ community of students, scholars, and activists on your campus:

1. *Seek out existing classes, or ask faculty to create a new course, that focus on reproductive justice.* Take the course and soak up all you can. Challenge yourself and others to consider the broad vision of reproductive justice, as encompassing any of the above issues, and more. If a course does not exist, create a petition signed by students who would take the course and present it to your favorite professor or student government. If it is only you, create an independent study that allows you to conduct quantitative and qualitative research on your classmates' experiences with, for example, abstinence-only sex education, crisis pregnancy centers, and slut-shaming or bullying. Or you can use an independent study to research particular nonprofit organizations that advocate reproductive justice and explore future career paths—such as grant-writing, legal advocacy, lobbying, research, grant management, budget director, communications director, youth training, or development.

2. *Attend an RJ conference for students.* If there is no way your university or college can provide an RJ course or if you want to extend what you learned in an RJ course, you have the right to seek out off-campus education. Ask your advisor, professor, off-campus study director, student government, or dean of undergraduate education to support you (and your friends) with funds to attend one of two annual conferences designed specifically for undergraduates. The first conference, called "From Abortion Rights to Social Justice: Building the Movement for Reproductive Freedom," but popularly known as "CLPP" because it is sponsored by the Civil Liberties and Public Policy program at Hampshire College, is held in Western Massachusetts every April (see Civil Liberties and Public Policy 2014). The second conference, called "Take Root: Red State Perspectives on Reproductive Justice," is geared toward empowering students from conservative places, and is hosted by the University of Oklahoma in Norman each February (see http://take-root.org).

3. *Expand the scope of standard writing assignments and events focusing on abortion with a broader RJ perspective.* A standard assignment in Composition and Philosophy classes asks students to defend or challenge *Roe v. Wade*, the 1973 Supreme Court decision that decriminalized abortion. Often, the anniversary of *Roe* is celebrated each January. Use these opportunities to promote an RJ view that recognizes how regulating abortion can be used

to harm any pregnant person, *regardless* of their moral, religious, or political position on abortion.

National Advocates for Pregnant Women (2009) supplies three ways to do this: show a five-minute video about how legislation regulating abortion adversely affected even antiabortion mothers. Cite a peer-reviewed scholarly article about the increase of arresting pregnant women to protect fetuses (Flavin and Paltrow 2013). Invite a reproductive justice activist or feminist attorney to speak on campus. For example, NAPW's Lynn Paltrow will deliver a lecture titled "40 years after Roe v. Wade: Reproductive Justice in the Age of Mass Incarceration" (Paltrow 2013). Additionally, many RJ organizations have resources and speakers for campus use. Spiritual Youth for Reproductive Freedom, Advocates for Youth, Choice USA, and Planned Parenthood's VOX are especially geared toward young people. Organizations designed to represent particular women of color include: SisterSong, National Asian Pacific American Women's Forum, National Latina Institute for Reproductive Health, and Native American Women's Health Education Resource Center. All can help transform mono-dimensional discussions of abortion into wide-ranging conversations.

In addition to celebrations of *Roe v. Wade*, there are routinely antiabortion demonstrations on campus, including a display currently promoted as "Justice for All" and featuring three-story-high graphic illustrations of abortion that falsely equate it with lynching, genocide, and the Holocaust. You can create a multifaceted, community-wide response to this by enlisting professors of GWS, ethnic studies, law, medicine, and history to serve on a panel that spells out the medical, philosophical, and historical flaws of this display, and by encouraging students to write letters to the editor and creatively stage a counterdemonstration. Examples and resources are included in the article "What to Do When They Say Holocaust" (Mason 2012).

4. *Apply for student government funds.* As a student, you can join an existing reproductive justice campus group or start a new one. As a registered organization on campus, your group is eligible to receive funds with which you can attend one of the aforementioned conferences, invite speakers, or host events. If a group already exists but is ineffective, think about having an RJ representative to serve in other student groups in order integrate the RJ perspective by discussing intersections of concern suggested by the bulleted list above.

Claiming an education can be hard work, as Rich said, and claiming your RJ education is no different. But when you join with others and take advantage of all the resources available to you, you transform yourself and your world.

And there is another important takeaway to her story—that the Women's and Gender Studies classroom provides an intellectually engaging form for emerging debates and issues central in students' lives. Not every class will lead you to mobilize others on behalf of a cause, but it will sharpen your ability to think and debate about contemporary critical issues that affect women and men's lives.

Learning about the issues and history of reproductive rights is often a core part of Women's and Gender Studies classes. Many students become aware and active on these issues during their academic career, and some become active on campus. In our survey, we found that activism on reproductive rights issues was a common thread across 1995–2010. In a thoughtful Point of View, Dr. Carol Mason, faculty member in the Department of Gender and Women's Studies and Director of Undergraduate Education at the University of Kentucky, discusses the multiple ways that students can become involved in reproductive rights issues on campuses.

### Finding Wo-mentors

We in Women's and Gender Studies are not the only ones to recommend mentors. Finding and cultivating strong mentors is something consistently promoted in business, leadership, and professional development circles. As part of our continued quest for professional development, both of us have participated in a number of leadership development and mentoring programs. Cheryl had the privilege of experiencing two New Leadership programs (Tri-State in Morehead, Minnesota, and in Las Vegas), as well as participating in the Mankato YWCA's Women's Leadership Program.[3] Michele participated in an academic leadership program at the University of North Carolina at Chapel Hill. Each of these programs highlighted the important role of mentors.

Sometimes, mentors are formally assigned to you as advisors, and you develop a working relationship that extends beyond graduation. Other times, we are adopted and nurtured by faculty members, professional staff, community members, or past graduates of the program who may encourage us in one or more of the following ways: listening to our concerns, giving us tough love when necessary, forwarding educational and/or professional opportunities, assisting in introducing us to others, helping us to think "outside the box," reigning us in, providing opportunities for research, activism, or publishing, and sharing in our joy in our accomplishments and/or providing support in the face of disappointments. Some mentors may be comfortable with "warm and fuzzy interactions" (where they disclose personal information about themselves and may invite you and other students out for lunch), whereas other mentors are comfortable with more formal, structured mentoring. Whether you actively seek a mentor, or if a mentoring relationship emerges organically, these relationships, like friendships, may be short-term and contextually bound. Some mentoring relationships may evolve into a decades-long connection. They are important to your development as a student, and can serve you well as you leave your undergraduate experience, continue your education, or enter the job market.

The role of mentors was important for graduates in our study. Many people reported that the mentors who have been most influential have been the professors, staff, and advisors they met in their classes, through formal internships, and in community work. These relationships have been robust for our graduates years after they have formally graduated. At your campus, there may be an official way to be mentored through a university program that focuses on college students' issues. Mentoring programs might be offered through the division of Student Affairs, Office of Residential Life, the Women's Center, etc. No matter how and where you find a mentor, their influence on your personal and professional life can be profound. Because we realize the importance of mentoring, we asked survey respondents about their experiences via the online survey.

Here are some of the responses we received to our mentoring question "Who are your current mentors? Describe your relationship to them."

- "Many of my former professors serve as my most influential mentors because I am a first-generation college student and they helped foster my education and showed me that I can live an intellectual life. Two of them are also my feminist mommas who showed me the light and have changed my life by giving a name to what I have already practiced."
- "My undergraduate advisors, one female and one male, with whom I still regularly e-mail . . . I met with them at least weekly on an informal and formal basis, especially in my final two years when we spoke about my graduate school prospects. I also worked

with the female mentor as a teaching assistant and a research assistant."

- "My mentor passed away in late 2008. Since that time, I have relied on close friends to discuss intellectual, emotional, and sociopolitical matters."
- "Former internship supervisor—provides professional guidance, wisdom, and best practice support within my chosen field of employment."
- "College professor—took classes on domestic violence and pornography with him and later [was a Teaching Assistant for] domestic violence course; former employer/college professor—worked at women's leadership center during college–took her Women in Politics course during college."
- "These people know me well and understand my strengths. Although different, they all have a good understanding of feminist issues and understand my passion for it."

Cheryl describes her unique and varied history as a mentee:

I had the fortune to be mentored by passionate and activist scholars at the University of Toledo while pursuing my MA degree. Because the department was fairly small in terms of faculty members and graduate students, it felt more like a family than a formal workplace. As a graduate student, I had access to the lounge, copying privileges, and felt comfortable visiting faculty members in their offices. When I first went back to school, I was unsure of my academic abilities after working for years in the nonprofit world. I was immediately befriended by Dr. Barbara Chesney, a sociologist whose work focused on health and medical issues. Not only did she offer me the opportunity to serve as her research and teaching assistant, but later she agreed to serve as my thesis chair. I feel I have emulated her style in my interactions with graduate students. Barbara and I would often go to coffee shops and other off-campus locations to grade papers and discuss thesis ideas. Aside from showing me the culture of academia, Barbara was there for me emotionally when my father passed away during the first week of my second year of graduate school. I knew Barbara would hold my confidences in my moments of grief, especially after I was surprised by her presence (along with two of my graduate colleagues and friends) at my father's funeral. Largely because of Barbara and later Barbara Brents—my mentor at UNLV—I feel that being a mentor is more than just imparting formal knowledge. A good feminist mentor listens to his or her students, is their ally and advocate, and continues the relationship after graduation. Another mentor at the University of Toledo was Dr. Patrick McGuire. Aside from intellectually engaging me in the topic of political sociology in the classroom, he was someone I could easily turn to when I had a question, concern, or just wanted to talk. I can remember stopping by Dr. McGuire's office to chat about ideas raised in class, to ask questions about graduate school and research, and to get affirmation about my choice to go back to school. Unfortunately, a few years ago Dr. McGuire lost his fight with cancer, but his influence on my life has been profound. Last, but not least, I had the honor of working with Dr. Cary Kart while at the University of Toledo. I was inspired by his medical sociology course and was able to work with him on revisions he was doing on his gerontology textbook. I can always count on Dr. Kart for his sense of humor, as well as his fierce grasp of sociological concepts. I also felt that Dr. Kart would fight for his department and students—a trait that I also try to emulate.

It was through Women's Studies and the mentoring that I received under Ellen C. Rose (the former director of the UNLV Women's Studies Department) that I was able to co-teach my first (and only co-taught) course, "Porn in the USA." Through fate or kismet, a newly hired assistant professor in Political Science and I met and found a connection over a multitude of ideas and issues. We bonded over a common interest in Sexuality Studies and were given the go-ahead to develop and teach a course on pornography. It was through this collaboration that Michele and I first worked together. Later, Michele continued to act as my mentor, collaborator, coach, confidant, conspirator, and friend. She not only served as one of my dissertation committee members, but Michele has always made herself available to me to discuss teaching issues in the classroom. She also helped me process the transition from graduate student to new professional while I worked as a visiting professor in Women's Studies at UNLV, during my time at Minnesota State, Mankato as an assistant professor of Women's Studies, and as a co-author on presentations. It was through these conversations, dialogues, gripe sessions, and my caffeine-fueled epiphanies that our concerns about Women's Studies and our students resulted in a book proposal for *Transforming Scholarship*.

We can highlight a few key points from Cheryl's story:

1. Professors are people, too—Cheryl talks about how accessible these mentors were, how you can have many of them, and how boundaries between school and life are blurred or even erased when mentoring relationships become friendships, too.
2. Personal is not a dirty word—Cheryl was able to develop several personal friendships with her mentors. See "10 Tips for How To Be A Good Mentee" on the evolution of mentoring relationship.
3. Two heads are better than one—Cheryl talks about how she came to her own realizations about school, work, life, book proposals through conversation, dialogue, and the company of mentors.
4. You can write your own book, too, or whatever big dream inspires you! Cheryl talks about living up to her potential with the guidance she received from these fabulous people.

Yet, as with any type of relationship, you need to be aware of your own conduct so that the relationship is one of reciprocity. Some mentees may not perceive interpersonal and professional boundaries of their mentors. They may unwittingly try to monopolize a mentor's time, expecting counseling or a therapeutic relationship. Much of the demanding work of being a professor happens outside the purview of what undergraduates see and experience. The demands on faculty time increase every year. Keep in mind that your faculty member has three jobs in their college or university: teaching, research, and service. Be respectful of the time that you work with a mentor. Think about how to be a good *mentee*.

It is as important to be aware of how you feel the mentoring relationship is going. You may feel grateful to receive support and help with your concerns and career planning, rather than feeling like it is an obligation that your mentor is fulfilling. But, unfortunately, mentors can sometimes possess unreasonable or unattainable expectations for mentees. If you feel bullied, pushed, or overly criticized, please trust your experience and find a way to extricate yourself from that mentoring relationship.

## POINT OF VIEW CONTRIBUTORS FOR CHAPTER 2

**Jennifer N. Fish** is Associate Professor and Chair of the Department of Women's Studies at Old Dominion University, where she also teaches in the Graduate Program in International Studies and leads annual global

## 10 TIPS FOR HOW TO BE A GOOD MENTEE

1. Help the mentor get to know you. Your mentor may ask you about your goals and aspirations, so it is wise to be prepared for such questions.

2. Maintain clear lines of communication with your mentor. For example, if you set up meetings, show up on time for appointments. If you must cancel, give enough notice as possible so as not to inconvenience your mentor. Also find out the best way to communicate with your mentor, vis-à-vis text, e-mail, or phone.

3. Be focused. It is fine to be interested in general conversation during time with your mentor, but, as a rule, be prepared to articulate what you would like help on.

4. If your mentor gives you an assignment or task to complete in order to achieve your goal, do it.

5. Do not e-mail five times a day or monopolize your professor's time during their office hours or break times.

6. Thank you notes are always appreciated. If your mentor has written a letter for you on short notice, spent additional time with you, or, taken you to a conference, a handwritten note or card is a nice way to acknowledge that person.

7. Respect the boundaries that your mentor creates. Be mindful of your mentor's time, their privacy, and their professional status. For example, some of your professors may be part-time or adjunct faculty, and may have different time commitments than full-time faculty.

8. Try not to put existing archetypical (and gendered) expectations on your mentor (e.g. surrogate mom, therapist, etc.). While these may occur unintentionally, try not to put unachievable expectations on your mentor.

9. Strive to develop reciprocity over time. Remember that while your relationship may start off as a one-sided relationship, this may change over time. Your mentor may rely on mentees to give them perspective on current trends on campus, in culture, and on your journey into a career.

10. Understand the changing nature of mentor and mentee relationships. Like friendships, some mentoring relationships are short-term and others may continue. Find a mentor that you can have a working relationship with and be willing to part when or if the goal of your mentoring relationship has been achieved. It is important to reciprocate, when appropriate, and realize that you and your mentor are complex people who can renegotiate the conditions of your relationship post-graduation.

studies courses in South Africa. Her research interests center on post-conflict development, with particular emphasis on women's roles in restructuring society.

**Carol Mason** is Professor of Gender and Women's Studies and Director of Undergraduate Studies at the University of Kentucky. She is an interdisciplinary scholar of twentieth-century American culture known for her research on the rise of the right since the 1960s.

## YOUR TURN: EXERCISES

### INVESTIGATING THE COMPONENTS OF YOUR EDUCATION

Now it is time for you to critically assess all of the components of your education. Find a time when you will not be disturbed and gather the materials for your program that you acquired based on the exercise in the previous chapter. Take some time and think about what kinds of questions and ideas excite you. Reflect on the following questions:

- Are there issues that you find yourself drawn to in Women's and Gender Studies?
- Is there a type of research that you have been exposed to that excites you?
- What kinds of courses will you need to achieve depth in your areas of interest?
- What types of internship opportunities are available to you through the program or department?
- What courses are being offered during the next two semesters?
- Are you interested in studying abroad? If the answer is yes, have you investigated the study-abroad office on campus?
- Have you begun preparing for your senior year?
- Have you identified a mentor(s)?
- Have you thought about what you most would like to learn as a mentee?
- What are the ways that you find yourself applying your interests in Women's and Gender Studies to current topics and informal and formal extracurricular activities at your campus?
- Are sparks that are happening related to jobs?

### IMPORTANT PROGRAMS FOR GLOBAL STUDENT TRAVEL

#### Gilman International Scholarship Program

The Gilman Scholarship Program is open to U.S. citizen undergraduate students who are planning to study and intern abroad. The program aims to diversify the kinds of students who study and intern abroad and the countries and regions where they go by supporting undergraduates who might otherwise not participate due to financial constraints. The Gilman Scholarship Program accepts applications two times per year. Ideally, students should begin their application one full semester before their study-abroad program or internship is scheduled to begin. All applicants will be notified via e-mail of the status of their application in May.

Web page: www.iie.org/Programs/Gilman-Scholarship-Program

## Rotary International Studying Abroad Scholarships and Programs

### District Grant Scholarships

District grants can be used to sponsor secondary school, undergraduate, or graduate students studying any subject, either locally or abroad. In addition, the scholarship may cover any length of time—from a six-week language training program to a year or more of university study. Districts may ask scholars to make presentations to local Rotary Clubs and participate in Rotary service projects, but such involvement is not required by the Foundation.

Web page: www.rotary.org/myrotary/en/district-grants

Additional information: www.rotary.org/en/document/899

### Global Grant Scholarships

Global grants support scholarships for graduate students studying abroad in one of the six areas of focus. Scholarships range from one to four years, and therefore can include an entire degree program. Prospective scholars must show proof of admission to the chosen university before the grant will be approved.

Web page: www.rotary.org/en/global-grants

Additional information: www.rotary.org/en/document/899

### Rotary Youth Exchange

Youth Exchange is a study-abroad opportunity for young people who spend anywhere from a few weeks to a full year as an international student hosted by local Rotary Clubs. Exchanges are for people ages 15–19 who: (1) have demonstrated leadership in their school and community; (2) are flexible and willing to try new things; (3) are open to cultural differences; and (4) can serve as an ambassador for their own country. Costs vary from country to country. Local Rotary Clubs generously host students and provide room and board with a host family and a small monthly stipend. Participants are generally responsible for round-trip airfare, insurance, travel documents (such as passports and visas), spending money, additional travel, and tour fees.

Web page: www.rotary.org/en/youth-exchanges

### Boren Scholarships

Boren scholarships provide up to $20,000 to U.S. undergraduate students to study abroad in areas of the world that are critical to U.S. interests and underrepresented in study abroad, including Africa, Asia, Central and Eastern Europe, Eurasia, Latin America, and the Middle East. The countries of Western Europe, Canada, Australia, and New Zealand are excluded.

Web page: www.borenawards.org/boren_scholarship

### Searchable Databases for Study-Abroad Scholarships and Grants

#### *Institute of International Education Study Abroad Funding*

This directory features detailed descriptions of hundreds of study-abroad scholarships, fellowships, grants, and paid internships for U.S. undergraduate, graduate, and postgraduate students and professionals.

Web page: www.studyabroadfunding.org/index.asp

#### *U.S. Study Abroad Scholarships and Grants List*

Web page: www.nafsa.org/Explore_International_Education/For_Students/U_S__Study_Abroad_Scholarships_and_Grants_List

## Notes

1.  This constitutes a partial list of such programs:
    Washington University's Women's, Gender and Sexuality Studies: http://ascc.artsci.wustl.edu/~women/wgs_undergrad.htm
    CSU Long Beach: www.csulb.edu/colleges/cla/departments/wgss
    Swarthmore College: www.swarthmore.edu/x19973.xml
    University of Kansas: www.womensstudies.ku.edu
    University of Cincinnati: www.artsci.uc.edu/womens_studies
    University of Minnesota: http://gwss.umn.edu
    Wesleyan College: www.wesleyan.edu/fgss
    New York University: http://genderandsexuality.as.nyu.edu/page/undergraduate
2.  "Tip Drill" (2003) is a video that depicts several misogynist and demeaning images of women, including a man holding a credit card and simulating sliding it through the back of a woman's thong.
3.  New Leadership refers to leadership programs originally developed by the Center for American Women and Politics at Rutgers University in 1981. Typically, these programs feature a weeklong residential experience in which college students and female activists in the community gain knowledge, experience, and mentoring in order to further their empowerment goals. For more information, see http://wrin.unlv.edu/new, http://appserv.mnstate.edu/whitede/conference/index.htm, or www.mankatoywca.org/womensleadership.php.

# 3
## HOW *YOU* CAN TALK ABOUT WOMEN'S AND GENDER STUDIES ANYTIME, ANYWHERE, AND TO ANYONE

Picture this: you have just arrived home for winter break after your fifth semester at school. As you sit down to your first home-cooked meal in weeks, you proudly announce to your family, "I've decided to switch my major from Premed to Women's and Gender Studies." Across the mac and cheese, your parents drop their forks and knives, eyes popping out of their heads, and remark. At first you are met with an uncomfortable silence, perhaps not the first one you have encountered since you have decided to declare this major or minor. Then you hear, "What the heck are you going to do with a Women's Studies major? And what *is* it anyway?!" Their Premed doctor-to-be has just transformed before their very eyes into a "bra-burning, man-hating feminist," and they want answers—now.[1] Good news—we are here to help!

You have made an academic commitment to Women's and Gender studies in your college career. We believe that given this unique area of study, your commitment to communicating effectively about it is very important. Although the dinner-table scenario may not fit your own personal experience, you may have struggled with how to explain your choice of academic major to family, friends, and the "nice old lady" sitting next to you on the airplane. And you may ask yourself why you should care about the person on the plane. Every opportunity to talk intelligently about Women's and Gender Studies is a useful thing to undertake, because that person you talk to may be a potential employer, chairperson of an awards committee, or philanthropist. By talking with them about Women's and Gender Studies in an easy, positive, and understandable way, you do your part to make this field of study visible and demystified. That random person you speak to may be, at some later date, in a position to make a decision that could affect someone with a Women's and Gender Studies background. We think that communicating well about Women's and Gender Studies creates a public ripple effect that has unknown positive ramifications.

You are not the first person to face these challenges. Many other students before you have had to talk to others about Women's and Gender Studies. In this chapter, we will hear from former students about their experiences meeting these same challenges. As we stated in the Introduction, we think it is important to communicate with others about the role and value of Women's and Gender Studies in your academic training, because it offers you an opportunity to provide a compelling and positive frame for your academic interest and issues of gender equality. Although an overwhelming majority of graduates found that many people supported their interest in Women's and Gender Studies, there were also students who reported otherwise. This chapter prepares you for communicating these aspects of your chosen field of study to others who are interested and supportive, and some who may be unaware of the existence of Women's and Gender Studies as an academic major, or who may hold misconceptions about Women's and Gender Studies.

We hope that you are eager to talk about Women's and Gender Studies, and that you will strongly value communicating both the concepts and skills that you are learning and the overall importance of your education. Language shapes who we are, how we see ourselves, how others perceive us, and our very actions and behavior. We want you to harness the power of language consciously to serve you.

We devote an entire chapter to this topic because we believe that communicating with others about one's field of study is a skill that is undervalued not only in Women's and Gender Studies, but in most undergraduate fields. In other words, students are not typically encouraged

## WGST PROGRAMS AND DEPARTMENTS RESPOND TO QUESTIONS ABOUT EMPLOYMENT

Women's and Gender Studies departments and programs have been proactive in responding to the question of what one can do with this degree through designated areas on their web pages.[2] For example, the Women's Studies department at the University of California, Irvine not only lists some of the skills that employers have found in Women's and Gender Studies graduates, but lists some of the special attributes that undergraduates bring to a variety of organizations and businesses:

Employers and graduate programs also know that your Women's Studies degree means that you:

- are well-rounded, with a wide breadth of knowledge;
- are prepared to work in diverse organizations, companies, and communities, and to be successful in our increasingly complex and connected world;
- stand out from the crowd, and have the creativity and confidence to major in an innovative field; and
- have expertise on gender, race, sexuality, and class relations, which are areas for which there is growing demand in a number of fields and professions.

The University of Massachusetts at Amherst's web page lists a "partial list" of some of the jobs that Women, Gender, and Sexuality undergraduates have obtained under specific topic areas such as "arts, business, administration and technical work, education, health, human services, library services, political action, research, and writing, editing and reporting." Portland State University's Women, Gender, and Sexuality Department's web page is similar to UMass Amherst's web page in listing some of the occupations that their undergraduates have secured after graduation, but they have also embedded links for "vocational biographies, professional associations, Internet sites with career-related information for Women's Studies majors, and Internet sites with job search information for Women's Studies majors."

or coached on how to discuss their chosen academic majors. One of the core goals of this book is for you to learn how to be your own best academic advocate. Being your own best advocate involves becoming comfortable with communicating. You will feel more confident about your choice, and others will experience that confidence when they interact with you.

In this chapter, we first discuss the kind of "constituencies" that you will be regularly speaking with about your Women's and Gender Studies education: family, parents and relatives, partners (e.g. husbands, wives, domestic partners, and significant others), friends, and the general public (e.g. potential employers, co-workers, professors, and, yes, the "nice old lady" on the airplane). Some of these folks may know a lot, while others may know nothing about Women's and Gender Studies in higher education. We highlight and help you anticipate some of the questions you may be asked, and the responses that you might receive from each group.

Learning how to communicate about Women's and Gender Studies takes practice, time, and, like most things, it is a process. Think of developing your communication skills as a type of workout. Just as it takes focus, practice, and determination to run a marathon or keep up in yoga class, these same characteristics apply when trying to become comfortable with various types of public speaking. If you can think of communicating about Women's and Gender Studies as a muscle to develop and flex, you are more likely to get inspired, to practice, and to get creative about your responses. It takes time to think through and answer different types of questions that may be posed to you by family, friends and the neighbor next door. The exercises at the end of this chapter are designed to help you practice communicating with others.

## The Five Questions

Drawing from our own experiences as educators in Women's and Gender Studies, we have identified five basic questions that are consistently posed to Women's and Gender Studies students. We explore them throughout the chapter:

1. If Women's and Gender Studies centers on women's lives, is it anti-male?
2. Given the enormous progress women have made over the past three decades, why would you need a degree in Women's and Gender Studies?
3. What kind of employment can you find with a degree in Women's and Gender Studies?
4. Is Women's and Gender Studies biased because it has a political agenda?

5. Does Women's and Gender Studies create victims by arguing that women are victimized in different ways?

Do any of these questions sound familiar to you? For clarity and ease of classification, we provide examples of how various groups of people might raise these questions. However, in your everyday experience, you are just as likely to be asked any one of them from any person. Let us see how these questions might emerge for you.

### Talking to Family

We begin our discussion with the important core group with whom you will most likely have to discuss your choices about an educational degree: your family. Family members tend to have a vested interest in our college experience. They often provide emotional, financial, and social support for us while we attend college. So, when you think of family, what people come to mind? Are you thinking of your:

- parents;
- husband, wife, partner, or significant other;
- teenage son;
- great-aunt; and/or
- godfather?

Get a clear image of that person or group of people. We would like you to keep their image in mind throughout this section. They are the people you will most likely talk with about Women's and Gender Studies at some point during your college career.

One of the most stressful experiences that some students have during college is sharing their decision of an academic major with family members. Why? Because, for some students, it can mean choosing a very different path than the one their parents thought they were taking. It can bring up a difficult conversation about family expectations that were perhaps, up until this point, implied but not explicitly stated. For example, if you were always strong in the sciences throughout high school and had taken lots of science classes in the early part of college, there might have been an expectation that you would pursue a career in medicine or the health professions. Much as with the scenario in the opening of the chapter, if you come home and announce that you are now a double major in Women's Studies and Anthropology, your family may be completely surprised and confused. Choosing a major with intention and purpose can feel both disorienting and exhilarating, because it marks perhaps the first time that you embark on a learning process that you have defined for yourself. It can be disorienting, for example, if you always thought of yourself as a Zoology student but have, over the past two years, become obsessed about the role of masculinity in nineteenth-century British novels. That kind of change can feel like a dramatic shift for everyone involved.

The challenging path for a student is to illuminate their decision-making process to someone who does not share the same day-to-day academic experience. Some students inform their families of their decisions about classes, majors, and minors throughout their college career. Others have longer conversations about academic matters over holidays, summer, fall, and winter breaks. First-generation college students may have the additional challenge of talking about the college experience to family members who do not understand or identify with that experience. This may be especially acute in working-class families, for students from countries where education is seen as a privilege and not a right, or in families where a college education is seen as tied solely to creating economic opportunity rather than personal self-development or fulfillment. If a family member is helping to pay for college, there may be significant expectations that they get to shape what you decide to major in and the opportunities that you pursue during college.

For students who are more financially independent, the concern over what a particular family member thinks may be less of an issue because the student may not live at home or rely on any monetary support from parents or extended kin. These students may find themselves having conversations with their intimate partners, which can produce some similar dynamics.

Many students find that when they talk to their family members about their interest in Women's and Gender Studies, they receive positive and supportive responses. This can be your experience, too. We will give you tools to increase the likelihood of a positive outcome.

Affirmative responses about Women's and Gender Studies from family members can feel deeply supportive. Carol shares her experiences of talking with her family:

As the first person in my family to earn a four-year degree, it has been rewarding to tell family members what I do as a Women's Studies student. Granted, my great-grandmother and great-aunts have no need for the jargon of academe (hegemony, discourse, constellation of identity, etc.). However, these women very well understand what it means to be discounted because of race, class, and gender. And when I tell them that part of my work is "acting like women count" through research and writing, for example, they care and understand and are, I am gratified to say, deeply proud of me.

(Carol, 2007, University of North Carolina
at Chapel Hill)

Marci,[3] a former student of Michele's, had a startling experience when she talked with her mother about becoming a Women's Studies major. Marci talked about her commitment to issues of sexual violence. It was then that her mother revealed a life-changing story to Marci. Marci's mother had been raped in a bar when she was in her early twenties, before Marci was born. Her mother lived in a small town and detailed the negative experiences that she faced in seeking support and justice. She felt that even the local support services aimed at sexual assault survivors were judgmental. Her mother explained that she felt judged because of her prior sexual behavior and also felt others looked down upon her because of her class status. She had a very difficult time bringing a case against her attackers. Marci had never heard this story before. Her mother was thrilled that Marci had found Women's Studies, and noted that she had taken some Women's Studies courses at a community college. Her father was also supportive of her decision, and encouraged her to conduct an internship at a rape crisis center near campus.

We have found that many students who have decided on Women's and Gender Studies have seen themselves as walking in family traditions of study. Carla, a Women's Studies minor, said:

My mother was a Women's Studies minor at SUNY-Geneseo in the late '70s/early '80s, so in a way I was continuing the tradition. Being a third-wave feminist was like being a chip off the old block. I am proud to come from such a forward-thinking family, men and women included.

(Carla, 2008, University of North Carolina
at Chapel Hill)

Graduates have also reported that parents make very supportive statements about their choice to pursue Women's and Gender Studies, such as: "I wish they'd had Women's Studies when I was in school. I would have taken it!"

It is completely normal for parents and family members to be interested in their loved one's education. If family members do not embrace your choice of Women's and Gender Studies, several factors may be involved. For example, family members do not always know or understand the changes that have happened over time in higher education. We have found that some parents, in particular, reflect back to their own experiences in college and project them onto understanding the choices their children make. People's expectations of what constitutes academic work are usually heavily influenced by their own personal experiences. This perspective can sometimes position perceived "new" majors unfavorably. Some parents may assume that if it did not exist "when I was in school," then the major or area of academic study is somehow less legitimate.

For instance, if a student's parents went to school during the 1970s, depending on what college or university they attended, they probably did not have campus departments and programs dedicated to the study of the environment, peace, or ethnic studies. However, these academic fields have emerged over the past 40 years and have thriving majors that are well established on many college campuses and universities. Another example: perhaps your mother attended a state university around 1990. It is likely that there was not a Women's Studies program established there at that time (or, if there was, she did not know about it), and it is quite possible that she never even had a female professor during her college career. If so, her experience might make her skeptical or less receptive to understanding why you have chosen Women's and Gender Studies. If this is the case, you may find yourself having to talk about how Women's and Gender Studies developed in higher education, drawing on material from Chapter 1.

Parents also feel an enormous responsibility to make sure that you are successful in the world. Sometimes parents ask, "How is this major going to help you find employment?" They obviously want you to graduate with a degree and set of skills that can benefit you in a fast changing global marketplace. Therefore, it may be useful for you to have a sense of what kinds of positions you can apply for with your degree. Finding this information in our book or on your school's website would be a start. It might also be useful for you to spend some time finding out who are the most successful graduates of your school's program—you will get lots of useful information from Chapters 5 and 6, which focus on employment and career pathways. Women's and Gender Studies graduates work in a variety of fields and succeed in the public and private sectors. Some parents and relatives may welcome such concrete information and be more supportive of your decision when this is included.

It may also be helpful to remind family members that you will enter into a very different labor market than the previous generation. Employ ment in one sector over the course of one's life is rapidly becoming a thing of the past. For example, your career path is most likely going to be a fluid experience as opposed to a stable one. It would be helpful to share with family members who may not know that nearly half of all graduates change their career plans after they finish college and the average person changes careers nearly five times in his or her lifetime. This trend will probably remain stable for the next several decades. You might also stress to your family that Women's and Gender Studies (as with other liberal arts majors) is preparing you to be adaptive and responsive to larger trends in the marketplace. It does not prepare students for one specific job, but is a way of preparing to harness one's individual talents and abilities in a broad variety of careers.

Talking openly about what Women's and Gender Studies means to you, why you value it, and what you think it might mean for your career can create a level of closeness between you and your family. It also means thinking ahead about how to tell the story of your experience of Women's and Gender Studies. We agree with best-selling author Mary Pipher about the importance of stories as "the most basic tool for connecting us to one another" (Pipher 2006: 11). Stories evoke strong emotions in our listeners and can trigger powerful stories from our audiences in return. We encourage you to become intentional in how you tell the story of your interest in Women's and Gender Studies. People often respond favorably when you tell them why this academic field of study has meaning to you. It also gives you time to reflect on its meaning, as it did Courtney, a double major in Journalism and Women's Studies, who discusses her experience talking with family:

## CHARTING CAREER CHANGES: RESEARCH AND MYTHS

When discussing future careers and the labor market, you may come across Information that says that the average person changes their career three to eight times over their life. Actually, there is no accurate statistic that charts workers' changes over time with that predictability. The problem with this estimate is twofold. There are not only issues with "operationalization" or how one defines and measure the terms one is using (e.g. an occupation versus a career; a shift within the same field to another job type or a promotion), but with collecting the data as well. According to the U.S. Bureau of Labor Statistics, there is a paucity of longitudinal data measuring the average number of jobs/careers held by the average citizen. A Bureau of Labor Statistics (BLS) news release published in July 2012 examined the number of jobs that people born in the years 1957–1964 held from age 18 to age 42. The title of the report is "Number of Jobs Held, Labor Market Activity, and Earnings Growth among the Youngest Baby Boomers: Results from a Longitudinal Survey." The report is available on the BLS website (see www.bls. gov/news.release/pdf/nlsoy.pdf). These younger baby boomers held an average of 11.3 jobs from ages 18–42 (in this report, a job is defined as an uninterrupted period of work with a particular employer). On average, men held 11.5 jobs and women held 11.1 jobs.

However, it is important to convey to worried friends and family members that the trend in employment is that workers need to be prepared to change jobs often. And many studies suggest that there is not a direct correlation between choice of major and a specific employment position post-graduation. Given our survey data and interviews conducted for this book, we strongly believe that training in Women's and Gender Studies prepares students to think creatively and dynamically about matching their skills and interests to the working world. Moreover, there is ample evidence that employers are seeking the kinds of liberal arts skills that Women's and Gender Studies students tend to possess. In a recent national survey of business and employment leaders, 93 percent said that "a demonstrated capacity to think critically, communicate clearly, and solve complex problems is *more important* than [a candidate's] undergraduate major" (Association of American Colleges and Universities and Hart Research Associates 2013). Also, more than nine in 10 of those surveyed said it was important that candidates that they hire demonstrate ethical judgment and integrity, intercultural skills, and the capacity for continued new learning. Moreover, in the five key areas that employers said they want more emphasis in Women's and Gender Studies students tend to excel in, these include: "critical thinking, complex problem-solving, written and oral communication and applied knowledge in real-world settings" (Association of American Colleges and Universities and Hart Research Associates 2013).

Information is power, and being informed of quantitative surveys of what employers are saying about the value of a liberal arts degree can add substance to your conversations with others.

When I told my parents I was a feminist, they had a lot of questions. Dad wanted to know if I was dropping my Journalism major, if I was planning to miss class to attend bra-burning rallies, and if I considered what a male boss might think in the future. Mom wanted to know if I was still going to shave my legs, if I had been to church lately, and if she was still going to have grandchildren—"not adopted ones—real ones." They both wanted to know if I had actually thought about this decision.

That was three years ago and, thankfully, my parents have a better understanding of what being a feminist means—and what it means to me. Though most of their original questions were thoughtless and unfounded, asking if I had thought about my decision was extremely relevant.

It wasn't until I enrolled in Introduction to Women's Studies my sophomore year that I began to think about anything. I consider myself to be an intelligent person, but until that point I was not an intellectual person. I had never considered motives or experiences before accepting information as "the truth." I had never thought about the ways in which I was privileged or oppressed. I had never thought about activism or agency. I had never even thought about my own racial identity as a person who is half-white and half-American Indian.

> (Courtney, 2010, University of North Carolina
> at Chapel Hill)

Although, initially, Courtney's parents were not supportive of her decision, Courtney was able to talk with them further about her academic interests, and in time the stereotypes that her parents held dissolved. Over time, they also could see the positive changes that occurred in Courtney's life as Courtney truly claimed her education.

Frank conversations about the role of feminism and Women's and Gender Studies will probably come up at some point with your parents. You can view discussing your interests with your parents as a process, one that can have an impact on yourself and your family in interesting and sometimes unpredictable ways. Diana Rhodes is a graduate in Women's Studies and Sociology from UNLV and is profiled in Chapter 6. Diana's experience provides a useful illustration of how conversations about Women's and Gender Studies can contribute to new ways that family members experience their own reality:

My mom always raised me as a strong independent person. My mom was raised in Texas and she came to the US in the early

1970s, from Vietnam, when she was 8 or 10. She came right at the end of the war and she was the youngest of 12 siblings. My mom is a badass!

At first, they [her parents] did not quite get it [her feminism and interest in Women's Studies], but they are now cool with it. I realized that my parents have always given me choices, they always let me choose what I've wanted to do. It was funny because my mom didn't identify as a feminist. I would buy my mom bell hooks books and stuff for birthdays and she would never read them. She was like, "it's not really my thing," which is interesting, because when I first started getting into my activism, my feminism and my Women's Studies world is when she more rapidly began moving up in her career. She works in gaming [in Las Vegas]. She started in the cage [as a cashier] . . . and now she's a senior shift supervisor. The more she got promoted and started moving up, the more she started seeing these very gendered things and how male-dominated her world is. She saw the choices and the compromises she would have to make. She stopped wearing skirts and started wearing suits. She would buy her pants a size too big so it would hide her curves. She shared with me these little things. We'd talk about it and now she tentatively identifies as a feminist. The more she got into higher positions, she started to see the things I'd talked about, which was really not good, and she had to face those things. But she started dealing with those things and asking why things were happening, [asking about] "this very power structure, patriarchy," the kind of words I was talking about, and now she's very, very proud of me.

(Diana, 2006, University of Nevada, Las Vegas)

You never know where a conversation about Women's and Gender Studies will take you!

---

### SPOTLIGHT: MOYA BAILEY

You met Moya Bailey in Chapter 2. Here, she reflects on her parents' understanding of her pursuit of Women's Studies and her passion and commitment to feminism—interests that do not easily map onto a traditional career path:

It's difficult because they [her parents] see feminism as a constant critique (which it is), but they see that as a negative thing. They say, "Don't you get tired of pointing out negative things on TV and in the newspaper?" And I'm like, "Don't you get tired of taking this in and it not being healthy?" But then we've joked about that and even my dad will sometimes say, "You think I'm this patriarchal man," and he'll say it in a joking way—it's a joke but with an edge. But I think my relationship with Women's Studies does challenge the way women are supposed to be, and he knows that. What's interesting is that as an only child, I think the way my mom and dad raised me was to be independent and take care of myself (not to depend on men), which is a feminist principle. It's interesting to me that they cultivated [that in me] but then they are surprised how that gets carried over—they didn't connect what they were doing to feminism explicitly.

Moya said in her interview that her parents believed that being a doctor was a very clear career choice for their daughter, so they were surprised when she changed her major (from Premed and Psychology to Premed and Women's Studies) and focus:

I loved science, it came easily to me, I did lots of summer science programs, went to hospitals and did lots of programs related to medicine, so it seemed like a big switch to them. But I couldn't really see the systemic change that would happen for me, becoming a doctor. I could be a practicing physician who did things differently as an individual practitioner, but in terms of the system itself, it didn't seem like [being a doctor] had enough impact, and that was one of the things that made me shift. So, they are concerned about my individual livelihood, but feminism made me think beyond myself in many ways. And that is one of the tensions that they have with feminism, that it is global and focuses on the big picture and community. And I think in a lot of ways they don't trust a lot of people, and rightfully so—they grew up in Birmingham [Alabama] during all of the social unrest [of the civil rights movement]. Those experiences have made them very interdependent upon each other and my family. I don't necessarily have that same sense, so my sense of "Let's change the world on a global scale" is not where they are.

Moya charts the evolution of discussions about Women's and Gender Studies and feminism with her parents, with these discussions encompassing humor, their concern, and her sense of what is right for her life. Moya makes an important connection between how her Women's and Gender Studies training and feminist practice encouraged her to think differently about career choices. We will come back to this point in Chapter 7. Your training in Women's and Gender Studies is going to encourage you to use a different lens to think about what is next after graduation. Moya found that this type of critical thinking led her down a new and interesting path.

Conversations about Women's and Gender Studies can become inflamed quickly when issues of sexuality or politics unexpectedly arise. Some family members may question your political beliefs and even your sexual orientation if you show an interest in Women's and Gender Studies. Respondents in our survey and interviews revealed stories of initially feeling harassed when talking to some family members about their choice to major in Women's and Gender Studies. Some graduates have felt that Women's and Gender Studies can be used as a scapegoat for parents and relatives to suggest disapproval for other beliefs and behaviors that they might feel are unacceptable.[4]

More specifically, some female students are concerned that a family member may accuse them of being a lesbian if they discuss an interest in Women's and Gender Studies. "Lesbian baiting" has had a long history in feminism and Women's and Gender Studies, and we live in a society where LGBT issues and feminism are still suspect. Graduates mentioned that being accused of being a lesbian was a response from some family members (and peers). It is our belief that this is a homophobic response, and can provide for a tense conversation. It can also be additionally challenging for students who feel that they *have questioned* aspects of their sexual and/or gender identity through the synthesis of material and critical reflections in their classes.

Suzanne Pharr (1988: 19) defined lesbian baiting as:

> an attempt to control women by labeling us as lesbians because our behavior is not acceptable, that is, when we are being independent, going our own way, living whole lives, fighting for our rights, demanding equal pay, saying no to violence, being self-assertive, bonding with and loving the company of women, assuming the right to our bodies, insisting upon our own authority, making changes that include us in society's decision-making; lesbian baiting occurs when women are called lesbians because we resist male dominance and control. And it has little or nothing to do with one's sexual identity.

Although we emphasize in this chapter the importance of face-to-face verbal communication, we also believe that other types of correspondence play important roles in communicating your ideas. If you find yourself accused and attacked about sexuality and/or political views after talking about your interest in Women's and Gender Studies, and you have tried to respond respectfully and cogently (using some of the techniques that we offer at the end of the chapter), it may be important to allow for a cooling-off period between you and that family member. During that cooling-off period, we suggest that you try writing them by e-mail, card, or letter some of your thoughts about how that person responded. Written communication allows for some time to elapse between strong feelings that might have been shared by you and a family member. Writing also helps to clarify one's thoughts and allows for reflection, unlike direct communication. If you decide to write a letter, you might want to express disappointment at the tone of conversation, about what allegations or assumptions were made, and about how that made you feel. You can use "I" language. For example, "I feel like 'X' when you say 'X'." Using "I" statements can help you express your feelings without blaming others. This allows for the person to look at their assumptions and to distinguish between what you would like to accomplish as a student and being labeled in a category that may or may not reflect your immediate experience. There is, of course, no guarantee that your letter will be heard and received with the intentions you meant, but it provides another way to communicate your ideas and feelings with someone who is very important to you.

If you do decide to have a conversation with peers or family members regarding stereotypes about your sexuality and your major/minor/concentration, you may want to model the ideas that are conveyed in the Women's Sports Foundation's "Special Issues for Coaches of Women's Sports" report (2009). They include a section that lists questions and responses for coaches regarding some parents' concerns that lesbians may be "present" in women's athletics as either players or coaches:

> You can also tell parents that one of the benefits of playing sports is the opportunity to learn to work with people across differences and that this experience is good preparation for living and working in an increasingly diverse world. Tell parents that you expect all of your athletes to treat each other with respect and to learn to work together as a team. Women's teams often include athletes and coaches who are different from each other in many ways— race, religion, class and sexual orientation, to name a few. (Women's Sports Foundation 2009: 13)

Whether you are currently a student athlete or not, we believe that this statement conveys to parents the very ideas of Women's and Gender

## STRATEGIES FOR DEALING WITH LESBIAN BAITING

The term "lesbian baiting," in this context, refers to the interpersonal experience some students who express interest in Women's and Gender Studies face from family, peers, and others who assume (or accuse) that the student identifies as a lesbian or bisexual person. The person might respond, "*No!* I'm not a lesbian!" and by doing so, she is validating that such a thing would be terrible. Indeed, it validates the homophobia that propels the comment. This is a very common strategy to shut down Women's and Gender Studies students.

> Lesbian baiting is tough. A guy at my work assumed I was "man hating" because he knew I was a Women's Studies major. I think the best way to deal with it is to train yourself to be calm and not get defensive over such things. Depending on the person, maybe you can ask them to explain how Women's Studies makes you a lesbian. Sometimes when people are forced to explain their ABC thought processes, they realize how dumb it sounds.
>
> (Tucker, 2008, University of North Carolina at Chapel Hill)

Studies: acceptance of others (and oneself), the importance of education, cultural competency, and teamwork in an increasingly diverse world.

The best preparation for family discussions is to take some time anticipating their responses. As you reflect on the person (and people) who constitute your family, can you begin to imagine what kind of response they might have when you tell them about your interest in Women's and Gender Studies? Will they be supportive or uninterested, or ask for more information? Have they expressed strong feelings about your career path throughout high school and college? By anticipating the types of responses you may encounter, you can begin mentally to script your answers to your family member's questions. Also, as you begin to create a ready answer for someone you know and love, you will be able to recycle and reframe your answer for other groups (such as friends or the general public). The exercises at the end of this chapter will help you to do just that kind of work.

### Talking to Friends

Learning from and being with other students who become your friends is one of the special gifts of a college education. In college, friends are often a mirror of our interests, academic and personal passions, likes and dislikes. Friends play a key role as sounding boards and advisors as we navigate both the academic and social life that is part of a college experience. We have heard a range of responses from our respondents about the role of peers in their college influences. For some students, many of their friends have taken Women's and Gender Studies classes and are encouraging of them to explore the field. Others had friends who had never heard of Women's and Gender Studies and made pointed remarks about choosing it as a course of study. Students can feel confused and isolated when peers are not accepting of their personal and academic choices. If you are not prepared for it, navigating the range of possible comments from friends about Women's and Gender Studies can feel overwhelming.

April, a double major in Psychology and Women's Studies, discusses her experience:

> While I was in school and had only taken a few Women's Studies classes, I didn't know what to say! Then I started to tell people to imagine taking a History class where the perspective was only from women—which I think was helpful, but it still confused some people. Now, I've added that it's more than just re-examining our past to include women's POV [point of view], but also examining how gender and sexuality shape all aspects of our lives.
>
> Also, I've found that male students tend to ask more [questions] than female students, and they assume that all we talk about [in Women's Studies classes] is feminism or man-hating ideas. Crazy!
>
> (April, 2009, University of North Carolina at Chapel Hill)

From peers, you might experience comments and questions that sound something like this:

- "Being a Women's Studies major—isn't that like being a double feminist?[5] That's going too far."
- "Isn't Women's Studies just for women? Isn't that against men?"
- "Doesn't Women's Studies just blame men?"

The idea that "man-hating" ideas comprise all of the discussion in Women's Studies courses is a familiar one. Lindy West (2013) addresses the complexities of labeling feminists as man-haters in "If I Admit to Hating Men is a Bad Thing, Will You Stop Turning it into a Self-Fulfilling Prophecy?" For West:

> Feminism is, in essence, a social justice movement—it wants to take the side of the alienated and the marginalized, and that includes alienated and marginalized men. Please stop turning us against you . . . It is nearly impossible to address problems facing women—especially problems in which men are even tangentially culpable—without comments sections devolving into cries of "misandry!" from men and replies of "misandry isn't *real*" from women.

Echoing West's sentiments, Jo T (2012), in a recent article in the *F-Word*, states:

> There's no denying that men are oppressed by certain cultural norms. These tell them (men) that they shouldn't openly express their feelings, that there is only a very limited way to perform masculinity in an "acceptable" way and that disagreeing with dominant tropes about what is and isn't "manly" can lead to very unpleasant consequences.

Yet, the issue for both West and T is when male-bashing claims are lobbed at feminism without exploring how the problem of alienation felt by many men is not caused by feminism, but by patriarchy or the systematic power structures/institutions that are still male-dominated. In other words, men are being oppressed by other men.

West goes on in the article to address some of the common refrains heard toward feminism, including: "why feminism has 'fem' in it or why we all can't be humanists," "why claiming sexism isn't real is a sexist thing to say," "why people being shitty to you does not mean that you are not systematically disenfranchised," "a list of the men's rights issues feminists are already working on," and "I'm sorry you are in pain but stop taking it out on women." Check out West's article for more information for your personal toolkit on how to respond to claims of "man-hating" (West 2013).

Many people may also conflate feminist political activism with the role of Women's and Gender Studies as an intellectual pursuit. And while it is clear that an aspect of inquiry in Women's and Gender Studies is concerned with change that benefits all, it is also an interdisciplinary field of study that is accountable to the standards of good scholarship and insights that govern work in colleges and universities. To this point, we think that reminding your peers of the academic outcomes and learning goals that Women's and Gender Studies seeks to teach would be helpful as a response to questions about its relationship to politics and activism. We like how scholars (and activists) Gwyn Kirk and Margo Okazawa-Rey grapple with this first question: "Good scholarship is about looking at analytical patterns and asking difficult questions" (2010: 5). During some point in your academic career, you may very well be interested in activism, but it is far from a given that all Women's and Gender Studies students define themselves as activists.

Unfortunately, feminists and women concerned with gender equity are often largely portrayed as being unfeminine, bra-burning man-haters. This distorted notion can affect how some friends may view Women's and Gender Studies and your interest in it. In Chapter 1, we documented the role of Women's and Gender Studies in demanding the inclusion of women into traditionally male-centered curricula—classes often centered on subjects that were ignored in other courses. Rather than addressing the lack of parity, some educators and the general public think that feminists and the Women's and Gender Studies community wanted to make men as invisible as women had been in the academy. Comments by friends questioning how Women's and Gender Studies addresses men's lives might mirror this same concern.

Yet, as Women's and Gender Studies has flourished in the academy, it has also opened up new spaces for examining the complexity of both women's and men's lives. Looking at men's lives and asking critical questions about gender has enabled scholars to examine the concept of masculinity and to develop Men's Studies. As Michael Kimmel states in his provocative essay "Men and Women's Studies: Premises, Perils, and Promise" (1996): "without Women's Studies there would be no Men's Studies." Women's Studies made gender a lens with which to understand the world. Through critically evaluating the roles of men in society, scholars could look more closely at how men also occupied multiple social statuses (including age, race/ethnicity, nationality, sexuality, ability) that affect their experiences with power and privilege in contemporary societies.

## THE MYTH OF BRA-BURNING FEMINISTS

If you have talked to someone about feminism and/or Women's And Gender Studies, there is a good chance that you will have heard the ever-famous phrase "bra-burning" at some point. This phrase might arrive in front of you as the question: "Do you want to be like those 'radical bra-burning feminists'?" Or as a phrase: "Those 'bra-burning feminists' were really angry way back when." In many people's minds, feminist activism of the 1960s is often reduced to women burning their bras. You will find in your studies that this idea is narrow, simplistic, and *untrue*. During the 1960s and 1970s, women and men were actively challenging gender roles and ideas about men and women in society in a variety of ways and places. Yet, the media framing of that decade of feminism was all about bras. So, what did really happen?

Although some people may equate bra-burning as a necessary adjective before the term feminist, there has been a lot myth-making between the two. Many second-wave feminists took aim at the normative standards of beauty, including critiquing the role of beauty pageants as ritual of reinforcing norms about ideal womanhood. A few days before the 1968 Miss America pageant, a number of women protested (including members of New York Radical Women) and threatened to burn all "instruments of torture" (i.e. girdles, curlers, bras, and issues of *Cosmopolitan* and *Playboy*). This was one of the first public, organized protests by women to critique a big and popular event. They did not, however, burn any bras (deciding in favor of fire safety). A reporter quoted Robin Morgan, an activist there, and she indicated that it had been a "symbolic bra-burning." Although no bras were actually burned at this event, the reports in the paper just a few days after the event connected feminists with "bra-burners." Most historians of this time period suggest that very few actual bras were ever destroyed during the women's liberation movement. However, once that symbolic frame was presented as a way to understand "women's libbers" and feminists, it stuck as a dominant one that did bring national attention to the women's liberation moment, thus creating allies. Indeed, women around the world began to protest beauty pageants. But the "bra-burning feminist" label created a frame for parts of the public to delegitimize and dismiss important concerns that many women were raising through the beginnings of a mass movement.

For more information on this topic, see Ruth Rosen (2000) *The World Split Open: How the Modern Women's Movement Changed America*, and Estelle Freedman (2002) *No Turning Back: The History of Feminism and the Future of Women*.

Concepts such as "hegemonic masculinity," as explored by scholars such as R. W. Connell and James W. Messerschmidt (2005), Michael Kimmel (1994), and Michael Messner and Donald Sabo (1994) have challenged masculinity as a universal experience, and instead presented it as an ideal type, which many men aim toward (due to multiple rewards and pressures), but few men can attain. As discussed in Chapter 1, besides Men's Studies, gender as the key organizing focus of inquiry helped in the creation of Gender Studies, Transgender Studies, and Queer Studies. Thus, rather than being exclusive or narrow, Women's and Gender Studies has advocated for and supported a more inclusive and complex analysis for all human beings.

So, if you are confronted with questions specifically about the role of men in Women's and Gender Studies, you might respond with a statement such as the one offered by Gwen Kirk and Margo Okazawa-Rey, who smartly addressed this topic (paraphrased and imagined here):

> Sounds like you've got a misperception that by focusing on women, men are left out of the picture. First, Women's Studies is about looking at gender, which includes women and men's roles in societies. Women's Studies doesn't blame everything on men of any particular background. That's anti-intellectual. I find Women's Studies personally empowering and useful in how to critically evaluate the ways that longstanding patterns of inequality affect us all. I see Women's Studies as committed to seeing how experiences of inequality and privilege shape people's everyday lives.
>
> (Kirk and Okazawa-Rey 2010: 5)

The benefits of Women's and Gender Studies classes are not only for undergraduates, but have applicability outside the classroom. Recently, on the *Chronicle of Education* blog, in "Confessions of a Community College Dean" (2012), Dean Dad discusses how his experience taking Women's and Gender Studies classes has been invaluable for his position as an effective leader. He states:

> Women's Studies courses were some of the most useful courses I've ever taken.
>     I'm not kidding.
>     Moreover, I can imagine them being incredibly useful for other men in management roles.

That flies in the face of cultural stereotypes, I know. Courses like those are usually held up—by those who like to make such arguments—as among the most self-indulgent of the purely academic enterprises. They elicit snickers from some. I get that. But there's a tremendous value in them that rarely gets expressed, even by supporters of courses like those.

At their best, the Women's Studies courses I took—yes, I used the plural—helped with two incredibly important management skills. They helped me learn to navigate complex and emotionally charged issues, and they helped me learn to depersonalize categories.

These skills are useful every single day.

Read more at Dean Dad (2012).

A slightly different way to respond to naysayers might be:

Women's Studies is not as narrow as you might think. Although it places women in a center of analysis, it does not ignore or diminish men. This analysis benefits everyone, regardless of their gender, and it looks at a range of issues. Women's Studies has

## THE WHITE RIBBON CAMPAIGN

In the early 1990s, a handful of men in Canada decided they had a responsibility to urge men to speak out about violence against women. Wearing a white ribbon would be a symbol of men's opposition to violence against women. In less than two months, 100,000 men across Canada wore a white ribbon, and many men found themselves talking about the root causes of sexual assault. This effort was incredibly effective and through it the organization was born.

The White Ribbon Campaign (WRC) is the largest effort in the world of men working to end violence against women (VAW). In Canada, the White Ribbon Campaigns take place throughout the year. In over 55 countries, campaigns are led by both men and women, even though the focus is on educating men and boys. In some countries, it is a general public education effort focused on ending violence against women.

The WRC is a small organization that encourages chapters to be started and run around the world.

taught me the ways that men have played key roles in promoting the advancement of women generally. For example, it was in my Women's Studies class that I learned about the White Ribbon campaign, which is about men fighting sexual violence. I've also discovered the ways that men have been actively fighting for fair pay for women and women's health issues.

The White Ribbon Campaign is a great example of how Women's and Gender Studies concepts can manifest into a social movement by men and for men to address sexual violence. Another example of how Women's and Gender Studies can be directly applied on campus can be found in Wantland's (2005) "Feminist Frat Boys? Fraternity Men in the (Women's Studies) House." Rather than expecting change to occur within the confines of the traditional Women's Studies classroom, the developers of the Fraternity Peer Rape Prevention Program collaborated with members of the Greek system to embed sexual anti-violence programs within the system. In addition, we would be remiss not to mention the work of violence prevention educator Jackson Katz, whose work in anti-sexist violence education has been the inspiration for many Women's and Gender Studies students and faculty who have read his books and watched his education films (*Tough Guise*, *Wrestling with Manhood: Boys, Bullying, and Battering*, and *Spin the Bottle: Sex, Lies, and Alcohol*). Katz and his colleagues have made important strides in addressing sexual violence perpetrated by men for male viewers/readers/audience.

## Men Talking about Women's and Gender Studies

Both heterosexual and queer men who take Women's and Gender Studies classes and choose to major or minor in it can face unique and particular challenges when talking with peers about their academic commitment to Women's and Gender Studies. For example, heterosexual men may face homophobic remarks from some male peers who question their sexual identity. Heterosexual men may also encounter skepticism from their female colleagues who question their motives about majoring in Women's and Gender Studies. Some comments that our respondents have heard concerning men in Women's and Gender Studies include: "They're just acting like sensitive men in order to get into women's pants" or "Because they're privileged as men, they can never truly understand a feminist perspective." We have also encountered heterosexual men who are trying to define themselves as men in a culture that often asks them to demean the very women who have raised them, women with whom they have raised families, women as partners who have survived sexual assault, and women who are their children

We turn now to Matt (whom you met in Chapter 1), who reflects on the comments he received from peers after he declared his Women's Studies major:

> A lot of the men in my life at the time I was getting into it [Women's Studies] had no idea of what to make of it. They would either say, "What are you going to do with that?," "What the hell are you thinking?," or, "It's a great way to meet chicks." It was always one of those three responses. Or, maybe not stated as directly to me as often, but raising . . . questions about my sexual identity. Of course, men learning about women's experiences means we want to sleep with men. That's not even logical! But lesbian and gay baiting is a common response to women or men who get involved in feminist projects.
>
> (Matt, 1999, University of North Carolina
> at Chapel Hill)

Homosexual men also must deal with issues of sexism, both within the larger social environment and within gay male culture. Homosexual or queer men might also be mistaken for or presumed to be transgendered individuals wishing to become transsexuals—since they are interested in "women's issues."[6]

In his thought-provoking essay "How Feminism Made Me a Better Gay Man," Zach Stafford (2012) reflects on his experience in Women's Studies classes:

> Sitting in classes where I was a gender minority was at first jarring. Between all the sports teams, gym rooms, and jobs I'd had in the past, I had never been around large groups of women before.
>
> I immediately became hyperaware of any comments that were degrading toward women, which led me to see the comments I myself had made in regard to how certain gay men performed their "gayness" (for example, the "flamers," whom many in the community attack for being "too gay") as particularly problematic and only further dividing us rather than uniting us.
>
> Feminism showed me that critiquing or making jokes about gay men for certain feminine qualities was essentially critiquing

women. It was a form of sexism that hurt more people than it made laugh.

As I went through school and learned more about feminism(s), I started having a hard time connecting with old friends and even family.

... Feminism is about liking women—more importantly, it's about seeing women as equal. However, feminism showed me that it takes more than liking someone to see them as equal.

You have to fight next to them to make them equal.

As a gay man, you are a man, and men have much power and privilege in the world (i.e. patriarchy), but being gay complicates that identity, making you seem less-than in many people's eyes.

Many bigots see you as being like a woman or wanting to be a woman, which gay men will internalize and see as negative.

Feminism looks at that thought and says, "What's wrong with being a woman?" and pats you on the back, and even may give you a pair of heels to strut in.

This part of feminism was and is to this day empowering. I needed to hear that message at 18, and I still need to hear it now.

Unfortunately, there are no easy remedies for challenges raised by peers. We hope that after discussing the importance of Women's and Gender Studies in your life with your friends that they are better able to understand your motivations and perhaps look at their own misperceptions in a new light.

### Talking to the General Public: Employers, Coworkers, and Casual Acquaintances

When I applied for the Marshall scholarship, I had to attend a panel interview on campus. I was interested in pursuing a master's degree in Gender Studies at Leeds University, home to the Centre for Interdisciplinary Gender Studies. I imagined there wouldn't be much competition for this particular degree in a college that was outside of London.

One woman on the panel asked me why I wanted to study gender [and] what the validity of the subject was. She asked in a respectful way, saying that as a person who had studied math, she really didn't know what to expect in such a course of study. I wasn't prepared for the question at all. [I thought] If Leeds and many other universities devote faculty and centers to the subject, then it must obviously have some validity beyond my mere opinion

---

### 🔍 SPOTLIGHT: MATT'S TIPS

As we have noted, men who are interested in Women's and Gender Studies issues might encounter open skepticism and hostility from other men (and some women). Matt has spent the past decade working on issues of sexual violence and motivating men to become allies in the struggle against violence. He thinks it is imperative for men to become active in feminist struggles. He provides these tips to encourage male students to deal with peer pressure:

- Find other men who are doing anti-racist, anti-sexist, and anti-homophobic work. It helps to build a community of supportive male allies. It is critical for men to do work within the communities of privilege they occupy so that they can be better allies.
- Become engaged in activist projects. Men in Women's and Gender Studies who might identify with feminism can deepen their commitments to feminist work by committing over a period of time to projects in which they are interested. This can support their interests and help build friendship and ally networks with both women and men.

---

on the subject, not to mention the effects of grassroots feminist movements across the planet.

I recovered quickly and gave a decent answer, but I was in no way prepared to defend the entire academic pursuit of gender studies. [I wondered afterwards] Are other masters programs questioned this way?

(Carla, 2008, University of North Carolina
at Chapel Hill)

You encounter many people in your life in a variety of situations. In this section, we want to spend some time encouraging you to think about how you will communicate with people who are not your family or friends. We mean casual acquaintances—potential employers, coworkers, people you meet on a plane, professors (not in Women's and Gender Studies), and passersby. In our experience, it is very common that students meet and casually talk about their academic interests with people outside their immediate family and peers. You may even meet people inside your university, other faculty members and staff, who do not know about the Women's Studies department or program at your college or university— as Carla's example above demonstrates.

We think it is important for you to gain some measure of confidence in talking about what Women's and Gender Studies means to you in brief exchanges with people you meet casually. Again, you may encounter people aside from your peers or parents who do not know much about Women's and Gender Studies. Many students have these encounters early on in their academic careers.

Tucker, a graduate whom you met earlier in the chapter, reflects on her experience:

> So when people have absolutely never heard of Women's Studies, I try to explain it as the study of all different types of people that have been historically left out of academics; that the [Women's Studies] degree is about raising awareness of the oppression of different races, religions, genders, ethnic groups, socio-economic backgrounds, etc. So, if I think people aren't going to be very receptive to hearing about Women's Studies, I try and explain it in a more all-encompassing way.

Thinking about how to talk to others about Women's and Gender Studies was very important to Tucker as she began interviewing for positions after graduation:

> When I applied to my current job at a technical college, they had explained to me that many of their students were from different socioeconomic and racial and ethnic backgrounds. Later on one of the people interviewing me asked me what exactly Women's Studies was. He made some joke about living with his wife for 25 years and if that counted, ha-ha. I explained to him that it was about being aware of the different types of people in this world and used it to support why I would be a good candidate for this position—because of my sensitivity and awareness of other people's differences.
>
> (Tucker, 2008, University of North Carolina<br>at Chapel Hill)

Meeting people who do not know what Women's and Gender Studies is can also happen if you travel out of your home country, as Katelyn, a Women's Studies major, relates below. She traveled to Guatemala both while she was a student and after she graduated:

> Whenever I told peers I encountered while traveling that I was a Women's Studies major, the most common reaction I would

receive was a blank face. They would look at me as though I had somehow misspoken and wait for the real answer. When I began to explain what a Women's Studies major was, they would continue to stare blankly until I finished, and then would say, "OK, but what is your career going to be?" This would then launch into a discussion of the numerous paths that you can take as a Women's Studies major and after I told them the path that I was planning on taking with my degree, they would tell me an anti-woman joke. It's amazing how after telling someone that you're a Women's Studies major, they think that the most appropriate response is to tell you a joke about how women belong in the kitchen. Yet, after many different times of hearing almost the exact same response, I've developed a pretty good answer for the blank stares [when people do not know what Women's and Gender Studies is], and have heard almost every anti-woman joke that there is. The answer that I almost always give people when they ask what Women's and Gender Studies is, is that it's the study of the past and current struggle of equality for women and men. It looks at our history from a gendered perspective and aims to gain a better understanding of what happened to all members of our population, and not just those writing the history books. It also integrates a social, racial, and economical lens when examining society. Women's and Gender Studies is not just about trying to rewrite history from a female perspective, as people often claim, but really a chance to look at our history and try to understand why certain inequities still exist today and how we can work to change these.

> (Katelyn, 2008, University of North Carolina
> at Chapel Hill)

Although we hope that your international experience will go more pleasantly, Katelyn's experience is a good reminder that it is important to be prepared to talk calmly and intelligently about Women's and Gender Studies.

## Bias

You may encounter people who believe Women's and Gender Studies does not constitute a real discipline, produce useful knowledge, or is inherently too political to be an "unbiased" discipline. Some people might hold the assumption that "Women's Studies is not 'real' scholarship but, instead, is feminist propaganda" (Kirk and Okazawa-Rey 2010: 5).

The word "bias" is one that you might hear occasionally when you talk about Women's Studies in particular. People may imply that it is biased to begin inquiry with questions that center on women, their experiences, and implications of living with inequality in a variety of forms. For example, Women's and Gender Studies classes often ask the question: "Why do we see different and negative global outcomes for women in the areas of health, economics, and political spheres?" Someone you meet might not like the starting point of talking about unequal outcomes. They might come from a research tradition that assumes an "objectively" knowable world where all questions are equally legitimate and are unconcerned with the "real world." So, bias can emerge as a type of critique that is used by some when all research is presumed to be conducted "objectively," or without reference to or interest in lived experience.

Women's and Gender Studies research in the academy emerged, in part, to counter truth claims by researchers who, on the face, seemed "unbiased," but systematically ignored or distorted women's experiences. Often, the neutral and unbiased observer was revealed to have power to direct and communicate research findings in specific ways suitable to them, and to not be neutral at all in portraying ideas about human history. Research that appeared on the surface to be neutral often reproduced sexist ideas about men and women. Women's and Gender Studies scholars instead enter research from the perspective that all knowledge has a type of built-in lens with which everyone enters the research process. Indeed, many Women's and Gender Studies scholars would argue that all research has a perspective that should be acknowledged and made transparent, and that all results must be questioned. The research process is thereby seen as a type of self-reflexive exercise, as well as inquiry—offering insight into your own self and your position as researcher. Women's and Gender Studies scholars acknowledge that their work comes out of a perspective that challenges power and assumptions that knowledge is neutrally pursued in research. Women's and Gender Studies makes an explicit claim that knowledge can never be neutral.

There is also a political dimension to how particular ideas about the role of Women's and Gender Studies in higher education have been formed in the public. In "Sticks and Stones," Martha McCaughey describes the attacks in the US against Women's and Gender Studies— conservative arguments waged by scholars who suggest that Women's and

Gender Studies is not intellectually rigorous. These attacks try to delegitimize research that exposes inequities along race, class, and gender fault lines. Other challenges to Women's and Gender Studies have emerged in political hearings from legislators who question the legitimacy and, ultimately, government-sponsored funding for what they would call feminism and sexuality research (McCaughey 2009: 70). While this is not a new phenomenon, economic downturns, as well as changes in legal and political environments, present ongoing challenges to Women's and Gender Studies faculty and students alike. Political and social attacks on feminism and Women's and Gender Studies in higher education are cyclical and often reflect broader attacks on women's growing political and social power.[7]

Norway's recent national debate and furor about the value of studying gender is an important illustration of how questions about the role of Women's and Gender Studies in higher education manifest in contexts outside the United States. In the early part of 2010, *Brainwash*, a television show, aired that proposed to take up topics about biological- and social-explanation models of human behavior, especially within the realm of gender and sexuality. The show proposed exploring questions that included: "Are men biologically destined to be rapists?" "Is one born gay or does one choose to become gay?" "Why are so few women choosing careers in male-dominated fields?" The show was heavily favored to present biological explanations over socially situated ones. And, although gender experts were consulted, they and other interviewees were seemingly kept in the dark about the overall motives of the show. Gender scholars offered answers that relied heavily on looking at gender as a type of social construction, and they minimized the role of biology as the sole factor in understanding human behavior. When the show was broadcast, it erupted into a national debate in Norway about gender and the role of gender studies programs in producing research. Many in the academic community believed that the scholars were unfairly presented (and then attacked in the media) as having no interest in science or biology, which was not accurate. Some citizens and political pundits called for the closing of research centers on gender and sexuality; others believed that the gender research was less legitimate because it did not explicitly rely on the biological sciences. Many in the scholarly community perceived this to be an unfair criticism, as gender research (in Norway and globally) is connected to the sciences, but the starting point for the types of questions being asked often differ. Gender scholars do not take science at face value when understanding human sexuality and gender arrangements. Jorunn Økland, director of the Center for Gender Research, was in the maelstrom of these debates and has written several blog entries about the outcome of these debates:

> The debates have focused on the importance of natural sciences in explanations of sex; other main theories about gender and sexuality; main topics in gender research—what falls outside its remit?; the role of gender scholars in a state feminist country— are they supposed to be in opposition to the government or help them introduce research-based policies? The debates have also raised issues of media ethics, and how to produce catchy popular science programmes. The debates have, on the one hand, shown all the characteristics of a scapegoat chase (after all, only 4–5 gender researchers were interviewed, altogether there are less than 50 academics, Ph.D. students included, working at gender research units in Norway). On the other hand, it has provided gender researchers with a unique opportunity to spread awareness about their existence and to convey some of their research to the general public.
>
> (Økland 2010)

In responding to a question or remark about bias, you could emphasize that Women's and Gender Studies is taught globally in over 700 different kinds of institutions. You might say something such as:

> Given the diversity and longevity of the many institutions that currently encourage and support work on Women's and Gender Studies scholarship, it's not likely that they could survive in the academy this long without presenting useful information to scholars outside of Women's Studies and the public. Academic research on women and gender is published widely in the academy and is often used by policymakers. These factors suggest that the academic community works hard to secure the highest quality work from scholars in their fields.

Talking and debating about gender and sexuality often makes people uncomfortable. Women's and Gender Studies scholars have argued for the past 30 years that gender arrangements are neither neutral nor without consequence. A critique of societal power has also been a component of

Women's and Gender Studies research. Therefore, as students pursuing work in this area, you should not be surprised that Women's and Gender Studies has fended off its share of attacks and criticisms. We do not feel discouraged by such cyclical issues, as they are part of being involved with fields of study that seek to challenge the status quo, and we hope that you are not disheartened either. Instead, we encourage you to be a well-informed student who can respond to sometimes pointed questions in a calm and thoughtful way.

*Creating Victims or Identifying Inequality?*

Another question that you might encounter from someone in the general public is: "Doesn't Women's Studies create victims by arguing that women are victimized in different ways?"

Many of our respondents faced this question at some point in their Women's and Gender Studies training and have provided interesting responses. Eva Marie, a Women's Studies major who you met in an earlier chapter, responds:

> From the introduction of terms and definitions, some studies use the issue of victimization as a self-awareness tool to inform students how to recognize the meaning [*sic*]. It is my belief that Women's Studies does not breed victims, but gives its students a way to explain why victimization occurs and how to prevent it.
> (Eva Marie, 2010, Minnesota State University, Mankato)

Beth, a former student of Cheryl's, builds on this point:

> The importance of Women's Studies is to recognize our place in the world, how we contributed to the current state of society, and to promote the option (through knowledge) to act. Furthermore, although Women's Studies may bring the acknowledgement to individuals that they have been victimized, it also gives the knowledge and strength to turn victims into survivors and to make oppressors (in many forms) aware of their contribution to victimization (of themselves and others).
> (Beth, 2008, Minnesota State University, Mankato)

Carol, whom we met earlier in this chapter, comments:

> Women's Studies equips women to critically engage the world by asking sometimes very simple questions like, "Why do people warn

their daughters about being out at night alone, but not their sons?" Such questions do not make women victims as much as equip them to interrogate the various discourses that (in this example) make parents' fears "real."

(Carol, 2007, University of North Carolina<br>at Chapel Hill)

We know that Women's and Gender Studies graduates are up to the task of finding skillful ways of responding to questions, concerns, and even skepticism about their academic interests. In Luebke and Reilly's (1995) study of the first generation of Women's Studies graduates, they found that the majority of students were undaunted when faced with indifferent or even hostile feedback about their choice of major.

As with anything, a new skill requires practice, practice, and more practice. You may go through cycles of working on your communication about your academic interests. It might be helpful to think of this as a process that will continue even after graduation.

Communicating about Women's and Gender Studies is not just your responsibility. We, as professors, find ourselves in similar positions because we encounter people who know little about Women's and Gender Studies or have uninformed perceptions of what we do as professors. In other words, your Women's and Gender Studies professors may confront the same kinds of challenges that you may face. We feel that communicating about Women's and Gender Studies in an accessible way is part of our role as educators. Just like you, we have had to practice and find ways to make communication fun for us. Michele has been inspired by Jane Burns, one of her senior colleagues, who makes a point to travel with a copy of the department's complete course listings. When Jane sits down next to her seatmate on the plane and is asked by her, "What's Women's Studies?" she pulls out the course listing and says, "Here are all the courses that we teach." She also rattles off information about how Women's and Gender Studies has courses cross-listed with every major school on campus at the university (e.g. School of Social Work, School of Medicine, etc.), how the department teaches over 250 students each semester in the "Introduction to Women's Studies" course, and the ways that Women's and Gender Studies contributes to the mission of the university. For her, having a visual reference is quite helpful and allows her to feel relaxed while talking about what she does as a Women's Studies professor. We have suggested some exercises below to get you started as you think about your communication of Women's and Gender Studies.

## YOUR TURN: EXERCISES

### 1. ELEVATOR SPEECHES

One way to become more comfortable and proficient in talking about your academic passions is to practice a technique of communicating that is called the "elevator speech." The elevator speech began in the world of business. It is used to help prepare people to sell their product in a short amount of time—usually the time it takes an elevator to ascend a few floors. An elevator speech presents a sizable amount of information in a compressed way. Having a short speech memorized can be very helpful when you meet different people and want to convey important information in a quick and concise way. We have adopted the elevator speech as a teaching tool in our classes. For example, we will suggest a role-playing scenario where the student imagines he or she is in an elevator with someone (perhaps the dean of the college), and they have just a few minutes to verbally explain a concept we are discussing in class using jargon-free language. In this scenario, one student plays him or herself and the other student acts as the dean of the college. Students have told us that this exercise helps them to think on their feet and learn how to talk about complex terms in everyday language.

The elevator speech is highly adaptable. You can use this tool as a way to introduce yourself, to build professional and personal relationships, and to have a confident answer to the potential questions that you may face. The elevator speech has a few key components:

- the speech is not longer than 30 seconds;
- the speech is usually under 100 words; and
- the speech is no longer than 10 sentences.

The best way to begin is to develop an elevator speech that centers on your interest in Women's and Gender Studies by way of self-introduction. One way to begin constructing your elevator speech is to think about what your academic study means to you. In order to do this, you may want to look over your notes from Chapters 1 and 2. You also might want to set aside about 30 minutes to play with the following questions, which are designed to help you reflect on some of your experiences in Women's and Gender Studies thus far.

In adapting this tool for your everyday interactions with others, reflect on the following questions:

- What benefits does a degree in Women's and Gender Studies provide you with as a student?
- How have you made connections between what you study and everyday life?
- Is there a vignette/story you can tell that would communicate your personal experience as a Women's and Gender Studies major (or minor, etc.)?

Once you have reached a place where you have some answers to the above questions and better know the information and feeling you want to convey in your elevator speech, we would like you to take each of the questions that we posed at the beginning of the chapter and create versions of your elevator speech for the different audiences that we have discussed in this chapter: family, friends, and the general public.

- If Women's Studies centers on women's lives, is it anti-male?
- Given the enormous progress women have made over the past three decades, why would you need a degree in Women's and Gender Studies?
- What kind of employment can you find with a degree in Women's and Gender Studies?
- Is Women's and Gender Studies biased because it has a political agenda?
- Does Women's Studies create victims by arguing that women are victimized in different ways?

Much of your communication style involves not just the words you use, but also your body language. To deliver an elevator speech effectively, you will need to be calm in your delivery. Be conscious of fidgeting and work on eye contact. Write your elevator speech out and, if possible, record it or film yourself. Practice on friends who do not know much about Women's and Gender Studies. Remember that in casual conversation, there will be some give and take, and you can always add to your response if someone asks you a question.

Remember Kendra from our introduction? She was having a hard time communicating with her mother about her interest in Women's Studies and what Women's Studies is. We have started some prompts for you to complete:

*Kendra*: Women's Studies puts women's concerns and experiences at the center of academic study. And, Mom, that's the great thing about this major, I can take all sorts of courses that are cross-listed between the Women's Studies department and the Political Science department. I can study women's political participation in Latin America or in the US, for example. Or, I could take a political theory class that focuses on what women have considered important about democracy and citizenship.

*Kendra's mom*: And you can major in that?

*Kendra*: Yes, definitely. Women's Studies is an academic major just like Theater.

- "The value of Women's Studies as a major is . . ."
- "Graduates in Women's Studies from my program go on to careers in . . ."

### Examples of elevator speeches

#### Cheryl's elevator speech

*Q*: So, you're a Women's Studies professor. What exactly is Women's Studies?

*A*: Women's Studies begins with the assumption that we are gendered, or that we are socialized to see and classify ourselves and others in often "masculine" or "feminine" terms. Gender is not only something we are assigned at birth, but something we constantly achieve and perform throughout our lives. It is also reinforced through laws, ideology, and language. But, even as gender plays a major role in our day-to-day lives, we don't often question it or its impact on our interactions. Women's and Gender Studies also considers the impact of other statuses on our identities, such as race, ethnicity, sexuality, age, ability, nationality.

### Michele's elevator speech

*Q*: So, you're a Women's Studies professor. What exactly is Women's Studies and what do you teach?

*A*: Women's Studies is an academic interdisciplinary field interested in producing new ideas that challenge existing ones about women's and men's lives. For me, that means that much of my teaching and research is about rethinking assumptions about women as political actors and examining issues of power and dominance. It is a solutions-based investigation tackling some of the most pressing global problems of inequality in our time.

You want to take your time in crafting different versions of the elevator speech. It will be important to practice the speech(es) until you feel comfortable with your delivery. There are a number of resources on the Web where you can find more information about elevator speeches.[8] Another benefit of crafting elevator speeches is that they are also great practice for job interviews!

## 2. WORD PLAY

So, when discussing Women's and Gender Studies with your various audiences, ideally you want to use language that is easily understood and connects with people's everyday experience. Talking about power, oppression, and intersecting identities in a simple and straightforward way is not easy! Think of this task in relation to something that is really fun, such as playing with magnetic poetry/word sets. You have probably seen these magnetic poetry refrigerator kits either in your or a friend's home. The kits are subject-specific (e.g. London, gardens, beat poetry, dogs, etc.) and contain a number of words that relate to the subject. These kits can be fun and allow for creative expression as you try out new sentences, word forms, or haiku. Unfortunately, no such magnetic word kit exists for Women's and Gender Studies.[9]

You can use this tool to kick-start your own innovative thinking. In order to do this, first think of approximately 200 concepts that you would commonly encounter in Women's and Gender Studies classes. This sounds like a lot, but you can quickly search through your class notes or the indexes in some of your favorite books. A good place to begin might be the texts that you used in your introductory classes. You will also need to add a few prepositions and other connecting words to your list (e.g. of, the, and, have, etc.). It may be easier to type these in a file and then, when you are ready, place the words in bold or use a large font size. Next, print your sheet and cut out the words. Spread the words around. Use your imagination. Move them around to make patterns and stimulate thinking. Look at the words. How would you use them in general conversation? What words are you drawn to? What concepts still feel too hard to explain in general conversation? This might be a fun and rewarding exercise to do with your Women's and Gender Studies classmates and friends.

## Notes

1.   Later in this chapter, we discuss stereotypes and assumptions about women's and gender studies and students who choose this as their major.
2.   Here is the list of web pages referenced. We encourage you to find other examples.
     University of California-Irving: www.humanities.uci.edu/womensstudies/undergraduate/ws_degree.php
     University of Massachussets-Amherst: www.umass.edu/wost/careers/whatcan.htm
     Portland State University: www.pdx.edu/careers/what-can-i-do-degree-womens-studies
3.   This name is a pseudonym.
4.   We will discuss the role of politics in the next section.
5.   This was an actual comment that was said to former research assistant, Sarah "Tucker" Jenkins.
6.   We are indebted to Christal Lustig for this insight.
7.   Susan Faludi (1992) was one of the first authors to examine the various social forces that converged in attacking feminism and women's studies in *Backlash: The Undeclared War Against American Women*.
8.   See, for example, www.speech-topics-help.com/elevator-speech.html.
9.   The closest kind of refrigerator magnet kit that might be suitable is one by Jessica Valenti, author of *Full Frontal Feminism*. We've heard that this kit exists but have not been able to locate one.

# 4
# DISCOVERING AND CLAIMING YOUR INTERNAL STRENGTHS AND EXTERNAL SKILLS

In Chapter 2, we devoted some time exploring some essential components of a Women's and Gender Studies curriculum, and asked you to assess where you are in your academic career and where you want to go. In Chapter 3, we discussed the many ways in which you can communicate with others about your experiences in Women's and Gender Studies, and provided you with techniques to enhance your own understandings of concepts you have learned in your undergraduate program. Now we want to explore how you translate all of the great training you have had into skills and strengths for the postgraduate and working worlds.

You may have been asked by parents and peers what are your skills. Or, you may be at a place in your academic career that you want to pay attention to your emerging set of skills and competencies as you move through upper-level coursework. You may have in mind that you would like to go to graduate school or a particular type of employment and are curious about what you have to offer. Questions about the particular skills and knowledge you gain through the course of your degree and how these can be applied in a job or your career are not unique to Women's and Gender Studies graduates; many students somewhere in their college degree have to grapple with these questions.

As we argue in Chapter 1, you are part of an intellectual tradition and legacy, one that produces a student with a particular set of skills, ways of problem-solving, and worldview. That intellectual tradition, like others, has produced a distinct set of ideas and concepts that students learn through coursework and other learning opportunities. In this chapter, we begin with a discussion of the top concepts that graduates identified in our survey as important to their professional work. They will look familiar to you, as they emerge from the feminist classroom. We also show you how these concepts are used in respondents' professional lives.

We suggest how you might begin to organize what you are learning (e.g. concepts, theories, frameworks, etc.) through the framework of "internal strengths" and "external skills." Skills and strengths grow out of the work that is done both inside and outside the classroom.

Here is what we mean. An "internal strength" is a quality, feature, or characteristic that is not always readily apparent, but perhaps feels like an inclination or talent. The term "external skill" or simply "skill" is probably familiar to you as the ability to do something well and/or something that requires training to do well (Stevenson, Elliot, & Jones 2001).

You might ask yourself: "What core skills and strengths have I developed during the course of my education?" "How do I begin to assess the skills I'm developing from my interest in Women's and Gender Studies?" "What kinds of topics and projects do I find most intriguing?" "What excites me?" "Conversely, what are the topics and assignments that make me want to down a triple espresso because they feel like chores?" "What are my core interests (e.g. do I love studying the 1970s feminist arts movement or prefer nineteenth-century colonial legal history in West Africa)?" "What kinds of information do I gravitate toward when given the chance (e.g. do I read every blog I can find about human rights issues in Latin America or do I follow the latest breakthroughs by female scientists)?" "What Women's and Gender Studies-related activities do I find myself pursuing in my free time?" "Do some of my passions outside the classroom overlap with concepts from—or were possibly even inspired by—my Women's and Gender Studies classes?"

These are questions that are important for you to consider as you move through your educational and professional career. They are the basis for thinking about future employment, post-baccalaureate education, lifelong advocacy, and long-term happiness.

## SKILLS OR COMPETENCIES?

Competency is a term that you might see in employment descriptions. A competency is an ability to do something, and is often measured against a standard. "Core competencies" typically refers to expertise that is fundamental to job performance and how an employee uses that in an organizational context. Some people use the terms skill and competency interchangeably. We prefer the term "skills." In this sense, skill refers to both the identifiable and measurable actions and behaviors that you are developing as a student, which you will take into the working world, and your own commitment to lifelong learning, which will lead you to your most promising and fulfilling future. Your future is defined by you and can include thinking about a temporary position, a career, continued education, leadership, and activism, or a combination of all of these activities.

Throughout this chapter, we ask you to reflect on your talents, interests, and abilities in order to clarify what your internal strengths and external skills are and how they might translate into professional and other contexts.

## Top Concepts Listed by Women's and Gender Studies Graduates

Recently, writer "JuniperBug" of Buzzfeed posted an animated feature titled "22 Things Women and Gender Studies Majors Understand." What is striking about this feature, besides the acknowledgement of stereotypes many in the general public have about the gender identity/sexuality of students, is that it highlights some concepts that are assumed to be "common knowledge" by Women's and Gender Studies students, particularly sex and gender as social constructs and performativity (Buzzfeed 2013).

Reflect for a moment on the concepts that you have been learning in your Women's and Gender Studies classes. What are some concepts that emerge as important and that perhaps you have found repeated in various classes?

For many students, it is difficult to narrow down the one most important concept learned during an undergraduate Women's and Gender

Studies education. Often, the concepts and ideas we learn are intertwined with other concepts and make it difficult for us to say which had the most impact on how we perceive ourselves, our daily interactions, and our world. In addition, the Women's and Gender Studies "canon" has been changing since the inception of the field, and existing key concepts have been affected by new theoretical perspectives and research that becomes incorporated into texts and classroom pedagogy.

Despite the challenges of a changing canon and of figuring out what exactly constitutes a "concept" (see the "Critical Thinking about Critical Thinking" sidebar on p. 155), we were interested in what aspects of Women's and Gender Studies training stays with graduates and is used in their professional and personal lives. In our survey, we specifically asked our respondents: "What is the most important concept that you learned in your undergraduate Gender and/or Women's Studies coursework?" When we think of concepts, we think about ideas and analytical frameworks or lenses that you might find in your coursework. Below, we discuss the top five concepts that participants in our survey indicated had the greatest impact on them.

*Gender* as an important category of analysis is one of the top concepts to emerge from our data. In all Women's and Gender Studies classes, there is discussion of why it is important to pay attention to the way social and institutional norms about gender and gender roles affect everyone's everyday experience. Gender as a category of analysis is a fundamental concept that has emerged over the past 20 years.

A subcategory of this concept involved responses that listed "the social construction of gender." The social construction of gender has been a dominant theme in the field of Women's and Gender Studies, especially within the past 20 years; Judith Lorber (1994), in fact, explicitly makes the case for the concept in her influential piece "Night to His Day: The Social Construction of Gender." Drawing upon the earlier scholarship of Candace West and Don Zimmerman (1987), Lorber believes that the process of engendering people is so commonplace that we only become aware of its impact when something is outside of the norm.

Similar comments received from students on our survey included:

- "For me, the most important concept is the social construction of gender, especially in science."

- "My concentration was on the history of sexuality and gender roles. The most important thing I learned is that these concepts are fluid and change over time and across cultures."
- "Gender is a creation, not a truth."

*Intersectionality* is another key concept that was mentioned by our survey's respondents. According to Berger and Guidroz (2009), race, class, and gender, as well as sexuality, age, ability, nationality, and ethnicity, are integral to one's position and status in society. Intersectionality approaches argue that individuals can locate their lived realities in relation to how structural forces and systems of oppression create and maintain differences based on these socially constructed identities (Berger and Guidroz 2009: 1). Intersectionality is an umbrella term to a host of theoretical and methodological approaches. This term emerged from the theorizing of women-of-color activists and theorists, who argued that gender could not be understood in isolation from other complex systems of oppression (e.g. race, sexuality). Analysis and activism are strengthened by an attention to approaching problems through an intersectional lens. Besides intersectionality, other terms have become synonymous with this concept, including race–class–gender matrix, multiple axes of inequality, the intersection, and the intersectionality approach. Our survey respondents echoed this multiplicity of terms associated with the concept of intersectionality, so we organized those terms under this concept.

Below are typical responses from our survey:

- "Intersectionality—how multiple oppressions can affect people and have to be considered by social justice advocates who want to achieve full equality."
- "That various axes of oppression intersect one another on multiple levels depending on the body, subjectivity, and position in society where they intersect."

The third concept is that of *inequality*.

Depending on definition of feminism, equality (or lack thereof) is the main organizing element of this modern social movement. According to Lorber (2012: 1), the basic goal of feminism is:

achieving equality between men and women. In many times and places in the past, people have insisted that women and men have similar capabilities and have tried to better the social position of women, as well as the status of disadvantaged men.

The concept of equality was first introduced in liberal political philosophy of the eighteenth and nineteenth centuries that argued for equal recognition and rights under the law for all people, regardless of race, social class, gender, and religion. While one of the first manifestations of equality under the law was voting rights (or suffrage for women), gender inequality is still experienced in a variety of institutional forms such as under the law (e.g. recognition of trans* identity for documents and medical care), the economy (the wage gap and differential gender representation of management and labor), the family (access to marriage, as well as different expectations for unpaid labor in the home and sexual violence), religion (belief systems that justify and maintain the unequal social organization of society), the state and military (unequal representation in leadership), education, arts, and media.

For many Women's and Gender Studies students, their readings and assignments make them more aware of the concept of inequality—how economic and social rewards are often distributed across a society unequally:

- "I learned that some issues I saw as personal shortcomings were actually the result of structural inequality directed at women. It also helped me to interpret the situations of other women in my family in this light. This was liberating, to say the least."

Undergraduate students stated that they learned as part of their Women's and Gender Studies education ideas about compassion, fairness, justice, and equality. We grouped these together under one umbrella that we are calling *equity*, our fourth concept. One respondent wrote, "the concept of fairness, justice, and treating people with equality and with respect, including the ability to understand other paradigms than the one you were raised with." In many Women's and Gender Studies classrooms, there is much attention given to discussing how to understand and remedy contemporary situations that have their roots in historic structural arrangements that favored one community over another. As Women's and Gender Studies curricula has maintained its connection with social movements and stresses applied learning through praxis, it is little wonder that many of its students have internalized notions of equity and justice.

## CRITICAL THINKING ABOUT CRITICAL THINKING: CONCEPT OR A SKILL

In many of your classes, you might have come across the term "critical thinking." Professors or teaching instructors might stress how important critical thinking is for the class. Critical thinking as a goal for the class may even be mentioned on a syllabus. When we think of critical thinking, we tend to categorize it as an activity—as something that students do in the way they approach and synthesize materials. We did not view it initially as a stand-alone concept because of its very broad definition. Many people in the survey, however, listed critical thinking as one of the most important concepts gained from their training—this got us thinking about the term. One reason why participants might list critical thinking as a concept is because Women's and Gender Studies introduced them to the role of critical thinking and its emphasis in Women's and Gender Studies classes. When conducting research, it is important to honor and make sense of information that participants provide. Related phrasings that we coded under critical thinking include critical analysis, critical writing, etc.

Here are how some graduates talked about critical thinking:

- "The ability to challenge a dominant/mainstream narrative—critical thinking."
- "How to think critically and question authority."

The fifth important concept listed by survey respondents was that of *empowerment*. Standard definitions of empowerment are: (1) give authority or power to; and (2) give strength and confidence to (Stevenson et al. 2001). Other terms associated with this concept include "agency," "self-determination," and "choice." Often, when a graduate listed empowerment, it was coupled with a reference to their gender identity (e.g. being a woman). As we stated in Chapter 2, many women students explicitly find Women's and Gender Studies useful in coping with some of the challenges and stressors of being a woman in sexist and male-dominated societies. Thus, we should not be surprised that we see this reflected in what concepts some students found useful. Moreover, with the emphasis that Women's and Gender Studies scholarship places on the importance of understanding and advocating for oneself and others through feminist and collective struggle, empowerment is a salient concept.

Other important concepts for Women's and Gender Studies graduates, as raised by our respondents, include: patriarchy (and capitalism), "internalized oppression," the "Birdcage" metaphor, collective action, choice, voice and active listening, respect for women, media bias, power (external, as well as perpetuated by women toward women), gendered violence, privilege and the politics of location, "the personal is political," omissions and silences, mind/body split, dichotomous thinking, and feminist research and knowledge production.

These concepts that the graduates identify are probably familiar to you. There is not a clean, direct one-to-one correlation between Women's and Gender Studies concepts and strengths and skills. Many concepts are difficult to disentangle from skills, as they are often learned through rapid application. By asking graduates about the concepts that have had the most influence on their thinking, Women's and Gender Studies faculty can better understand these ideas as shaping problem-solving skills in students. It also gives students and professionals an indicator of what ideas have longstanding power, what concepts are being challenged, and what ideas are emerging in the field.

## Internal Strengths and External Skills

Our research builds upon prior work that demonstrates that people who major in Women's and Gender Studies see themselves graduating with distinctive "skills" (Luebke and Reilly 1995; Dever 2004). However, we believe the term "skills" does not capture the complexity of what you have learned, because the term "skill" focuses on the more tangible and quantifiable aspects of your training, and therefore we make a distinction between internal strengths and external skills. An education in Women's and Gender Studies helps build both internal strengths and external skills in different ways. This discussion is grounded in how graduates talked about the strengths and skills they learned through their Women's and Gender Studies education.

At this point in your academic career, you have probably gained some feedback about the kinds of things you do well. You may not, however, have received any acknowledgement, or even be aware of your potential internal strengths. As mentioned earlier, internal strengths are those core talents you may possess but are not always aware of. An internal strength, however, is not always a preference or a talent. It may develop through the course of your training. Internal strengths can create a feeling of positive behavioral change inside a person that might not easily be measured. The internal strengths that are difficult to quantify accurately are reflected in graduates' understandings of how they interact with the external world because of the training they received.

Identifying internal strengths may take a process of reflection through self-administered tests or the verbalization by family members, peers, professors, employers, or others to make you aware of an internal strength. Strengths can be overlooked or neglected because they are taken for granted. Often in educational and occupational environments, we are critiqued on our deficits. Our "faults" are readily pointed to as areas for improvement. Yet rarely are we praised for our internal strengths and/or preferences. Here are some questions to start you thinking about your strengths:

- What kinds of feedback have you received on your research papers, activism projects, and/or internship memos?
- What areas have you been encouraged to pursue and by whom?
- In what areas do you consistently receive the highest ratings when evaluated by your supervisor at work?
- In what kinds of situations do you tend to thrive?

Unfortunately, we are seldom reminded of how important and valuable our inner strengths are in relation to the types of occupations in which we are interested. For you, your inner strengths might be amplified by your experiences in the Women's and Gender Studies classroom. With conscious recognition, you may be able to translate your internal strengths into a launching pad for the development of your external skills.

Everyone has inner strengths; they simply differ from person to person. Ideally, instead of focusing on our shortcomings, we should be promoting our inner strengths as areas to draw upon within an organization or cause. For example, you may have always been comfortable meeting new people and like to connect individuals with others. According to Buckingham and Clifton (2001), you may have the gift of "WOO" ("winning others over"). You may have been that young student who was never too shy to give a speech in the school auditorium or would gladly run for class president in high school. You may have a knack for motivating others in any activist work that you are currently doing. You may find it easy to speak often and persuasively in your classroom settings. On the other hand, you may not be as comfortable meeting new people, but prefer instead to work with smaller groups with whom you are familiar, or maybe you prefer one-on-one encounters or even working alone. This internal strength, of being "deliberative," allows you to approach situations strategically and weigh the various elements carefully. So, you might also think of an inner strength as a tendency, preference, or a leaning toward a particular behavior. In order to explore your own inner strengths, you may want to reflect on the following questions on everyday aspects of your life:

- Do you like to study alone or with a group of others?
- Do people tend to describe you as independent and self-reliant?
- Do you tend to seek help when confused with classwork, or do you prefer to try to figure it out before asking for help?
- Have you sought out mentors or have people actively engaged you as a mentee?

Knowing one's internal strengths is important. Not only will this knowledge guide you in looking for employment opportunities that (ideally) match your internal strengths and talents, but finding a good fit can also complement those external skills of your colleagues, collaborators, and employers. Utilization of your inner strengths will not only help you professionally, but as you learn to maximize your inner strengths you will be able to bring out the best qualities in those around you. This seemingly simple understanding can bring you much success and happiness.

Now, let us move from reflecting on your own personal inner strengths to looking at the internal strengths and external skills that many Women's and Gender Studies students generally possess. First, we will address internal strengths, including: critical self-reflection, self-confidence and empowerment, leadership, and ability to create community.

## Internal Strengths

### Critical Self-Reflection

An important internal strength is the ability to engage in *critical self-reflection*. Knowing how to engage in critical self-reflection helps you to assess your interests and talents accurately, as well as identify interpersonal areas that still need development. Your training in Women's and Gender Studies encourages a deep self-awareness about how one makes decisions in the everyday world and how they are connected to ideas of equality, fairness, tolerance, and social justice. Moreover, it illuminates the different institutions that shape how we experience the world.

At this point in your academic career, you have probably spent time thinking about interlocking oppressions. This ability to view the ways in which institutions and systems are interconnected and how they impact one's experiences based on social status is a powerful tool with which to view the world. Yet, as Patricia Hill Collins states, "we all live in social institutions that reproduce race, class, and gender oppression" (Collins 1993: 727). To be critically self-aware is to understand how one is complicit in perpetuating inequality. Critical self-awareness helps to reveal our blind spots in judgment, prejudices and the stereotypes we hold that help to maintain oppression.

You might want to pause for a moment and think about the role of critical self-reflection in your life. Have you come across this term in your Women's and Gender Studies classes? If so, in what ways have you found it useful for navigating the social world?

When we asked graduates about how they have used their degree since graduating, many respondents noted how important critical self-reflection was in their personal and professional lives:

- "Oh, I use it [my Women's Studies training] all the time in the way I interpret situations and act in them. Professionally, I created a staff training for an environmental education program utilizing feminist and queer theory and activism."
- "[I found self-reflection useful for] the ability to examine my own privilege, my own assumptions, and the part I play in broader systems of oppression."
- "[I use self-reflection] to analyze my relationship, guide the way I raise my children, and form the basis of my analysis of family law, and inform my interpretation of media.

As our respondents indicate, critical self-reflection is not only vital in their personal lives, but in their professional environments as well. As many Women's and Gender Studies graduates work in careers that have an impact on the lives of women and multiply-oppressed communities, it is especially important to assess the impact our work has on others. By internalizing the famous feminist mantra "the personal is political," Women's and Gender Studies graduates are cognizant of putting theory into practice and of avoiding the dangerous territories of "do-gooding" or meddling (rather than supporting individuals and groups) in order to gain the tools and resources they need to succeed.

*Self-Confidence and Empowerment*

Another important internal strength is the combination of *self-confidence and empowerment*. Having self confidence means you are able to listen to your inner voice, which tells you "you can do this" and "I want to do this"—rather than listening to the sometimes well-developed and loud self-defeating dialogue that prevents us from acting or from listening to less-than-supportive others. Self-confidence is also the ability to understand one's needs and articulate them. It means speaking up when you believe that you are right and taking an unpopular stand for something you believe in, too. We have partnered self-confidence with empowerment because they work together. A sense of feeling empowered can lead to more self-confidence. Self-confidence tends to foster healthy risk-taking. There are many jobs and careers that encourage and reward risk-taking.

One graduate surveyed said, "Because of my training in Women's Studies, I am more willing to take risks that will enhance my professional development."

> Another life skill that I received from my Women's Studies major was self-confidence and self-respect. It was absolutely amazing to

## A "SHOUT OUT" TO A STUDY THAT INSPIRED US: WOMEN'S STUDIES GRADUATES: THE FIRST GENERATION

Luebke and Reilly's (1995) groundbreaking study demonstrates that the first Women's Studies majors (1977–1992) credit their field of study with "increasing their self confidence and esteem, finding their voices, greater awareness, courage, self sufficiency, pride, dignity, and self worth" (Luebke and Reilly 1995: 2000). In our global study, we found that many of these same themes are still salient for more recent graduates.

be learning about incredible empowered women in an environment of self-motivated women who all believed that we could do
anything and how each one of them had dreams that they were
going to fulfill. I feel that oftentimes women's education is pushed
under the rug and Women's Studies is seen as a fluff major, but
even if I hadn't learned anything from a book during my time
[in Women's Studies], the environment that I was learning in
was so nurturing and encouraging that it helped my confidence
and motivation more than any other time in my life.

(Katelyn, 2009, University of North Carolina
at Chapel Hill)

Although Women's Studies and Gender Studies attract both women
and men, women students still feel that Women's Studies (in particular)
helps them develop internal resources that aid them in navigating a
sexist world, specifically by building confidence in themselves. There were
many comments that were similar to this one we received from a financial
consultant for hospitals who said why confidence was important to her:
"I'm not quiet, I'll speak up about issues."

Here are some responses we received:

- "Women's Studies 101 was the first class where I felt comfortable
  jumping in and speaking my mind (at 18); it translated to all of
  my other classes and jobs. Thank goodness."
- "Being with other smart, ambitious women in small classes really
  gave my confidence a huge boost and it helped me come out of
  my shell. I learned to speak with conviction in my Women's Studies
  classes."
- "[I have gained] an awareness of my rights as a woman . . .
  empowering me as a person. I have gained confidence and a greater
  sense of self. I am aware of the workplace challenges that women
  face."

A reporter with a nonprofit magazine said: "I believe it [self-confidence]
makes me a smarter woman, and has helped me to speak my mind and
stand up for who I am in both my work and personal life." Others stated
the following:

- "For the first nine years of my career, I worked in the sports industry
  as a publicist. I think my Women's Studies degree gave me a huge

boost of confidence just because it allowed me to study the discipline across economics, the arts, history, and yes, even sports."

- "Being confident makes advocating for what I believe in for my institution easier; I'm a curatorial assistant at a university art museum. I research and help curate exhibitions. Feminism has become connected to multiculturalism for me and in terms of the museum world it helps me to evaluate/rethink inequality in terms of the art world/art historical canon."

- "I am significantly more confident in my professional and personal life. I know who I am and focus on the important aspects of my life. I truly believe in helping others. With friends and coworkers, I showcase many core feminist values: nonviolence, collaboration, mentoring, service, and more. I learned about myself and what it actually meant to be a woman and feminist. It's the core of my identity."

## Leadership

We argue that *leadership* begins internally before it is manifested in actions in the external world. Leadership is an important internal strength. In Chapter 1, we discussed the learning components and philosophy that makes the Women's and Gender Studies classroom unique. In "What is Feminist Pedagogy?" Carolyn Shrewsbury (1993) identifies the core elements of feminist pedagogy or the application of feminist ideals into the teaching and learning process. According to Shrewsbury, these elements include community, empowerment, and leadership. Some of the inner strengths associated with leadership include: the development of negotiation skills not only in the professional arena, but in personal relationships as well; that we, as individuals, are responsible for our actions, as well as taking responsibility for any decisions we have made that have an impact on others we supervise or who are dependent on us; and that we are responsible for the success (or failure) of our efforts. Because of the emphasis on collaborative learning and the importance of praxis, Women's and Gender Studies classrooms are often an arena where students begin to see leadership characteristics modeled for them. Throughout your training, you may have opportunities to learn about leadership through internship and activism opportunities. In our survey research, graduates discussed how their training helped develop their capacity for leadership in everyday situations, as well as in specific leadership roles or positions:

- "My coursework in Women's Studies, as well as the on-campus activities in which I participated, helped me develop leadership skills I never knew I had, and probably never would have developed without those classes and that environment."

- "I work in politics, so a systemic understanding of gender, race, and sexuality issues has been extremely helpful, especially in coordinating coalitions. It has also been personally helpful in helping me navigate workplace sexism. I've noticed that I have a level of confidence in dealing with sexist co workers and supervisors that, unfortunately, many of my female colleagues do not."

- "For one thing, I work with families and young women, and I am better aware of their challenges in terms of access to resources, repercussions in many cases of physical or sexual abuse, and gender role expectations. Many of the individuals I work with are struggling with gender and/or orientation identity, and I feel my degree has aided me in working with these issues. More importantly to me these days, as a mother, I have used my knowledge of women's rights in helping to secure the first job share at my company—this allows me to be the primary caregiver for my children and to breastfeed—a women's issue not generally covered (I think) by most academic programs."

A graduate student in Social and Cultural Psychology credits the leadership and presentation skills she received as an undergraduate to her current success in front of groups: "I am comfortable giving presentations to peers and superiors." The director of fundraising for a nonprofit group working on the issue of human trafficking names strengths-based leadership through collaboration as one of her important skills: "I've always been able to build really strong teams—whether they were work-related teams or to gather a group of friends to participate in a volunteer project."

As another respondent stated:

The skill of leadership provides the confidence, assertive attitude, integrity, accountability, and ability to collaborate with others in order to succeed on any chosen path. As a Women's Studies major, I was empowered to take control of my future through learning about the presence of strong women in history, and my experience working with feminist groups/Public Allies (an AmeriCorps program, which is a 10-month nonprofit apprenticeship and leadership training program). The nonprofit I am working with is the ACLU of Delaware.

The importance of leadership as an internal strength is also evident in the leadership opportunities that graduates often created for themselves, which we discuss in Chapter 1.

### Community

Inner strengths that are connected to *community* include the ability to build connections and relationships inside and outside of our workplace, family, and neighborhoods. An example would be facilitating discussion among groups in conflict. This may involve leaning toward consensus-building practices rather than a stance of majority rule. It may include being the voice that calls for inclusion of a wide variety of perspectives rather than those of a select few who appear more powerful or who seemingly have the most "rational" argument. This inner skill may also draw upon your own code of morality. While our morals are shaped by our family, our social institutions, and even our disciplinary perspectives (or professional code of ethics), we often need to act in ways that support our inner sense of what is right and wrong. It may also mean stepping outside our comfort areas and becoming an advocate or an ally for a cause or group that may have been an adversary in the past.

Our survey respondents gave many examples of how their training in Women's and Gender Studies expanded their sense of community and how they utilized the concept of community as an inner strength that is valuable in a variety of day-to-day interactions:

- "The importance of listening to others, and being able to sometimes not know exactly why someone feels the way they feel, but to listen to what they have to say and show empathy [toward] their situation."
- "I recognize gender power struggle in both my personal and professional life. I doubt I would be aware of such struggles without having majored in Women's Studies. Knowing what's going on power-wise informs my decisions professionally and personally.

Knowing how to read between the lines and find out what's really going on is such a big part of working for any organization; Women's Studies has helped me tremendously in learning to do this. Even if there's nothing I can do about a particular situation, knowing that what's really going on involves power, and possibly gender power, means I am informed and ready to respond. It also calms me and reassures me that the situation may not be about me at all."

- "One person matters. Each of us is one person until we come together for a common cause, and that can evoke radical change. In addition, we can't remain stagnant—keep up the evolution of the women's movement in order to keep up with the times. Also, it's important for feminists to be vocal in the community, home, and workplace. Sometimes these big changes begin with our families and friends."

- "Presently, I am involved in Public Allies, an AmeriCorps program, which is focused on bringing positive social change to local communities. We work for local change through our involvement with local nonprofits, public service days in the community, and team service projects with community members. This is also the reason I am involved with Planned Parenthood's Young Advocates group. We plan and attend events to inform the local community about sexual and reproductive issues."

- "It helps me remember how the public health work that I do must be tailored to the community I'm working with; it also helps me as I evaluate my own approach to healthcare, especially prenatal care, and it gives me reason to participate in a variety of programs that I feel give other women the opportunity to explore new experiences and perspectives on life.

In this way, Women's and Gender Studies graduates are often in a position to enact positive and effective engagement with diverse populations. In sum, several of the internal skills associated with a Women's and Gender Studies education facilitate a broad sense of involvement and leadership by: (1) engaging with how you are connected to the world, as well as to other people; and (2) inspiring you to better yourself and the world through facilitating active engagement and activism in its many forms. Now we will discuss the external skills that can develop through your coursework and interest in Women's and Gender Studies.

## External Skills

External skills are learned and refined through knowledge, experience, and practice (Buckingham and Clifton 2001: 30). Often, skills are formalized into a set of steps or procedures that, through repetition and consistency, become refined (Buckingham and Clifton 2001: 45). Here is a list of external skills that Women's and Gender Studies students tend to possess:[1]

- thinking critically;
- developing interdisciplinary dexterity;
- developing critical reading and analytic skills on the variety of theoretical perspectives on sex/gender, race/ethnicity, social class, and sexuality;
- developing and cultivating openness, awareness, and respect of individuals, groups, perspectives, and experiences that may differ from their own;
- considering an issue from multiple perspectives;
- constructing arguments with evidence obtained from research;
- an ability to engage in research and analysis in order to gather information to either support or refute concepts and ideas;
- locating, evaluating, and interpreting diverse sources, including statistics;
- connecting knowledge and experience, theory and activism in Women's Studies and other courses;
- communicating effectively in writing and speaking;
- using gender as a category of/for analysis;
- discerning the importance of interlocked oppressions;
- applying cross-cultural and global awareness to "big questions" about women and gender; and
- applying knowledge for social transformation and citizenship.

Women's and Gender Studies skills are both overlapping with other disciplines and also distinctive in their application.

*External Skill 1: Thinking Critically*

Many students in our research valued that Women's Studies training gave them technical skills, but also encouraged them to read deeply and perceptively. Here is what Katelyn, a student quoted earlier, says:

> A very concrete skill that I learned while a student, particularly in my Women's Studies classes, was the ability to think critically and analyze works. We employed this in every class, and it was necessary to learn in order to write effective papers and get the most out of my classes. But more than simply getting good grades, this skill has translated quite well into the "real world." When reading articles in newspapers, magazines, or online, I find myself using the skills that I learned as an undergraduate and questioning the authors and wondering why they did not choose to include certain facts or where they had gotten some of their information. This skill has helped my confidence in debating with people and also appearing as an intelligent person to my peers.
>
> (Katelyn, 2008, University of North Carolina
> at Chapel Hill)

Another graduate from our survey responds:

> My job involves working with a lot of quantitative data, which is very different than my undergraduate interest in qualitative research, including ethnography. Still, I use the skills taught to me by my Women's Studies program. I have to work within a very rigid system of data collection and reporting (a main part of my job is translating raw data into data that can be used on an international, statistical scale). The way I examine and critique hegemony in the research field is that I closely examine every piece of data before coding it. I make sure that a patient's true experiences and conditions are being reported. I monitor any general oversight done by the healthcare providers who are working with them.

*External Skill 2: Critical Reading and Analytic Skills on the Variety of Theoretical Perspectives on Sex/Gender, Race/Ethnicity, Social Class, and Sexuality*

While you may be predisposed or have an inner strength that makes you interested in people of different statuses or positionalities, your Women's and Gender Studies courses also inform your perspective. Through dialogue and debate with feminist theories, your Women's and Gender

Studies classes encourage you to apply this lens to a variety of different situations. For example, you may have been asked to analyze or "unpack" visual representations of a particular community. You may be asked to do a similar assignment using Michael Kimmel's or R. W. Connell's concept of "hegemonic masculinity," or Adrienne Rich's "compulsory heterosexuality." You may have supported your position through a literature review of feminist authors.

*External Skill 3: Discerning the Importance of Interlocked Oppressions and the Ability to Apply Concepts to New Situations*

The concept of intersectionality or interlocking oppressions is a central one in Women's and Gender Studies and one that you are probably already familiar with. As we noted earlier in the chapter, this was the concept that graduates ranked as a top concept. This concept translates into a skill through applied use in professional situations. This ability is extremely useful. For example, perhaps you are seeking a job in the real estate industry. Not only must you be familiar with laws and regulations affecting the industry, but your ability to understand the relationships or intersectionality between race, class, and gender and other social identities may enable you to help clients find housing that fits all their needs—not just square footage. Perhaps your clients are differently abled and need access to support services or need to live close to public transport, or perhaps they need a floor plan that allows them to maximize their activities of daily living. How might housing's proximity to schools be important or the racial or age composition of the neighborhood? All of these factors play into your ability to work with your clients and their specific needs. Not only is this important for your client's well-being, but if one of your inner strengths is building community, you may be very aware that a happy and engaged neighbor is a benefit for everyone.

*External Skill 4: Developing and Cultivating Openness, Awareness, and Respect of Individuals, Groups, Perspectives, and Experiences that May Differ from Our Own*

The ability to understand others' viewpoints while still advancing our ideas is a skill that many graduates listed as important. Many graduates reported how important this skill was in their professional and activist endeavors. This comment echoes many respondents: "I feel very flexible in my way of thinking and able to engage with many different people and approaches." Many graduates said that treating people with "respect, consideration, and understanding" was an important skill they used. Several graduates also said that being a "thoughtful listener" was an important skill.

No matter what type of employment you plan on pursuing, you will, in some way or another, interact with others. Whether working face-to-face or not, we live in a complex, multicultural world, and it is essential to work with others who may differ from us. While many workplaces have some formal recognition of equal opportunity mandates and provide yearly training for employees so as to stay in compliance, your own ability to work well with others is an asset to any organization. Your Women's and Gender Studies (and any multicultural curricula) courses, as well as any experiences you have had learning about diverse cultures, may give you invaluable insight into working with others who grew up in a culture that differs from the mainstream. In fact, you may have had classes on social movements or collective action, where you were required to work together with others in a group setting despite your differences. To your professor's great delight, you probably learned to appreciate your differences and integrated these into the final product. This is a talent that can be used by you and your employer to create a just and open workplace. This brings us to one of the ethical perspectives often associated with feminism—that of "an ethic of care." Not only do we take care of ourselves, but we learn to be advocates and allies for our colleagues and to demand social justice and equal opportunities for others. One respondent listed "awareness of people's experiences" as important: "It made me able to deal with obnoxious 'good old boy networks' in a way that most feminists would have balked at, but, in the real world, you don't always get to wear a Capital F on your shirt."

Here are some comments that exemplify how people thought about and utilized this external skill:

> Within both professional and personal life, it *is* important to be culturally aware of where people come from and their situations . . . even more so in a professional situation because then you are dealing with clients (in my case, social work) and do not want to be judgmental of their situations or say something offensive.

How this helps them professionally: "My office is a safe space in every aspect of the word."

Another comment was:

> People can have different beliefs and I can still respect them, but at the same time work to preserve my beliefs.

How this helps them professionally: "Because my organization produces research on reproductive health issues, I work in a field that is emotionally charged. I have to remind myself that those that disagree with me are people too."

One respondent, a consultant in children's mental health, university lecturer, and health data manager, listed "trying to be inclusive of everyone" as one of her important skills: "I teach Psychology of Women, a course cross-listed with Psychology and Women's Studies. I have also used information on gender studies in my therapy." This graduate also said this skill was used in a professional context as a reminder to "use person-first language when talking to and about therapy clients."

A critical care nurse noted the importance of the skill of being able to empathize with different groups of people:

> If I'm not able to empathize, I'm not able to do my job effectively and the patient then suffers. By being able to see them as individuals and accept their lives as they are, I am able to accomplish more and I have had many people come up to thank me for making their (or their family member's) experience of being in a critical care unit bearable.

A film studies graduate student and educator said that "listening and respecting diversity" is an important skill:

> People often forget to listen to others these days; therefore, people only listen to—linear story—what they want to hear. Women's Studies encourages you to listen to others, which is becoming the most valuable action we need.

A project operations assistant and research coordinator for a nonprofit stated that: "I feel very flexible in my way of thinking and able to engage with many different people and approaches." This graduate performs grant research and writing (website, newsletter, and brochure), and said this skill helped, in that: "It aids interpersonal relationships and helps me adapt to any situation."

*External Skill 5: Ability to Engage in Research and Analysis in Order*
*to Gather Information Either to Support or Refute Concepts and Ideas*

An ability to examine an idea from a different perspective or to challenge
the prevailing collective wisdom takes strength, empowerment, and self-
confidence. Challenging prevailing assumptions and authority is difficult,
especially when one feels threatened (directly or indirectly). Yet, as we
have seen with several recent national and economic disasters, people who
challenge prevailing ideas are needed not only for a democracy, but it is
just good business. Often, it is not enough to challenge an idea, but one
must back up the challenge, utilizing a variety of viewpoints, research,
and standpoints. Therefore, core external skills of Women's and Gender
Studies undergraduates include researching and gathering information
from a variety of resources, standpoints, and perspectives. Also, these
skills can make your own perspective more rich and perceived by others
as more valid. Your training also helps develop your ability to see
connections between unlikely issues and develop arguments and positions
that take into account hidden or marginalized perspectives.

One graduate responded:

> I used it [research skills] regularly while coming up with a strategic
> plan for our Government Relations department at Planned
> Parenthood, and while planning the best methods for grassroots
> organizing. I am aware of the human rights critiques and power
> disparities when I discuss international human rights programs
> at my law school. I look for silent perspectives alluded to in our
> casebooks, in cases populated by and judged by wealthy white
> men.

Cheryl feels that she uses this external skill constantly. She teaches
about the history and theories related to HIV/AIDS. It is not enough to
be familiar with the current epidemiological and biomedical perspectives
about HIV as a retrovirus, or how it is thought to enter and interact with
the immune system. Cheryl finds that it is helpful to use metaphors of
the virus that make it more familiar and easier to understand. Cheryl also
discusses how the very metaphors we use in relation to HIV and AIDS—
plague, military metaphors (invading army), pollution (punishment for
sin or sex)—are the subjects of study by feminist scholar Susan Sontag
in her text *Illness as Metaphor and AIDS and its Metaphors* (2001). In
addition, by referencing pop culture (e.g. films and books, including *And*

*the Band Played On, Angels in America*) and addressing popular theories about the origins of HIV/AIDS, the topic of HIV/AIDS becomes less medicalized and more accessible to the general public. Its impact and understanding can then be supported through the arts, social sciences, journalism, etc.

## Putting the Pieces Together

You might not be aware that you may have already been evaluated on your external skills in Women's and Gender Studies courses by your professors, colleagues, and peers. For example, part of the process of assigning grades to students is through exams, journal entries, quizzes, oral presentations, papers, and other assessment tools (e.g. portfolios). These tools attempt to capture the degree to which you are exhibiting proficiency in the standards established by your program or department's curriculum committee, the university, and even those informally mandated by the Women's and Gender Studies scholarly community.

There are many places in your education to begin to assess your inner strengths and skills:

- examining components of your study: coursework, internship/ externship, honors and awards, study abroad, praxis project, honors thesis, and independent study;
- talking with people: conversations with peers, mentors, and parents; and
- reflecting on passions, hobbies, interests, and activist history.

---

### 🔍 SPOTLIGHT: STACY HUNTINGTON

In this spotlight, Stacy reflects on the skills she gained through her Women's Studies education, participating in the undergraduate research conference held at Minnesota State University, Mankato, and how it informed her thinking, research, and postgraduate life:

> The words "critical thinking" are often bandied about in academic settings, yet one person's idea of critical thinking is seldom comparable to another's. I experienced many types of academic settings, most of which prided themselves on enhancing the student's critical thinking skills, before I encountered the feminist classroom. The feminist classroom provided me with a setting in which

critical thinking was truly, in its most honest form, not only encouraged and enhanced, but sincerely represented. The professors who facilitated my Women's Studies classes did not engage in demeaning debate with a student over a concept, but encouraged the student to explore the idea more thoroughly through a different lens, the feminist lens. This was done all while empowering the student to explore not only what they thought and felt, but why that was their perception. Thus, I developed what I like to call on my cover letter and resume "a truly unique perspective," which not only identifies multiple aspects of a situation, but also allows me to analyze and discuss the implications of each. I do not always represent the most popular opinion or simplest solution, but my voice is always heard and I know that when I speak, people listen.

One of the very first concepts introduced during the WOST 101 Intro to Women's Studies course is the "invisible knapsack." Peggy McIntosh wrote the essay "White Privilege: Unpacking the Invisible Knapsack" in 1988, and it resonates just as loudly 22 years later as it did then.

My research project for the URC was titled "Deconstructing the Slut," and explored the ramifications of sexually active young people in a small Midwestern university. While constructing the survey questions, my professor encouraged [me to] incorporate questions that explored sexuality, gender identity, race, ethnicity, and age. While I found it difficult to adequately construct applicable questions that would provide an opportunity for each of the issues to be addressed, I feel that my research provided a reasonable representation of the demographic. The results of my research suggested that young, white, college-aged, heterosexual women who are sexually active with more than one partner are more likely to be considered sluts than young, white, heterosexual men, young, black, heterosexual men, young, white, gay women, young, black, gay women . . . and so on.

Currently, I am a church secretary and contract writer for a small-town, weekly newspaper. More than anything, my Women's Studies education provided me with a skill set more conducive to living a meaningful, insightful, tolerable life. My feminism cost me one job, but at the same time gave me the courage and empowerment to be steadfast in my opinion. My feminism does not make me popular or well liked, but it does enable my voice to be heard, which is a voice that is willing and able to speak for those who cannot. My success at the URC empowered me to openly and confidently discuss those nasty "taboo" topics such as sexuality and gender in public settings. And I honestly felt people walked away happy to have listened.

(Stacy, 2008, Minnesota State University, Mankato)

The exercises below will help you get started on this exciting work.

## YOUR TURN: EXERCISES

### 1. RATE YOURSELF ON INTERNAL STRENGTHS AND EXTERNAL SKILLS

Below we have listed all the internal strengths discussed in this chapter and eight of the external skills based on the longer list above, each worth 10 points. If you feel you have an internal strength or external skill that is just developing, give yourself five points. If you have a well-developed internal strength or external skill, give yourself eight points. If you feel that you have a fully developed internal strength or external skill, give yourself 10 points. If you feel your strength and/or skill is not developed at all, do not award any points. Tally up your points. Scores of 70 and above are in the target range—congratulations, you possess some key strengths and skills that will serve you well in work and life! Scores below 70 indicate where you might want to continue to improve or may indicate a lack of interest in this area—no worries, you now know what you need to build on and can move ahead.

Use your results to create a plan that moves in the direction of your long-term goals. In other words, if you are lacking in an area, seek professors, mentors, training, or coaching to fill in your gaps or weaknesses. Most importantly, however, take pride in the internal strengths and externals that you do possess and then take time to practice communicating those to others.

#### Examples of some internal strengths and external skills

- critical self-reflection;
- confidence;
- feeling empowered;
- leadership;
- ability to build community;
- applying cross-cultural and global awareness to "big questions" about women and gender;
- considering an issue from multiple perspectives;
- thinking critically;
- locating, evaluating, and interpreting diverse sources, including statistics;
- connecting knowledge and experience, theory and activism in Women's Studies and other courses;
- effective verbal communication;
- discerning the importance of interlocked oppressions; and
- applying knowledge for social transformation and citizenship.

### 2. WRITE YOUR OWN LETTER OF RECOMMENDATION

It is not uncommon that during your academic career you will ask someone—a professor, teaching assistant, internship advisor, or employer—for a letter of recommendation. Letters of recommendation are used to assess students for a variety of programs, jobs, honors, etc. You may have already asked someone you know who can discuss your assets to write a letter of recommendation. One technique for learning how to communicate the knowledge and skills you have gained through Women's and Gender Studies is to craft your own "letter of recommendation." Cheryl reaped the benefits of this activity when her advisor asked her to create a letter of recommendation as a self-reflective exercise in preparation for a job application. Not only did this activity give Cheryl's advisor a better idea of her student's talents, knowledge base, and experience, but in the process of writing the letter, Cheryl had to learn how to promote herself, frame her talents in a manner that corresponded with the requirements of the position, and actively acknowledge her strengths. The act of writing often allows us the opportunity to reflect, edit, and compose our lives into scripts that we internalize and ultimately believe. You might share your letter with your mentors and people you name as references and see whether they would describe you in similar terms.

## Note

1. We have developed this list after looking at a wide array of assessment reports on the field of Women's Studies (see Levin 2007).

# 5
# SO, WHAT *CAN* YOU DO
# WITH YOUR DEGREE?
## EXPLORING VARIOUS EMPLOYMENT
## AND CAREER PATHWAYS

What kind of career do you dream about? Do imagine yourself as a lawyer fighting for issues of equality? Or a diplomat? Or an artist? Or some combination of all three? In Chapter 4, you took some time assessing your interests, skills, and strengths in Women's and Gender Studies. We hope that you came away from that chapter eager to find out more about how others have used their degrees in obtaining employment and developing satisfying careers. In this chapter, we provide an overview of the range of career pathways and employment opportunities that WGST students have pursued over the past 15 years. In this chapter, we also introduce you to a diverse number of employment sectors, some that you may not have considered before. We think it is important for you to be informed about the great breadth of employment sectors in thinking about what interests you. We also highlight graduates' experiences in law, higher education administration, the health professions, academe, and entrepreneurship as many in our survey worked in those arenas. Taking time in this chapter to identify some key areas of interest should spark curiosity and raise areas of discovery you may not have thought of before when thinking about career options. We hope to encourage a sense of wonder (as opposed to dread), when thinking about the kinds of jobs and careers that you might pursue. There's so much to explore!

## CAREER SERVICES RESOURCES ON THE WEB

As you read through this book, you have gotten some tasty hints of what skills you are developing while pursuing your degree, and some areas that you may want to explore in terms of jobs and careers. In Chapter 2, Katharine Brooks provided some perspective on approaching career services, the value of a liberal arts degree, and ways to approach employers. Before, during, and after visiting your campus's career services office, you may want to do your homework and utilize the resources that are currently on the Web. For example, the University of California Berkeley's Career Center website (University of California Berkeley 2014) has some great resources regarding internships and graduate school, as well as links to explore career options. With topics such as "career fields," "What can I do with a major in . . ." and "employer and industry guides," these resources may illuminate career fields you may have never considered, and also allow you to brush up on the best way to present the knowledge and skills you possess. For example, the section "Architecture, Planning and Environmental Design" is broken down into a variety of subsections, including career profiles and guides—"Inside Jobs" is an interactive website that allows you to choose an area of interest (job category and what are you good at)—and see different jobs and the training/experience that is needed (with a Berkeley graduate picture beside it). Additionally, this section also lists student organizations for the career field and a listing of the field's professional organizations. If you are a student at UC Berkeley, you have additional opportunities to reference materials that list alumni and the career paths they have chosen. You may want to check with your own university to see if similar resources are available.

Another website that has information about employment options is Everyday Feminism (http://everydayfeminism.com). In particular, Melissa Fabello's (2014) article "So You Want a Feminist Job" offers five ideas for looking for a feminist job (e.g. "Narrow down feminism" and look in the right places) (Fabello 2014). Other helpful articles on this website for maintaining oneself (and perspective) in the job search include "How to Weather Post College Unemployment" (Slavin 2013) and "Gainful Unemployment: 5 Acts of Self Care While Job Hunting" (Uwujaren 2012). Additionally, the section on work offers support and resources for those in careers/jobs that may be fulfilling in some ways but problematic in others (Adamson 2013; Kim 2013). You will find more resources as you start exploring the Web. As you encounter these sites, you may want to bookmark them and share them with others in your network. Often, what may be helpful to you will be helpful to someone else. Later, he or she may "pay it forward" and help you (or someone else) on the career path.

## Employment and Career Pathways from the Survey

Graduates have held a variety of diverse and interesting employment positions: everything from professors to stage managers. You are definitely not going to starve pursuing work in Women's and Gender Studies! We found that there are several professional areas that graduates clustered in over the past decade and half: higher education administration, entrepreneurship, law, academe, the health professions, and nonprofit work.

Some trends we note are the high number of medical and health professionals in our survey, especially those working on issues of women's health and HIV/AIDS issues. There were many doctors and surgeons in our survey, and several of them specialized in women's health. There were also a high number of nurses of different credentials (i.e. registered nurse, nurse practitioner, etc.) in a variety of settings (e.g. psychiatric, operating room). Additionally, many graduates worked in the health professions through research and clinical opportunities.

We see this finding as particularly interesting, in that it perhaps is a result of the second-wave women's health movement that began in the mid-1970s, which fought for more women health practitioners and created new opportunities for women in the health professions. This U.S. trend also mirrors the international increase in employment opportunities in the health professions.

There were many graduates who worked in the area of HIV/AIDS— specifically counseling and testing services. Moreover, there were graduates who worked in the HIV/AIDS field through community-based organizations, local, state, and national government, or who are fighting for the civil rights and dignified treatment of HIV-positive people through law or nonprofit advocacy work. It stands to reason that HIV/AIDS has emerged as a prominent issue for Women's and Gender Studies communities. Not only does the epidemic affect people across a wide spectrum of identities (gender, race/ethnicity, nationality, social class, age, and sexuality), but as it emerged, the way that state actors and public health entities reflected long-standing patterns of inequality toward marginalized communities. The activism and utilization of social movement tactics by those infected and affected by it challenged the medical establishment. This pandemic also emerged in concert with the gay liberation movement, as well as second- and third-wave feminism.

Another important trend that has less to do with a specific career but is about broader intellectual and employment trajectories is the high number of graduates who have pursued advanced degrees after graduation. Over 70 percent of all graduates who completed our survey had or are pursuing advanced degrees since completing their bachelor's degree. We think that this finding signals that a few things are unique to the training that Women's and Gender Studies students often receive:

- *Intensive and individualized mentoring.* Given the structure of many programs and departments, students often receive support and outstanding mentoring during their education.
- *The "interdisciplinary advantage."* In Chapter 1, we highlighted the importance of interdisciplinary training in Women's and Gender Studies. This kind of intellectual dexterity and synthesis may create competitive advantages for students seeking graduate training in a wide variety of fields.
- *The Women's and Gender Studies classroom.* In Chapter 1, we discussed how the emphasis on peer-to-peer learning, critical engagement with texts, and participation are features of many Women's and Gender Studies classrooms. It could be that this type of training produces a student who has very strong writing and communications skills that also provide an advantage when seeking advanced degree opportunities.

## Employment Worlds

Women's and Gender Studies students in our survey work in a variety of fields and occupations. This is not only the case in the United States, but internationally. According to Silius (2005: 118), the Women's Studies graduates who participated in the project Employment and Women's Studies: The Impact of Women's Studies Training on Women's Employment in Europe (EWSI), who came from nine countries (Finland, France, Germany, Hungary, Italy, the Netherlands, Slovenia, Spain, and the UK), were predominately employed in five employment sectors: research and education, government, journalism and media, health and human services, and diversity/equal opportunity initiatives. Yet, there are Women's and Gender Studies graduates, as indicated from our survey, who have a variety of different career aspirations and pathways.

There are many "worlds," so to speak, of employment. Below, we list brief descriptions of the several categories. We then focus on a few of these worlds in depth. As you do research, you will find what careers provide entry-level positions and which would require additional training, certification, or degrees. Keep in mind that this list is *not* exhaustive!

## The Corporate World

There were a number of graduates who worked in "corporate America" in their careers. A standard definition of a corporation is that it is a legal entity or structure created and empowered through laws of a state. Corporations typically have a group of people called shareholders who benefit directly from the success of a corporation's actions. A corporation has rights and privileges that are separate from its members—shareholders and founders of the company. Here, we use "corporation" to refer to large-scale businesses. Corporations come in a wide variety of sizes, from those that employ over 100,000 people inside the US (e.g. Starbucks), to those that employ 8,000 people in the US (e.g. Qualcomm, a company specializing in technology innovation).

Employment opportunities in the corporate world includes entry-level and management positions in a small or large company that makes and sells goods or services designed to meet the goals and more often than not produce a profit for shareholders. Corporations vary by size and type, but generally are organized into several types: "G," "general," "S," "Close," and LLC. In the corporate world, the power structure is multi-tiered, which means that you, as an employee, must report to a manager, who also reports to a manager, etc.

Corporate America means different things to different people. It can conjure up images of complex global entities or a brutish work environment that includes high competition and 80-hour work weeks. Images are different from reality, and you probably do not want to write off this "world" without a fair shake. Working in corporations can be meaningful, financially remunerative, include a wide variety of benefits and/or incentives, and help you develop a broad range of skills.

There are many job classifications/employment categories that may involve working for a corporation, which are listed below under other specified areas (e.g. medical and allied health, legal, science and technology). For example, you may be a nurse practitioner working for an HMO.

The Bureau of Labor Statistics is a great resource to examine different job categories and the level of education generally required, as well as the average salary for these positions. For the category of business and financial operations (which many may associate with the corporate world) the following are some examples of some positions you may want to explore while looking for employment: accountants and auditors; budget analysts; claims adjustors, appraisers, examiners, and investigators; fundraisers; human resource specialists and labor relation specialists; insurance underwriters; logisticians; market research analysts; meeting, convention, and event planners; and training and development specialists (Bureau of Labor Statistics, U.S. Department of Labor 2014d).

For many WGST graduates, working for a corporation may be perceived as contrary to the ideals and ethics of your degree itself. For example, in Campbell and Orr's (2010) interview with Hester Eisenstein about her book *Feminism Seduced* in *Socialist Review*, Eisenstein is concerned about the mainstreaming of feminism without critical analysis of capitalism:

> I felt that in the process of selling globalization, corporate leaders and other elites have been systematically trying to seduce women into embracing the expansion of capitalism ... There are academic feminists who say that the way to get out of patriarchy and women's role in the family is to get women into production, into paid work. This is all very true but not if you're working 14 hours a day and being stripped and tested for pregnancy.

You may fear that working for a corporation is the same as "working for the man," being in the belly of the beast or part of an "evil" empire. One way that you might be able to address your concerns is to see how a corporation ranks in corporate social responsibility. According to Buchholz (1991), most definitions of corporate social responsibility have the following elements:

> Corporations have responsibilities that go beyond the production of goods and services at a profit, responsibilities involve helping to solve important social problems, especially those they have helped create, corporations have a broader constituency than stockholders alone, corporations have impacts that go beyond simple marketplace transactions, and corporations serve a wider range of human values than can be captured by a sole focus on economic values.

In addition to a potential employer's ranking on corporate social responsibility, you may want to investigate how a corporation ranks in terms of its diversity. The environment for women and underrepresented groups in corporate America has been slowly changing. As corporations see themselves vying for capable and desirable workers, they have been pushed (through activism by workers) to think about creating an environment that supports and values diversity, women's experiences in the workplace, and health and wellness issues.

Patel (2012) gives some additional reasons why a job in a corporation may be the right move for a career seeker. In particular, there are many benefits to working in a corporation for Women's and Gender Studies graduates who want to make a difference. The first benefit is the ability to operate in a "massively scale driven environment." This notion refers to the ability to see an idea or change in a procedure, or new product that you have been advocating for, take root, and when it does, the results are massive and can potentially impact the day-to-day lives of a large number of people globally. Not only is this potential self-satisfying, but to know that the changes you have put into action may impact the lives of people around the world may be extremely motivating. The second benefit to working in a corporation is learning how to use influence over authority. For many Women's and Gender Studies graduates, one of the skills that was enhanced during their degree was leadership. In a corporate environment, one must learn how to influence authority and balance the competing demands of stakeholders, supervisors, and consumers. Third, rather than using top-down management, organizations such as Zappos are trying new organizational forms (e.g. "holacracy"), which they believe helps to fuel innovation. A holacracy, according to Gosfield and Sweeney (2014), is an organizational form in which authority is more evenly distributed and "workers are seen as partners; job descriptions are roles; and partners are organized into circles." In a sense, in this organizational form, workers can operate more like entrepreneurs who fulfill multiple roles and ultimately are responsible (and accountable) for achieving and advancing the organization's main goal. Thus, one idea builds on another, which not only may impact your organization's culture (and earnings as well), but society at large. Last, but not least, a benefit of working for an organization is harnessing the power of an ecosystem. Because you must depend on a variety of people with specific roles to accomplish your overall goal, you will not only gain multiple perspectives, but the ability to work with a variety of folks who have different personalities and talents than you. Workplace diversity should not only be seen in terms of positionality (e.g. gender, race, class), but learning styles, personality types, etc. Ultimately, while corporate culture may not be your ultimate career destination, it may provide a working environment that will allow for further skill development.

You may be attracted to a corporate environment for these reasons and because you are interested in the services and products that a company provides to the general public. Our graduates have worked in corporate America in a wide variety of positions including: marketing director, research and design staff, consultant, and manager of reporting and analytics for a sales team. We also have seen that, in several cases, women's and gender studies students have found themselves in corporate environments in positions that support creating a more inclusive and diverse workplace, including those that involve human resources. If you do find a position in a company and would like to continue to grow there, we highly recommend that you find on-the-job mentors to help you successfully advance in your career.

Some examples of Women's and Gender Studies graduates who participated in our survey and who worked with corporations include:

- Manager of Reporting and Analytics ("I work for an IT media company and analyze the lead generation campaigns, lead delivery, and reporting for our sales team and clients.")
- Certified Public Accountant.
- Director of Business Development and Scrum Process Mentor ("I work with small businesses to help take them to the next level. This could mean increasing their revenue, software quality, or employee satisfaction. Most of my work falls in the field of Sales, Marketing, and Organizational Transformation Coach.")
- Claims Examiner ("I examine workers' compensation claims.")
- Director of Public Relations at a unique grocery store with four locations in NY/CT.
- Government Services Executive ("I'm a consultant/advisor to government entities that provide health and human services, namely child welfare, workforce development, and public assistance and housing.")

## FOR YOUR LIBRARY

Trudy Bourgeois (2007). *Her Corner Office: A Guide to Help Women Find a Place and a Voice In Corporate America.* 2nd ed. Dallas, TX: Brown Books.

Jessica Faye Carter (2007). *Double Outsiders: How Women of Color Can Succeed in Corporate America.* St Paul, MN: JIST Books.

### The Health and Medical World

According to the Bureau of Labor Statistics, the North American Industry Classification System groups the health and medical world under "the Health Care and Social Assistance Sector":

> The Health Care and Social Assistance sector comprises establishments providing health care and social assistance for individuals. The sector includes both health care and social assistance because it is sometimes difficult to distinguish between the boundaries of these two activities. The industries in this sector are arranged on a continuum starting with those establishments providing medical care exclusively, continuing with those providing health care and social assistance, and finally finishing with those providing only social assistance.
>
> (Bureau of Labor Statistics, U.S. Department of Labor 2014b)

Like the corporate world, Women's and Gender Studies students may have some concerns about having a position in the medical-industrial complex, an arena that many feminist science scholars and feminist health advocates have critiqued as being discriminatory and exclusionary. Yet, historically, healing, health, and medicine have been areas where disenfranchised groups have been able to hold some positions of power and authority (midwives, herbalists, nurses, etc.). It is also a field that has seen a lot of radical change in terms of the diversity of personnel who occupy positions within the field. The health field is constantly evolving and so if this is an area of interest, it would be good for you to read about current micro and macro-level trends.

Positions in medicine and health include becoming a doctor (MD, DO (Doctor of Osteopathy), chiropractor, optometrist, dentist, pharmacist, veterinarian), physician's assistant, nurse (registered nurse, certified medical assistant, home health aide, pharmacist assistant, etc.), and dental assistant. But other important jobs within this field include audiology dietician and nutritionists, athletic trainers and exercise physiologists, EMTs and paramedics, genetic counselors, massage therapists, speech and language pathologists, occupational health and safety specialists, health educators, and disease investigators/public health investigators/epidemiologists. There are also a variety of medical administrative positions in clinics and hospitals available (many of which also may have been listed previously under "corporate world"), as well as technology related jobs (e.g. medical informatics technician, diagnostic medical sonographers and cardiovascular technologists, medical and clinical laboratory technologists and technicians, medical records and health information technicians, medical transcriptionists, nuclear medical technologists, orthotics and prosthetists, and phlebotomists). The rise of integrative medicine has also created several positions under the label of "alternative health practitioner," including acupuncturist, homeopath, and biofeedback specialist. Also, as the Affordable Care Act has been initiated, other job categories such as benefits specialists and patient navigator positions have emerged. Another avenue for those who are interested in pursuing careers in the medical field is a career in the military.

The different branches of the U.S. Military (including Reserves) offer career opportunities for those who are enlisting and will either be trained by the military branch itself (e.g. medics with the U.S. Army are trained in a 16-week course) or who will have their education supported with the caveat that reimbursement will be in the form of a prearranged term of employment for the military. Per the U.S. Army website, allied health professionals may work either under the Medical Service Corp or the Medical Specialist Corp. The Medical Service Corps is "home to medical administrative, scientific and provider specialties from direct patient care to management of the U.S. Army's health service system. Disciplines that fall under this branch are the behavioral sciences, health services, laboratory sciences, optometry, pharmacy, podiatry and preventive medicine." Medical Specialist Corp contains four specialty areas: "physical therapists, occupational therapists, clinical dietitians and physician assistants." For those who purse Allied Health in the U.S. Army, there is a variety of settings and roles that you may occupy in your service, ranging from:

> direct patient care in a hospital setting, administrative work in a staff headquarters or practicing your specialty in a field environment in the United States or overseas. You may serve in

## SPOTLIGHT: CATHERINE "KATIE" CASHETT (DISEASE INVESTIGATOR AND INTERVENTION SPECIALIST)

Cheryl first met Catherine as a new Disease Investigator and Intervention Specialist who was employed in the same program/office. During the course of a general conversation, Katie disclosed that she had majored in Women's Studies. Katie graciously agreed to share how her background and training in Women's and Gender Studies impacted not only her course of study, but her career pathway as well:

I earned my Women's Studies degree from the University of Washington in 2003 and at that time, my department required students to focus their interest in a particular track, for example Women and Law, Women and Health, Women and Education, etc. This allowed the student a way to focus their upper level undergraduate Women's Studies coursework in an area they were specifically interested in pursuing, perhaps as a career or in graduate school. In addition to this track coursework, both an internship and a senior thesis were required for graduation. My track was Women and Health, and my internship was seven months as a counselor at a women's health clinic that provided a "Well Woman" program and abortion care. The internship allowed me the opportunity to gain valuable experience and skills in reproductive health, such as direct patient care, clinical coordination, and client-centered counseling techniques. This linked to my first paid position after graduation in the clinic as the Well Woman Coordinator, where I worked for four years.

Since that time, I have continued to pursue work in reproductive/sexual health, working for a midwifery practice as the office manager and currently as a disease investigator in HIV/AIDS/STDs for a local health district. In addition to the practical experience I gained during the completion of my Women's Studies degree through my coursework and internship, I gained external skills of critical thinking, understanding diverse communities, oral communication, and being able to recognize the complexity of a problem. These are all key to my current work. For example, as a disease investigator, I am asking the people I work with to divulge very personal information to me about their sexual lives so that I can help them get tested, treated, get their partner(s) treated, and prevent the spread of infection in the community. In order for me to effectively do my job, it is important that I recognize the diverse communities the people I serve come from and the types of interlocking oppressions those individuals and communities may face, particularly where it intersects with obtaining services from a public health entity. Critical thinking and being able to analyze complex problems are also important in tracing the spread of infection in groups of people and in interpreting data, research, and outcomes from our work. My background in Women's Studies gives me a firm understanding of all of these skills, both from a theoretical as well as a practical perspective.

a variety of command, staff or clinical positions with assignments at one of the Army's medical centers, community hospitals, rehabilitation centers or research laboratories.

(U.S. Army 2014)

Many Women's and Gender Studies graduates who responded to our survey worked in the health and medical world:

- Health Center Assistant at Planned Parenthood in Louisiana ("an office assistant trained by the company to counsel women on birth control and STIs.")
- HIV Counselor/Educator/Phlebotomist ("I test individuals for HIV using a rapid finger-stick test. While the test is running, I educate people on the basics of HIV, prevention, and risk reduction. I also counsel clients and link them to services if they test positive.")
- Licensed Mental Health Counselor.
- Psychiatric Nurse.
- Editor and Project Coordinator at a breast cancer nonprofit that provides medical and quality-of-life information for women affected by breast cancer ("I write articles and edit a newsletter.")
- Research Manager in Hematology/Oncology and Genomic Medicine.

## *The Social and Human Services, Criminal Justice, and Legal Worlds*

The occupations that are typically associated with criminal justice and law are often limited by the media portrayals of police, federal agents, and lawyers that we have seen typically in movies and TV. Yet, this field, like many others, is becoming more diverse (race/ethnicity, gender, sexual orientation, ability, religiosity, country of origin), and its practitioners come from a variety of backgrounds, including business and accounting, social sciences, computer sciences, and engineering. Additionally, to be culturally responsive to the communities that are served by these entities, those employed in this larger field must be able to meet people where they are at and possess an awareness of the multitude of perspectives that the public holds. As Women's and Gender Studies students, you have a unique perspective to understand not only the barriers that individuals face due to historical and contemporary experiences of oppression, but also that some of the most recent civil rights victories have been a result of challenges and changes to the law.

For example, in spring 2007, *Ms.* magazine asked Women's and Gender Studies students: "What Can You Do with a Degree in Women's and Gender Studies?" Nancy A. Turner shared how her graduate degree in Women's Studies (and background in Policy Studies) led to a career working in the criminal justice field:

> I have had great experiences and opportunities afforded by my master's degree in Women's Studies and Public Policy earned at George Washington University in 1990. For the last eight years, I have been a project/senior program manager at the International Association of Chiefs of Police, responsible for several million dollars of federal funding aimed at enhancing law enforcement's understanding and response to crimes of violence against women. This work has included the publication of three national model policies for law enforcement agencies on the proper investigation of the crimes of sexual assault, domestic violence, and domestic violence by police officers. Most recently, we created a guidebook and roll-call training video for first responders on the crime of human trafficking, thus influencing the ability of individual officers to recognize and investigate these crimes in a manner that protects the dignity and rights of the victims while holding perpetrators accountable.
>
> Before this, I was employed by the National Coalition Against Domestic Violence as their (only) public policy advocate working to involve the grassroots network of advocates in the passage of the original Violence Against Women Act. I also worked in a non-profit shelter program creating a transitional housing program for battered women and their children. I also serve on city commissions (as a volunteer) addressing human rights, HIV/AIDS, and mental health—all issues related to violence against women.
>
> (Turner 2007)

Additionally, we find that these fields dovetail very well with people who may identify as "sustainers" (see Chapter 2) from our career pathway rubric of "sustainers, evolvers and synthesizers." Sustainers often develop expertise in these fields through their activism and internship experience.

The criminal justice and legal world has several career sectors within its broad term, including protective services, community and social services, and law. Community and social service jobs that may work in tandem with the criminal justice and legal world include: mental health counselors, rehabilitation counselors, social workers, substance abuse and behavioral disorder counselors, and social and human service assistants.

Protective service occupations have a variety of jobs that may interest Women's and Gender Studies graduates. These include accounting and computer forensics, correctional officers, customs officers, probation officers, fire inspectors, firefighters, police and detectives, private detectives and investigators, and security guards and gaming surveillance officers.

There are a variety of positions in the legal field, including: lawyers, court clerks, paralegals and legal assistants, stenographers/court reporters, legal secretaries, arbitrators, mediators and conciliators, consultants, and judges and hearing officers.

Many Women's and Gender Studies graduates who responded to our survey worked in the social and human services, criminal justice, and legal worlds:

- Civil Rights Lawyer.
- Administrator at Equal Rights Advocates—a nonprofit women's rights legal organization.
- Sexual Assault Victim Advocate.
- Adolescent Continuing Care Case Manager.

---

### SPOTLIGHT: VANITA GUPTA

Vanita Gupta (WS '96 from Yale) is a civil rights lawyer and the Deputy Legal Director of the American Civil Liberties Union (ACLU), where she oversees the ACLU's national criminal and drug law reform advocacy efforts. Gupta is an Indian-American, but was raised in England and France. After Yale, she went to New York University Law School, from which she graduated in 2001.

According to Gupta:

> Going to college at Yale was an intellectual feast. I came to Yale already interested in issues of power and inequality and searched for courses that investigated these issues in greater depth. WS courses gave me the opportunity to think about race and gender and how society structures inequality. The interdisciplinary approach was very exciting and I explored these issues through courses in history, literature, sociology, etc. It broadened my horizons.

For more information about Gupta, her career path, and personal life, see Chanda (2011).

- Research Director for Office of Indigent Defense Services.
- "I am the leader of the educational division at a national domestic violence organization."

### The Science and Technology World

While for some the idea that Women's and Gender Studies and STEM concentrations (Science, Technology, Engineering, and Mathematics) are incompatible, for many (feminist science scholars, college administers, and employers), these areas are, in fact, the locations that WGST graduates and/or traditionally underrepresented students should be. In a recent interview on *PBS News Hour* in 2013, the host Gwen Ifill questioned the current president of Spelman College, Dr. Beverly Daniel Tatum, about her administration's decision to encourage women to pursue studies and careers in STEM and drop college sports in favor of student health. In response to a question President Tatum was posed about the refocusing of academic goals at Spelman and its applicability, she replied:

> Well, let me begin by saying that at Spelman, we have been focused on STEM education, as well as a broader liberal arts focus, for many years. And that doesn't begin with me, but I'm happy to say that since I have been president at Spelman, we have been able to keep moving forward at a time when we see national interest in STEM declining.
>
> We know there are many young women of color interested in pursuing science. A third of our students are STEM majors. And we want to insure that they can move into fields where they are underrepresented and make a difference to our economy and to our nation.

When asked if this indicated a shift or a move away from a traditional liberal arts education, Tatum stated that:

> Spelman College is, in many ways, a traditional liberal arts college, in that we emphasize the skills that come from a strong liberal arts education, critical thinking, problem-solving, quantitative reasoning, communication skills.
>
> But, certainly, a third of our students come with an interest in moving into science. They may be thinking about health careers initially. But once they start to explore biology, chemistry, physics, computer science, engineering, they see a wider range of options.

And I think that's one of the things about Spelman, that when they come to Spelman, they are exposed to faculty who represent a very diverse group of faculty, men and women—52 percent of our STEM faculty are women. A third of them are women of color, so that they're a broad range of role models and they see that the sky really is the limit. There is no limit, excuse me, to their opportunities.

(PBS 2013)

This interview highlights the core values at the center of a Women's and Gender Studies education, which was voiced by many of the respondents as the core skills they gained through their degree, specifically critical thinking skills and communication skills. Also, it challenged prevailing sentiments that women and/or under represented groups are not interested in STEM, either as a subject of study or as a career path.

According to McGraw-Hill's Education website "Career Site: Career Clusters in Science, Technology, Engineering and Mathematics":

Jobs in the science, technology, engineering, and mathematics career cluster involve planning, managing, and providing scientific research and technologies. Other jobs also involve professional technical services (e.g. physical science, social science, and engineering), laboratory and testing services and research and development services.

(College and Career Readiness Career Center 2014)

Careers that can be categorized through science and technology are numerous. This world includes computer software engineers (these are the people who often create very popular "apps"). Computer systems analysts help businesses stay on the cutting edge of technological development.

The researching, tracking, and storing of information is part of the skill set someone uses when they work with information technology. If you have an interest in information technology, you could find yourself working on issues of bioinformatics in the field of medicine or using information technology in tracking climate change.

## The Government and Politics World

Positions in the world of government and politics include working for a federal/state/local government (or one of its many agencies), service as a staff member for a legislator or representative, political action committees (PACs), political parties, an executive agency, and local councils. A career in this world could encompass International work in diplomacy, nongovernmental organizations (NGOs), and Foreign Service. These positions can vary from working as an assistant town manager to grant-writing for the U.S. Agency for International Development (USAID). Sometimes, this world may seem intimidating and rather unapproachable to Women's and Gender Studies students. There are a variety of ways that you can not only enter this world, but be successful at it as well. For example, if you are interested in running for political office, you do not have to run for a Senate position immediately (if you do not want to). Perhaps a library board is more your speed. For example, Cheryl was able to enter into the world of academic politics first as a representative for the Graduate and Professional Association at UNLV. Later, she continued her university service as the chair of the Faculty Improvement Grant Committee. She also served (in a non-paying capacity) for the HIV Prevention Planning Group for Southern Nevada. Each of these experiences gave her the opportunity to learn how committees operate, and network and interact with colleagues and political power players with the institution/community. Michele ran for the Pittsboro Town Board in 2007, while simultaneously working as a professor for the University of North Carolina at Chapel Hill. Through their experiences with politics on a local and/or institutional level, both Cheryl and Michele were given a taste of running for office and achieved a degree of success that could be translated into future political service.

If you are considering working for the U.S. Federal Government (in a civilian or non-military capacity), there is a multitude of agencies that you can work for as an employee or often as a contractor. Additionally, U.S. Jobs further delineates federal careers into three categories: competitive service, excepted service, and senior executive. For more information on the difference between these categories and some of the agencies that fit under each, see USA Jobs Resource Center (2014).

Some agencies and positions you may not have considered, but that are listed under the category of excepted service, include: the U.S. Patent and Trademark Office (patent examiner), National Park Foundation (community partnerships program manager), international work (U.S. Foreign Service, U.S. Mission to the United Nations, and the Peace Corps), and the Library of Congress (materials handler).

For local and state jobs, you should look at the particular state or local municipality you are interested in working for. Another resource may be organizations such as the American Association of University Women (AAUW) and/or the non-partisan League of Women Voters who may have compiled resources that assist their members in advocating for their interests.

If you are considering a career in politics, be aware that you may have to put in your dues with unpaid volunteer opportunities or internships. Judi Brown discusses her experiences with political campaigns in the next chapter. The Career Center at UC Berkeley has a great web page on a career in politics and public policy, and some of the knowledge you should have as you consider this field. Some of the paying positions within politics include: legislative aids, field representatives, legislative correspondents, and campaign staffers (University of California Berkeley 2003).

Edwina Langenberg-Miller (2007) was another person who replied to *Ms.* magazine's question about what you can do with your degree:

> After graduating from George Washington University in 2003 with a double major in History and Women's Studies, I was hired by Sen. Lisa Murkowski of Alaska. As a member of her staff, I worked on a number of legislative initiatives, including recognizing Rosie the Riveters, legislation to authorize the Women's History Museum to use a building in Washington, DC, and the reauthorization of the Violence Against Women Act.
> I worked for Sen. Murkowski for four years before taking a job at a local lobby/litigation firm in Washington, DC. The client focus is primarily Alaskan, and I am the firm's legislative director.

Many Women's and Gender Studies graduates who responded to our survey worked in the government and politics worlds. Some of the positions held included:

- Deputy Director, Affiliate and National Programs with NARAL Pro-Choice America ("developing offline activism opportunities for pro-choice activists and organizational development support for our affiliate network.")
- "I work at the Democratic National Committee doing political research."
- Gender and Development Specialist ("freelance, mostly for the United Nations and some NGOs.")
- Field representative for a member of the state assembly.

### SPOTLIGHT: LINDSEY DERMID GRAY

Although they have never met face to face, Cheryl feels as though she has already met Lindsey. Due to her work at the local health department, Cheryl met Lindsey's partner through their work with Nevada's HIV Prevention Planning Groups. As a Facebook friend, Cheryl gets to see updates and snapshots of Lindsey's family. In fact, it was through social networking that a mutual friend reposted a request Cheryl made asking people to direct her to WMST graduates that have gone onto to careers in law, business, government, etc. Lindsey's partner, Gerold, contacted Cheryl and stated that Lindsey has a BA in WMST. In their phone conversation, Lindsey conveyed how she became a Women's and Gender Studies major, and how she found her current position as the Breastfeeding Coordinator for the Nevada State Division of Public and Behavioral Health:

> When choosing colleges, they would ask about what major you want to choose. On one of the lists was Women's Studies, and I checked that, knowing nothing about it, just having a sense that I craved what I might learn when women and minorities took center stage in my education. I went away to U of A (Arizona) and for whatever reason there were no Women's Studies classes (either could not take as Freshman, not offered, etc.). So I tried a few different majors (English, Political Science) and took a variety of classes, all under the sun. When I returned to the University of Nevada Reno (UNR) in my sophomore year, I took Women's Studies classes and settled firmly into the degree. My first instinct was correct, and I became completely enmeshed in Women's Studies.
>
> After I finished my WMST degree, I had a lot of philosophical awareness, but I felt I had no way to apply my knowledge into a career. In 2006, I began my degree in public health. At UNR, I had a graduate assistantship working on HIV/AIDS research. Yet, I elected to do my professional project (like a thesis) on alternatives to traditional prenatal care in the US. In other words, I researched maternal and childbirth outcomes. I questioned why a country like the US spends the most money on healthcare, including antenatal care, and has a prenatal care model that requires more visits than any other developed nation, yet our birth outcomes are so much worse.
>
> I found public health to be the perfect marriage for my background, and research interests, in Women's Studies. I wanted to find a way to apply what I learned about inequity based on race, ethnicity, class, and gender. WMST informed all that I know about these inequities, which was the foundation of my MPH studies. I was able to apply all that I learned in Women's Studies to more fully comprehend the ways in which our environment (neighborhood, peers, schools,

family) shape every choice we make and every opportunity we have in life. For my interests, an MPH degree proved to be the best compliment to my WMST degree.

Lindsey, like many Women's and Gender Studies graduates, was able to infuse her feminist perspective and critical thinking skills from her degree into her course of study for her graduate degree in Public Health. But she also had to balance her career goals with the demands of her personal life, including her relationship with her partner and parenthood:

While I was pregnant with my daughter, I worked as a community outreach worker for a hospice in Reno. The hospital was attached to a major hospital and the nonprofit hospital was sold to a major for-profit corporation. During the change, each worker had to reapply for their job, and consequently at nine months pregnant, I found myself laid off and without health insurance. The for-profit company didn't have experience with operating a hospice, and didn't see value in having an outreach person for a hospice program. It was really stressful. As you know, at that time, many insurance companies viewed pregnancy as a preexisting condition. Plus, it was nearly impossible to look for a job being nine months pregnant. Luckily, the HR person at my partner's job was able to circumvent their company's rules and regulations and had me placed on my partner's insurance. This was important, in that originally we were going to do a home birth (a decision that was made based on my MPH Professional Project regarding the deficits of traditional prenatal care in the US and benefits of the midwifery model), but for non-emergency reasons we had to go to the hospital for the birth. Without insurance, the cost would have been astronomical. After the birth, I stayed home for 10 months. I could not work with the idea of leaving her (my baby). The positive outcome of the situation was that I was able to stay home with my daughter and experience being reborn in my breastfeeding relationship with my daughter. It was this experience that led to the perfect marriage between my Women's Studies degree and my MPH.

At the time I was at home, the Statewide Breastfeeding Coordinator for Division of Public and Behavioral Health (who was dearly loved by the community) was moving to Austin. Thus, I became the Breastfeeding Coordinator for the Nevada State Division of Public and Behavioral Health, a position I have been in for several (four) months. Every day (at my job) is a dream! Basically, I work with policy at the state, and the reach of this position is endless. My main focus in this position is to oversee Nevada's breastfeeding support program within each of the state's WIC (Women, Infants, and Children) clinics. For those who may not know, roughly half of the babies born in the US are eligible for WIC. The population served in the WIC program stand to benefit the most from breastfeeding, as they likely are underinsured with little or no paid sick leave. Not only is this cost-effective for people with limited resources, but for those who breastfeed, less time is needed to take off from work for sick days or doctor's appointments, as research has shown that babies who are breastfed have fewer oar infections, GI issues, asthma, obesity, type 2 diabetes, childhood leukemia, and SIDS. Research has also shown lower rates of chronic health conditions for the mothers, such as type 2 diabetes and reproductive cancers. One of the challenges of working with WIC is that the program supplies free formula, which is a hurdle when my program supports breastfeeding.

A success of our program (within three divisions in the DHHS) is our "bringing your baby to work" policy. Employees of participating divisions are able to bring their infant with them to work until they're mobile—typically nine months. I have promoted this policy in a variety of settings, including other Nevada DHHS Divisions, other states' public and private workplaces, and at national webinars. My worksite has seen 25 moms (in four years) participate in the program and bring their children to work for up to nine months, and 95 percent of those moms breastfeed for at least three months. We encounter a lot of reservations about the "bring your baby to work" policy. It was even hard for me to contemplate bringing a new baby to a new job. Yet, the initiative has been very successful. All the coworkers involved with the moms in the programs have been supportive, including becoming part of the child's extended family (e.g. grandma, grandpa) and taking the children for walks, etc. This policy is a wonderfully progressive way to promote mother-baby bonding and breastfeeding, and serves as a much-needed tool to successfully combine women's home and work life responsibilities. I also promote events like "Big Latch On." This event (to raise awareness about breastfeeding) occurs at 10 a.m. (depending on the time zone), and the goal is to set the world record for most consecutive number of women breastfeeding at the same time. In Reno, we had 80 moms at UNR who all breastfed their children at 10 a.m. for at least a minute. Another goal for our department is hopefully soon to join forces with the Division of Child and Maternal Health to encourage breastfeeding to the other 50 percent of the population not on WIC.

Another policy initiative we are pursuing in Nevada regards changes in hospital maternal policies, specifically a "baby-friendly designation." This initiative (supported by WHO and UNICEF) makes suggestions for hospitals to be baby-friendly. The best start for a baby is to be skin to skin post-birth, and to use formula only when needed, and if the mother requests it. Babies are also to "stay on the mom and with the mom." The "baby-friendly designation" lays out 10 steps for hospitals to achieve. It's a huge movement, but there is a lot of pushback. In California, the legislature has called for all maternity centers with a certain number of deliveries to be baby-friendly by 2025. Nevada is looking to get there by taking steps in that direction. Another initiative we are working on is "breastfeeding-friendly" designations for businesses, restaurants, and other public spaces, and to build a public awareness and social marketing campaign.

Lindsey's degree in Women's Studies is credited with not only impacting her perspective on the world, but helped direct her in her course of graduate studies, as well as to find a job that was able to combine her passion for women's health issues with her role as a new mother and breastfeeding activist/advocate. She not only describes how her degree shaped her life, but also gave advice for those considering a degree in Women's and Gender Studies:

> A WMST degree shaped my worldview . . . I feel like it made me more compassionate and empathic. I now take time to observe privilege (my own and others) and understand why others don't think or behave the way I do. I've always believed that the most important thing I learned in my WMST program was that if you are not the victim of discrimination, it's likely that you aren't even aware it exists . . . it made me take a step back and consider when you perceive things around you aren't happening to you; they are in fact happening . . . one's environment impacts decisions . . . especially if you don't have someone who believes in you.

> If you find yourself drawn to a WMST degree, there is something inherently unique about you and your desire to see the world through an honest and unfiltered lens—to deconstruct the experiences of people who have systematically been treated differently through no fault of their own. Follow that desire to unearth these things and you will find that along the way, you will be carving out your own interests and identity with which you can most completely, genuinely, be a force in the world. The world needs people who know what WMST majors know.

## The Nonprofit World

The nonprofit world—as with the corporate world—is a career world that people often make assumptions about. Nonprofits can be categorized in a broad range of organizations, from churches, to foundations (e.g. the Kellogg Foundation, the Bill and Melinda Gates Foundation), to arts organizations. Although we stratify academe and government work, they could also fall into this category. The engine that drives the mission of nonprofits usually relates to serving a specific community or cluster of interests rather than a community of shareholders. Despite what you might have heard, the nonprofit world can often pay salaries for employees close to what private firms can pay, especially beyond entry-level positions. Positions in this world include utilizing the specialized skills of musicians and artists, as well as employees who perform functions such as fundraising, research, proposal writing, finance, community outreach, website development, marketing, and accounting. A great resource you may want to check out if you are interested in the nonprofit world is www.idealist careers.org. This website not only allows job seekers to receive updates on internships, volunteering, and job openings, but also has an area for nonprofits to posts vacancies and opportunities. In addition, it has sections devoted to job search tips, webinars on topics ranging from "Tips for Marketing Yourself on the Job Market" (Jones 2013) to "Join the Idealist Careers LinkedIn Boot Camp" (Jones 2014), and career resources (resources for your job search, resources for your career, and resources about nonprofits, social enterprises, and the sector at large). Additionally, to gain experience, you can also become a contributor for the website.

### The Information World: Broadcasting/Journalism/News Media/New Media Online

According to the Bureau of Labor Statistics and the North American Industry Classification System, much of what we know as media is classified under information:

> Information sector comprises establishments engaged in the following processes: (a) producing and distributing information and cultural products, (b) providing the means to transmit or distribute these products as well as data or communications, and (c) processing data. The main components of this sector are the publishing industries, including software publishing, and both traditional publishing and publishing exclusively on the Internet; the motion picture and sound recording industries; the broadcasting industries, including traditional broadcasting and those broadcasting exclusively over the Internet; the telecommunications industries' Web search portals, data processing industries, and the information services industries.
>
> The Information sector groups three types of establishments: (1) those engaged in producing and distributing information and

cultural products; (2) those that provide the means to transmit or distribute these products as well as data or communications; and (3) those that process data.

> (Bureau of Labor Statistics, U.S. Department
> of Labor 2014c)

Positions in this world can include blogging for a company, working as a radio producer, or working as a proofreader for a book publishing company.

Many Women's and Gender Studies graduates who responded to our survey worked in the information world. Some of the positions held included:

- Internet entrepreneur.
- Researcher ("I work with two nonprofit organizations based in Colombo, Sri Lanka. One organization works on women's rights while the other works on LGBT rights.")
- "I am an editor at a progressive women's magazine based in the southeast."
- "I am a novelist. I write lesbian romances. I've published two books and have two more completed and scheduled for release."
- Marketing Associate/Graphic Designer and Editor for a garden store.
- Research Analyst for an HIV/AIDS policy and economics research group.

### The Small Business/Entrepreneurial World

Have you ever dreamed of running your own business? Starting or owning a business is a dream for many individuals. Entrepreneurs fill specific needs in society by creating new goods and services. Whether one is challenged by the constraints of a structured, formalized workplace, intrigued by the possibility of "giving birth" to an opportunity, or encouraged to start a business by friends or family, entrepreneurship has been a growing trend, not only in the United States, but throughout the world.

Access to the workplace and debates over the private and public spheres have been long-standing issues with feminist theory and Women's Studies curriculum. Yet, an often overlooked and underappreciated aspect of the job market are those who create their own business or drop out of the "nine to five" environment. We think Women's and Gender Studies helps prepare graduates to work for themselves—at some point in their lives—given the confidence, support, mentoring, and creativity that the training fosters. Women continue to constitute a majority of new entrepreneurs (Duffy and Kan 2013). It is estimated that in just a few years, women will create over half of all new small business. Women entrepreneurs are often dissatisfied with traditional workplaces and want to balance work and home interests (MacNeil 2012).

Many entrepreneurs are interested in social justice and living in an equitable world. For example, the magazine *Fast Company* profiled the personal philosophies that shaped emerging entrepreneurs. Daphne Koller's (the cofounder of Coursera) sentiments reflect many of the convictions that Women's and Gender Studies graduates have in their career plans:

> I've always felt that we should try to live our lives so as to leave the world a better place. Or, to quote Steve Jobs, we should "make a dent in the universe." I also believe that this obligation only increases for people who are more fortunate.
>
> I try to seek out opportunities where a small amount of resources, time, or effort can make a disproportionately large contribution. I particularly value efforts with a ripple effect, where one action sets off an entire cascade of responses whose overall impact can be really huge. That's a major reason I chose to enter the field of education and went on to found Coursera. Educating even a single person can have a profound effect not only on that person's life, but also on the many people whose lives that person touches. By applying a relatively small amount of resources, we have the opportunity to transform the lives of millions of people, and indirectly of many more.
>
> (Nasri 2014)

Entrepreneur and small business owners come in many different forms and have different visions. One Women's and Gender Studies graduate who responded to our survey stood out. She claimed the label of entrepreneur ("I have a small popsicle company"). Jennifer Pritchett (Smitten Kitten) is profiled as a Women's and Gender Studies graduate who was able to parlay her knowledge and activism regarding sexuality matters into an independently owned feminist sex-toy store in Minneapolis.

### SPOTLIGHT: JENNIFER PRITCHETT AND THE MAKING OF THE SMITTEN KITTEN

The Smitten Kitten, a feminist sex-toy store based in Minneapolis, is one example of how Women's and Gender Studies students have become entrepreneurs. According to Jennifer Pritchett, the idea of the store resulted from a combination of factors: an unfulfilling work experience exacerbated by a hostile work environment in a university student services office, knowledge gained from courses (such as ones on collective action, feminist research, and feminist theory), and experience working in a variety of university offices and organizations during undergraduate and graduate school (e.g. Minnesota State University, Mankato's LGBT Center and Women's Center).

The Smitten Kitten was conceived and eventually opened as a feminist-oriented sex-toy store in 2003. The store advocates a sex-positive approach, as well as raising awareness about sexual health and environment, as evidenced through their Campaign Against Toxic Toys (CATT). Currently, the Smitten Kitten employs both full-time and part-time workers, has a physical location in Minneapolis, and also has a strong presence on the Web (see www.smittenkittenonline.com/).

Besides serving the sexual health needs of its clients, The Smitten Kitten also gives back to the community through its support of LGBT youth programs and intimate partner violence prevention and care efforts, as well as being the sponsor of a Gender and Women's Studies scholarship at MSU Mankato. While the end result of this feminist-inspired business relationship is a success, Jennifer is quite open about the challenges she and the business faced prior to opening. These ranged from long hours, raising funds for start-up costs and working with the available resources, negotiating with distributors, and little to no real income for a few years, as well as some resistance from the community, which was concerned about sexually oriented businesses. An important insight that Jennifer has for feminist entrepreneurs is to follow:

> a "one step at a time" approach . . . don't dream up the perfect business, just go with what you have. I started with $33,000 initially and went from there. Rather than dream an amount, start with what you have . . . and go from there.

Jennifer also believes her experience as a graduate assistant gave her applied and practical experience and knowledge that she could translate into her business: "I learned to make do when you don't have that much in terms of resources . . . making do with what you have and utilizing your resourcefulness, it is women's work." Jennifer's applied work experiences have also influenced her decisions in regards to hiring practices: "As a person who hires folks with WMST degrees, specifically what you do (and have done) makes a difference." Jennifer also believes in the importance of mentoring. A major influence on her, besides Deirdre Rosenfeld, Associate Dean of Students for Gustavus Adolphus College (and former director of MSU's Women's Center), was Megan Hooglan, the owner of Cactus Tattoo in Mankato, Minnesota, a successful woman working in a male-dominated field (see www.cactus tattoo.com/cactustattoo.html). Not only has Jennifer benefitted from mentoring, but she believes reciprocity is an important aspect of feminist mentoring: "Part of the mission of the store is to help people start feminist businesses." In fact, Jennifer has welcomed the opportunity to be available as a feminist advisor/feminist consultant:

> I work from a philosophy of abundance. The Smitten Kitten makes new clientele as we go. I give advice and welcome people to call and ask questions. It can be hard to be taken seriously, especially as a young woman in business. I always take people seriously and am always willing to help as part of my feminist mission.

The Smitten Kitten is but one model of entrepreneurship for Women's and Gender Studies students. If you produce products, there are a host of different physical and virtual areas in which you can advertise and sell your goods or services. You might also consider becoming an independent contractor. However you decide to pursue your goals, we recommend seeking assistance and guidance with representatives at organizations that support women-owned businesses, including the National Association of Women Business Owners (for local chapters) and the U.S. Small Business Administration, which sponsors a national network of Women's Business Centers. These organizations can illuminate some of the opportunities for being an independent business owner, helping you design a business plan, as well as helping with tax and legal considerations.

## The Education and Academic World

According to the Bureau of Labor Statistics, the educational services sector has been defined by the North American Industry Classification System as:

> establishments that provide instruction and training in a wide variety of subjects. This instruction and training is provided by specialized establishments, such as schools, colleges, universities, and training centers. These establishments may be privately owned and operated for profit or not for profit, or they may be publicly owned and operated. They may also offer food and/or accommodation services to their students.

Educational services are usually delivered by teachers or instructors that explain, tell, demonstrate, supervise, and direct learning. Instruction is imparted in diverse settings, such as educational institutions, the workplace, or the home, and through diverse means, such as correspondence, television, the Internet, or other electronic and distance-learning methods. The training provided by these establishments may include the use of simulators and simulation methods. It can be adapted to the particular needs of the students, for example sign language can replace verbal language for teaching students with hearing impairments. All industries in the sector share this commonality of process, namely, labor inputs of instructors with the requisite subject matter expertise and teaching ability.

(Bureau of Labor Statistics, U.S. Department of Labor 2014a)

Positions in the education and academic world include teaching at the K-12 (public or private school) locally or internationally, language school, or at the college level. For some positions, you may have to obtain a particular licensure or credentials; other jobs do not make these a requirement for the position. You might also be an educator as part of your position within a corporation (corporate trainer), freelance (sexuality educator), substance abuse and treatment center, or as part of a nonprofit (Planned Parenthood, Boys and Girls Club, etc.). There are numerous administrative positions in the education and academic world, including in admissions and enrollment, library and information services, psychological counseling, Greek Life, student recreation and/or athletic services, career services, student affairs, and cultural-specific services (e.g. women's centers, LGBT centers, international student associations, writing centers). If you are interested in a job within academia, there are several great resources for job seekers, including www.higheredjobs.com and the *Chronicle of Higher Education*. In fact, the *Chronicle of Higher Education* (besides being a *great* insider resource on all the issues, contemporary debates, and politics in higher education) has a job listing area called Vitae. It categorizes jobs into four large categories: faculty and research, administrative, executive, and jobs outside academe (Vitae 2014).

For example, when *Ms.* magazine asked Women's and Gender Studies graduates what they could do with their degree, a 1977 graduate from the University of Michigan showed how much her life and career paths had changed. According to Arlene J. Frank:

> I was one of the first Women's Studies major graduates at the University of Michigan, but in 1977 there were not many jobs available in fields where I could use my newly minted knowledge. My parents looked distressed; I was frightened. As the years went by and Reagan became president, my prospects seemed to dim even more. I was employed in two hospital settings, performing clerical work and organizing women into unions. When I had my son, I left the paid workforce and chose to stay at home with him for a few years.
>
> Fifteen years ago, when I decided to return to work, I wanted to make use of my academic and practical Women's Studies skills. I applied for and was offered my current job, directing a women's resource center at a community college. I have utilized all I learned back in the 1970s ... and living my dream job—to work to empower women.
>
> (Frank 2007)

Your life experiences may come in handy for many administrative academic positions. For example, if an academic advisory position targets international students, your double major in Women's Studies and Slavic Studies may be extremely useful for a college that does a lot of recruiting in Eastern Europe. In addition, as this is a university setting, your potential employer may be familiar with Women's and Gender Studies and the skills that your academic training brings to their position.

Many Women's and Gender Studies graduates who responded to our survey worked in the academic and education world. Some of the positions held included:

- Middle School Literacy Specialist ("Reading and Writing teacher for struggling 6th–8th grade students and literacy coach.")
- Project Manager, Webpublisher, and Public Relations Manager responsible at the Universities of Bern and Basel, Switzerland.
- Special Projects Coordinator at the Public Education Foundation, a nonprofit that seeks to improve K-12 public education in southern Nevada ("I write grants, manage programs, assist with special events, etc.")
- Assistant Professor, Psychology and African Diaspora Studies.
- Cataloging Services Specialist (library cataloger) and Crisis Worker at a domestic violence service organization.

## SPOTLIGHT: BRAD J. FREIHOEFER

Cheryl had the fortune to work with Brad while he was an undergraduate student at Minnesota State University, Mankato. Brad was not only a thoughtful and engaged student, but an activist as well. In fact, Brad's research project on gender-neutral bathrooms for his feminist research methods class was also presented at the Undergraduate Research Forum. The foci of his research, along with his engagement with MSU's LGBT Resource Center, were seemingly important foundations for his later employment at Iowa State University:

> In my sophomore year of college, I made the decision to change majors towards a Bachelor of Science in Women's Studies from Minnesota State University, Mankato. Gender and Women's Studies coursework provided a space to enhance my passion for social justice and transformed my understanding of the world and myself. Through research, theory, volunteering, internships, and group projects, my coursework provided a solid foundation in feminist theory and social justice, encouraged me to explore and apply critical lenses, and allowed the space to challenge preconceived ideas of my own privilege and power. My Gender and Women's Studies degree expanded my own skill set to better address individual, institutional, and systemic privilege and power, which shaped my career and propelled me toward my current role as the Coordinator of the Lesbian Gay Bisexual Transgender Student Services Center at Iowa State University.

> It has been an exciting and challenging transition into full-time LGBTQA higher education work. A few big highlights that have happened while I have been in this position include: Iowa State hosted MBLGTACC 2012, the largest student-run LGBTQA college conference in the country; we expanded the LGBT Center in 2010; increased student use of the space exponentially; and are working on creating greater access and equity for students regardless of gender identity and expression.

> My experience in Gender and Women's Studies focused on feminist theory within the broader social justice context. Through feminism and social justice, I began to recognize the power and value in interdepartmental initiatives to address inequities, build community, and enhance the student experience for all members of the university community. The coursework provided me the opportunity to explore the complexities of multiple intersecting identities, enhance collaboration across various communities, and examine the impact of my own privilege and power. The complexities of interlocking systems of oppression provided a framework in which to view and improve programs, policies, collaborations, and individual student support. Volunteer and internship experiences, both successes and especially failures, assisted to expand my

understanding, through the applied practice of working within intersections of identities. After my Gender and Women's Studies coursework, the feminism that I embodied and practiced was no longer only about sexism, but rather the interconnection to other forms of oppression, privilege, and power.

The combination of coursework and internships assisted in developing various critical lenses from which I evaluated programs, policies, initiatives, and campus climate with a multifaceted approach that more thoroughly addressed equity and inclusion. Although my current work focuses on sexuality and gender, I found value in applying social justice models and lenses to the development and creation of new programs, policies, and resources. Listening, paired with dialogue, can create inclusive, equitable, and effective programs, policies, and structures that challenge institutional oppression and act on intersectional inclusion.

One of the lasting outcomes from my Gender and Women's Studies degree encompassed the process of self-reflection and challenge that continues to lead to better recognition and action to address my own privilege. The self-reflective process was critical in my development and played a role in my comfort and ability to navigate challenging conversations as a professional. Through internships and volunteer experience that ranged from crisis sexual assault support services to event coordination, the Gender and Women's Studies degree provided avenues to examine real-world situations and to work toward equitable solutions that were based in theoretical frameworks that I learned during my coursework. I continue to repeat this process daily as I further read, listen, review, reflect, critically analyze, and apply principles that lean toward equity.

Each of these key components is interconnected and used daily in my current work. To begin a process toward social justice, I have found the majority of the work begins within. Self-reflection based in reading, researching, listening, applying, and developing ways to address the expanse of my own privilege has proved critical as I continue to improve and create a better path toward justice. Specifically, the white, male privilege that I examined throughout my coursework played a crucial role in approaching others for whom the questions of privilege, power, and oppression may be new.

One of the internal strengths that grew during my undergraduate education is my passion for social justice, equity, and positive change. The passion to make a difference provided the energy and motivation to get through the long days and challenges that one encounters navigating the world. From a core drive for equity and the freedom to be myself, the skills and knowledge obtained in a Gender and Women's Studies department enhanced my passion for social justice by providing a solid foundation and a skill set to create real and positive change, no matter what roles I undertake. My recommendation for future Gender and Women's Studies graduates: find your passion, listen, challenge your preconceived notions of yourself and the world, and expand collaboration with others to enhance social justice and equity in our global world.

## BOOKS TO GUIDE YOUR PATH

There are many publications available in the mass market that may be useful for you in researching career pathways. Two publications that we believe are extremely helpful and useful include Richard N. Bolles's (2014) *What Color is Your Parachute? A Practical Manual for Job-Hunters and Career Changers* and Katharine Brooks's (2009) *You Majored in What? Mapping your Path from Chaos to Career.* Bolles's text is the classic reference for job searchers. Brooks's text stands out as a paradigmatic shift in the career counseling field. Her book argues for the shift from a deficit model to one of strengths and experiences in searching for employment and assessing educational experiences.

*What Color is Your Parachute?* is a standard guide about finding a fulfilling career and is an extremely accessible and easy-to-read resource chock full of helpful advice and development activities. Cheryl appreciates the author's guiding idea that job seekers need hope and tools for developing their own ideas for their professional lives. Bolles also addresses job seekers' positionality and how who we are (age, race or ethnicity, class background) may impact our job search, and he acknowledges social inequalities in the marketplace. Yet Bolles also encourages readers to focus less on positionalities as factors in limiting your ability to get hired. Instead, Bolles recommends developing a list of transferable/functional skills that you possess and promoting these to potential employers. His book uses an inspirational message to convey his concerns.

Katharine Brooks's book challenges traditional ideas that one's major has a linear relationship to the occupation or field one will obtain work in. Brooks maintains that vocational researchers of the early twentieth century sought methods to link individual skills, interests, and talents with possible occupations. They developed a variety of tests and measures for these purposes, which reflected the epistemology and social context of the time—including institutional access and the power structure of academia. As Women's and Gender Studies students know, theories for explaining the world change over time. In order to address the needs of students completing their education in the twenty-first century, Brooks's text utilizes a more contemporary theory to assist students in assessing their skills and talents: chaos theory. A major idea within chaos theory is the "butterfly effect." The butterfly effect contends that seemingly unrelated events can produce a complex outcome affected by often unrelated but interconnected variables. Brooks argues that by exploring one's hidden talents and taking inventory of various skills, graduates can better adapt to the unpredictability of changing job markets (Brooks 2009: 11).

As with *What Color is Your Parachute?*, *You Majored in What?* offers readers exercises and activities in order to assess individual talents, interests, and skills. Cheryl likes that the book gives space for readers to assess their talents. Brooks also has readers consider areas or qualities in which they already are strong or well developed that can be marketed to employers. Brooks's examples tend to reflect traditional liberal arts majors (e.g. English, Anthropology, History), but Women's and Gender Studies majors/minors can certainly draw a connection between Women's and Gender Studies and liberal arts.

## SPOTLIGHT: SARAH "TUCKER" JENKINS

How does one land a "dream job"? We asked Sarah ("Tucker"), Michele's student and our former research assistant, to talk about how she went about it:

> In the fall of 2013, I became the Program Coordinator at the Women's Center and LGBT Center at Ohio University. I have one of those jobs that people who major in Women's and Gender Studies dream about. It's a job that I dreamed about. However, the twists and turns that my life has taken on the way to this moment have been far from what I expected five years ago. After I had graduated from UNC-Chapel Hill with my bachelor's degree in Women's Studies, I felt very lost and confused. I couldn't find any jobs related to my Women's Studies degree. I worked for three years, doing various jobs that paid the rent but did not fulfill my passion for social justice (the exception being my work as a research assistant on the *Transforming Scholarship* book!). During those three years, I learned that neither barista nor library assistant were dream careers of mine. I knew that my ultimate goal was to work in a nonprofit or education setting with feminist principles and I knew I needed to go back to school in order to gain the qualifications to be attractive to those kind of jobs.
>
> First, I decided to apply to Master of Social Work programs. This choice was based not on wanting to become a "social worker" specifically, but on trying to

find a degree that I thought would be most marketable. Although it was a blow to be rejected from the social work programs to which I applied, It was ultimately the best thing to happen. It gave me the opportunity to reconsider my options and revaluate what I would most enjoy. Although I had believed the MSW program to be more marketable, I knew that my passion still lied in Women's and Gender Studies.

I enrolled in the Women, Gender, and Sexuality Studies master's program at Florida Atlantic University and poured all of my focus and ambition into that program. I chose FAU because their program was highly recommended to me by a good friend and they offered me a graduate assistantship, which made it much more affordable. Where I had been relatively unengaged in campus activities during my undergraduate degree, I took a completely opposite approach to my academic engagement at FAU. My graduate teaching assistantship allowed me to T.A. with several professors for a year before teaching my own introductory level undergraduate Women's Studies course. This allowed me to learn about the basics of teaching Women's and Gender Studies courses before I had to get up in front of the students myself. I can honestly say that teaching Women's Studies changed the way I thought about other people, about myself, and about the way I wanted to live my life. It gave me the opportunity to practice patience and generosity with my students, many of whom were not necessarily interested in Women's Studies. Teaching allowed me to begin cultivating a spirit of acceptance toward folks, to make an effort to give them a "benefit of the doubt" not necessarily for their sake, but for my own.

In addition to teaching, I also decided to engage in a number of extracurricular activities on campus. I became involved at the newly formed LGBTQA Resource Center, a volunteer experience that gave me key expertise and skills that helped me land my current position. When I noticed that FAU had no current feminist student organization, I got together with some friends and we started one. Starting this organization and planning and implementing the various programs we put on provided another invaluable experience that I utilized during my job interviews. Along with this, I assisted the Women, Gender, and Sexuality Studies department with any programs they hosted, such as guest speakers, our annual Women's Studies conference, and Women's Equality Day. However, in spite of all of these activities, I made sure to prioritize my coursework over my applied campus related activities, a skill I had not mastered during my undergraduate years at UNC. Part of the reason graduate school was so successful for me was because of the time I took off before returning. Those three years allowed me to grow and mature, while also giving me the opportunity to appreciate how much I had really loved school.

After I graduated in May 2013, I felt similarly lost as I had after finishing my BA, I wasn't sure if I wanted to continue on to a doctoral program, or if I wanted to start looking for jobs. In the meantime, I was working at a grocery store and not enjoying the experience. I searched around my area for months, mostly going forward with the idea that I would find a job to work for a year while I applied to doctoral programs (although I wasn't sure what programs!). In the meantime, the Program Coordinator position came across my desk in an email forward from my department director. I applied to the program on a whim, thinking I would probably never hear about it again. My concern was that although I had all of the right qualifications for the job, I was not sure I had anything that would make me stand out from all of the other applicants. However, I was mistaken. I did hear back about a month later. Although I had applied to the job on a whim, I threw myself into the interview process wholeheartedly. First, I was invited for a phone interview. I spent hours researching phone interview tips online and made sure my computer had all of the necessary documents (resume, job description, website, etc.) opened before the interview started. I also read a suggestion online to send my LinkedIn page to my interviewers so they could put a face with my voice during the interview, personalizing the experience. LinkedIn is a professional social networking site that allows you to upload a photo of yourself along with your professional and volunteer activities. The phone interview was definitely nerve-wracking, but also fun. It was a new and enjoyable experience to be asked about feminist theory in a job interview. I was nervous, but overall felt adequately prepared for the questions. During the interview I was told that the nine phone interview applicants would be whittled down to three to be invited to Ohio University to interview in person. I was so nervous waiting to hear my fate! I was ecstatic when I got the call inviting me to come to Ohio. The interview was a full day; I was excited but also exhausted by the end of it. Although it was torture to wait for an answer, I had also come to a valuable realization. I decided it was not time for me to continue on for a doctoral program, instead I knew that if I did not get this job, I would start applying to more of the same around the country. However, I did not have to use my Plan B; I was offered the job the very next business day. From this experience, and many others like it, I know that the universe wants me to learn to accept what is best for me, not what I may think is best for me.

**YOUR TURN: EXERCISES**

Choose two or three new employment sectors that you have just learned about in this section and research them. What possibilities might they offer you with the skills and training that you will have by the time you graduate?

# 6

# WOMEN'S AND GENDER STUDIES GRADUATES AS CHANGE AGENTS

## SEVEN PROFILES

In Chapter 5, you got to see the multiple kinds of employment opportunities that exist for WGST grads. We hope that you came away from that chapter feeling empowered about the variety of possibilities available. You will discover more pathways here—some graduates pursue positions that directly utilize and apply their knowledge and understanding of gender issues, whereas others may work in environments in which a Women's and Gender Studies degree is a benefit, yet not always actively acknowledged. There is no one model or way to use one's Women's and Gender Studies degree! These employment paths are marked with trial and error, inspiration, passion, serendipity, creativity, and tons of hard work.

The graduates' employment profiles presented here grew out of our survey analysis and interviews. Our research demonstrates that Women's and Gender Studies graduates go on to find fulfilling work in a variety of fields. You will find how they talk about their journey into their current occupation useful, not so that you can replicate that same path, but so that you can understand the process by which they got there. These seven profiles also provide a context for living one's ideals and values of Women's and Gender Studies.

We present a framework of "sustainers, evolvers, and synthesizers," designed to highlight unique ways to think about how graduates have found their way in the professional world and build on our idea of Women's and Gender Studies students as change agents. You will read the profiles of seven individuals who exemplify this framework. They are change agents in small and large ways through their paid employment and commitments outside of work. Their struggles and triumphs provide useful models for you as you think about how you will use your training after you graduate. We think you will find yourself inspired by their commitments to gender equality and creativity in pursuing meaningful work. You may hear people say they do not know what you will do with your Women's and Gender Studies degree. And that Women's and Gender Studies does not seem to have as direct a line to a career as, say, going into Accounting. We think that perspective does not tell the full story, nor agree with the findings of our research. The perception that one's undergraduate major will lead directly to a job in a specific field is a falsehood that is not unique to Women's and Gender Studies, but most academic majors. We found direct paths to several career areas with a Women's and Gender Studies degree. Moreover, your training in Women's and Gender Studies allows you to assess the job market in new and different ways that lead to creating opportunities that go beyond "getting a job." Also, as Dr. Reger notes in her POV later in this chapter, there are lots of ways to conceive of developing and applying one's talents in various occupations that lead to a fulfilling career and personal life.

### Sustainers, Evolvers, and Synthesizers: Seven Profiles

There are three groups around which we have categorized our seven respondents. Their experiences represent a more general pattern that we have seen through interviews and survey data. The first group is called "sustainers." This group has two key features: the graduates in the group have pursued career paths that involve working on gender issues directly and in types of employment where the Women's and Gender Studies degree is often a complementary fit for the skills required for the position. There is a well-established track record of using a Women's and Gender Studies degree in these professional fields. The road is well traveled and there are lots of landmarks. In choosing the path of a "sustainer," you would follow the career journeys of many other Women's and Gender Studies practitioners (such as by becoming a domestic violence or sexual assault counselor, a coordinator at a Women's or LGBTQ Center, or even a WGST professor).

The other key feature of sustainers is the role of activism, which is central to their stories and undergirds how they find their career paths. Activism helps sustain interest in both the paid and unpaid worlds. In fact, activism helps some sustainers find employment, and is often a requirement of their jobs from inspiring action in the community, to organizing protests and other community awareness events. Activism helps some sustainers find employment, and is often a requirement of their jobs from inspiring action in the community, to organizing protests and other community awareness events.

The second group is called "evolvers." The three profiles that you will read in this "category" share two features: (1) these individuals have taken Women's and Gender Studies into arenas where it previously was not, either in terms of finding or creating new employment opportunities; and (2) they are highly adaptable and innovative, and are continually taking risks that support their inner vision.

The third group, "synthesizers" move back and forth between these two categories. As with sustainers, they are connected to career paths that tend to emphasize gender issues. As with evolvers, they have high energy and passion for trying new ideas. Synthesizers have an ability to move among and between careers that involve gender issues directly and utilize their activism in both their paid and unpaid work, as well as being creative in exploring new areas for taking risks with their vision.

This framework is a heuristic tool and not meant to create mutually exclusive categories. Indeed, we invite you as you read these wonderful graduate profiles to consider similarities and differences between them that might suggest other ways of organizing them.

*Sustainers*

*Rebecca Mann: Becoming a Paid Feminist*

Michele met Rebecca during a career services night at her university. During Rebecca's presentation on how to go into community organizing, she heard Rebecca say she had learned how to become "a paid feminist." Michele had never heard that term before and was very intrigued and asked if she could hear more of Rebecca's story. Rebecca Mann is currently the director of community organizing and outreach for Equality North Carolina, a statewide group dedicated to securing equal rights and justice for lesbian, gay, bisexual, and transgender (LGBT) people.

She is a lifelong North Carolinian and holds a BA in English, with a minor in Women's and Gender Studies, from North Carolina State University and an MA in Women's and Gender Studies from the University of North Carolina at Greensboro She graduated from college in 2000. Rebecca has worked as an advocate and organizer with the YWCA of High Point and Planned Parenthood Health Systems, and in the communications departments of IntraHealth International and the international reproductive rights organization Ipas.

Rebecca was one of the first people to minor in Women's Studies when it was first offered at her university, which to us makes her a "mini-pioneer." She stumbled across Women's Studies and she believes that she connected with it because it mirrored some of her interests developed in high school. She always believed in principles of fairness and equality: "Since the first [Women's Studies] class, I realized I want[ed] to do this." In her English and Journalism projects, she remembers trying to infuse those assignments with Women's Studies interest and content.

During her first semester in her sophomore year, Rebecca became involved in a local chapter of the National Organization for Women (NOW). She got involved with NOW as a manifestation of her activism. Little did she know that this involvement as a student activist was going to shape her career choices in small and large ways. She believes that it is important for students to apply what they know outside of classes:

> Coursework is great, but if you aren't connecting it to something bigger outside, I would find it hard [for] it to be meaningful. You're learning about stuff, but you're learning about systems, but seeing how that is impacting women is important.

Her parents were supportive of her minor in Women's Studies—it helped that she was also focused on editing and journalism. During the first year of being educated in Women's Studies, she also accepted a broader label for herself: "A roommate that I wasn't getting along with during an argument called me a feminist and stormed out of the room and I thought, 'Is that the worst thing you can call me?'"

She sometimes found the campus climate challenging as an activist for women's issues:

> At the time it was hard, but I think that after pushing through that for a little while, I realized it was so much better to be in that situation, because I feel like if you can stand up for what you

believe in, when a lot of people around you aren't in your immediate core and even the ones who are—I definitely had a lot of friends who just didn't get it—I feel like if you can do it in that environment, then when you get out, everything else is just cake. For a while I daydreamed about transferring to [a] campus where there was a strong feminist presence. But, I'm glad that I didn't because part of the learning process is to have that opposition . . . I wouldn't have been prepared for real life activism.

Rebecca believes the challenges she faced as an activist on campus prepared her for the challenges of activism and community organizing after college. Her first job after graduation was as a technical editor for a firm that contracted with top *Fortune* 500 companies. It was extremely well paid, though not very interesting or challenging to her. She was laid off during the "dotcom" bust, and she called it a blessing, because it allowed her to stop pretending that technical writing was the work she really wanted to do. All during this time, however, she continued her activism with NOW. While she was laid off, she used her connections through NOW, who knew her and could vouch for her, to gain several nonprofit positions. Because she had been a committed volunteer and organizer for so many years, it was easy for Rebecca's friends to call potential employers (that they often knew at other nonprofits) or write compelling reference letters for her. That allowed her to get a position at Ipas, an international reproductive rights organization. She attributes her success in getting in the front door and eventually landing a position with them to her personal connections. Her friends, mentors, and fellow

## ABOUT NOW

The National Organization for Women was founded in 1966 by a small but determined group of women's rights advocates. NOW is a leading progressive U.S. feminist organization. Feminist activists, scholars, and policymakers have been a part of its long history. NOW has devoted itself to issues of changing policy and public opinion on major issues including: reproductive rights, sexual violence, equal pay for women, gay and lesbian rights, employment discrimination, civil rights, and support for more elected women in political office. For more information, see www.now.org.

activists called on her behalf, which helped move her into a more competitive position to be considered for a job. The position was in the communications department, and this was a stepping stone position that led her to other positions with non-profits, including a position at a local Planned Parenthood doing policy work and organizing.

On her resume and in job interviews, she highlighted her minor in Women's Studies. She had devoted time to work in community organizing and advocacy, which helped compensate for the lack of skills she had in specific areas. Her activism augmented her resume, although she did not have direct paid work experience. Since she had been with NOW for several years during and after college, she gained an impressive list of external skills: event planning, community organizing, data systems, phone banking, canvassing, etc.

She also credits her activism with keeping her "sane" for the times that she was not in work that she loved. While an activist at NOW, she did research on timely issues, including pay equity and reproductive rights. This kept up her skills and she could show nonprofits that she was well read in a variety of areas.

When Rebecca talks to students, she tries to dispel the notion that you have to have a certain type of job with a Women's and Gender Studies degree: "Any job you have will be a feminist job if it's done with intention, if you're being aware."

She went back and decided to pursue an MA in Women's and Gender Studies because she wanted to deepen her work, and she also saw that positions in several areas of interest were looking for candidates who had postgraduate degrees. She chose a program that was very connected with the public policy world. The transition between being an activist and graduate student was a bit challenging at first. Despite this, she was able to deepen her knowledge of feminist theory and sociology.

For several years, she pursued her interest in lobbying, policy, and organizing, and became the Director of Community Organizing and Advocacy for Equality NC. This job opened serendipitously as she was finishing her master's program. Equality NC works on state policy affecting lesbian, gay, bisexual, transgender, and questioning (LGBTQ) North Carolinians. The organization works with the state legislature to pass bills that positively affect the LGBTQ community and also conducts grassroots campaigns in communities across the state.

In her interview for this position, her long-standing work with NOW was noted. During her interview, she discussed how NOW had also helped her concentrate more specifically on LGBT issues. As a straight, married woman she felt incredibly privileged to do this work. She also credited her work in her master's program, which concentrated on theory and gender and gave her a broader foundation. She believes if you are part of a majority group, "that it is an onus on you [to make sure] that other people are being treated equally."

## POINT OF VIEW

### SIX DEGREES OF FEMINIST SEPARATION

#### Jo Reger, Oakland University

For my research on feminist communities, I have traveled around the United States talking to young people who identify as feminists and activists. Many of them took Women's Studies classes in college and are graduates of Women's Studies programs. As the director of a Women's and Gender Studies program, the most common question I get from everyone (i.e. students, students' families, other faculty, administrators, and the woman who cuts my hair) is: "What can you do with a degree in Women's Studies?" To think about that question, I decided to re-examine the relation between college, feminism, community, and careers. To do so, I selected one community in the Northwest United States, where most of the people I interviewed had graduated from college. Looking at their lives, I find they enter into four basic types of occupations: *feminist/political*, *social service*, *professional/research*, and *other*. For example, three of the women interviewed worked in either overtly feminist (i.e. a feminist bookstore) or political (i.e. election campaign manager) jobs. Three worked in social service agencies doing a variety of work ranging from serving as a sexual assault advocate and volunteer coordinator to coordinating an Americore Service Learning program to organizing tenant services for a program working with the homeless. Another group worked as professionals, one as a schoolteacher, and the other as a public health research analyst. The final category was "other," with jobs such as nanny and UPS management. These career paths largely align with what I see Women's Studies majors doing at my university.

Looking at this list, one could conclude that about half of these feminists have feminist careers. This is true for this community, but I also found that *all* of them had feminist lives. In addition to asking about jobs, I also asked them what groups they belonged to and what did they do with their time outside of work. Again the answers fell into a variety of categories ranging from being members of feminist established organizations such as the American Association of University Women (AAUW), National Organization for Women (NOW), National Abortion Rights Action League (NARAL); political organ-izations such as the Green Party, Move ON, and the Democratic Party; arts and creative-oriented groups such as 'zine symposiums; LGBT rights organizations both local and national such as the Human Rights Campaign and PFLAG (Parents of Lesbians and Gays); and feminist groups with a specific focus such as Wiccan groups and fat positive organizations, as well as labor organizations and animal organizations such as the Farm Sanctuary.

Talking to them, I could see how they had integrated their feminism into all aspects of their lives, in ways that simply asking about their jobs did not show. For example, the nanny was extensively involved in issues of fat oppression and performed as a drag king. The feminist bookstore workers embraced established groups such as AAUW, as well as making 'zines and working with the Green Party. Almost everyone I spoke to was engaged in both the work that supported them as well as working in their com-munities in multiple ways. As a result, they were often connected to each other through one organization or another, creating a network of feminists that spread throughout the community. For example, the UPS manager worked in the same organizations as the nanny, the political campaign manager, and the tenant services coordinator. I call this creating "six degrees of feminist separation." Laurel, one of the women I interviewed, described the life after college she had created. She said, "[My] community is rich in feminists. Most all my friends [are] . . . They're who I [have] been attracted to and who have been attracted to me." This is what sustains Women's Studies graduates; not the specific job title, but the submersion into an engaged feminist community and these communities of activists, connected through jobs and organiza-tions, are filled with people pursuing interesting and fulfilling lives. This, I think, can make a better answer than a specific job title.

She most recently began her own consulting firm, Engage NC, that combines her expertise in fundraising, grant-writing, "message crafting," and advocacy work on behalf of socially progressive nonprofits.

### Matt Ezzell: Radical Teacher and Scholar

You met Matt in earlier chapters. By the time he arrived at UNC's campus, he had seen his older sister struggle, at an early age, with eating disorders and also later pursue a minor in Women's Studies when she was at college. He had also witnessed his mother find fulfillment going back to school for a master's degree in Literature with a concentration on contemporary fiction written by African-American women. Discussing issues central to women's lives was not a foreign experience to Matt. The first semester he, like most students, looked at different majors, including Business. Matt says that "Introduction to the Sociology of Gender," which he enrolled in during his first semester, changed "the course of [my] academic, professional, and personal trajectory."

He was amazed at how the class was structured to emphasize co-facilitation between students and instructor, and he reveled in the small group discussions, as well as the emphasis on critical thinking and that "the material is grounded in the lived realities [of people] . . . it wasn't abstract discussions of the social world." The instructor also invited students to share their lived experiences through the prism of gender, race, and class. Situating himself in relation to the concepts he was learning was new and exciting: "I didn't know that education could be like this."

His experience in that class provided him with tools to think critically about masculinity. After that class, he changed his major from Business to Women's Studies. When he told his family about his major, his mother and sister were supportive "that I had stumbled into Women's Studies." He was worried about what his dad would say, given that his father had been in business for most of Matt's life and was looking forward to his son following in his footsteps. He said, "Do you enjoy it?" and when Matt said he did, his father said to follow his interests.

When asked about pushback from his peers in the community after he announced his major, he said it was not so difficult: "Most of what I experienced was positive, partly because the deeper I got into Women's Studies, the more I surrounded myself with a self-identified feminist community."

As he discussed in Chapter 3, Matt had to navigate being the only male-identified person in the Women's Studies program. He was keenly aware of the challenges of the privileges he had as a man and the necessity of using that privilege to confront male bias. Soon after he took the class, he wanted to do an internship and work on issues of sexual assault and violence, an interest that emerged strongly for him:

> The more I started thinking about these issues and having conversations with people in my life about these issues, the more of my friends, particularly women friends, started to disclose issues of sexual violence; I was realizing very quickly that I didn't know any women who didn't have some experience of men's violence that they could connect to immediately. It was part of the experience of being a woman. There is this shared experience of

being targeted within a rape culture if you are a woman. And I was starting to approach a realization of what that meant. And I felt like I wanted to do something about this because I knew too many people that I care about who are struggling with this . . . and I hadn't really thought about this much before and I want to be active. I felt like I got the benefits of the targeting of women just because I'm a man. So, it's our responsibility to do something.

Matt called the local rape crisis center and said, "I don't know if you have male volunteers, I understand if you don't. The last thing I would want to do is be a trigger for someone who walks in the door to get help just because I am a man . . ." The person who answered said, "We do have male volunteers. We think it's really important to have male volunteers. And there is definitely a role here for you." He was able to volunteer at the rape crisis center, which included 63 hours of training; he decided to do an internship there, and as part of the agreement with the agency, he also had to commit to volunteering an additional semester after he was finished with the internship. Becoming involved with the rape crisis center became a total immersion into the topic of sexual violence and working at such a center.

As a volunteer and as part of his internship, he became a community educator. He did a number of training sessions in the area: "a lot of material was geared toward elementary school kids," but also high schools, community colleges, four-year universities, and community organizations. His focus became how to get men involved as allies with women against sexual assault. He would make a point of speaking to any organization that wanted to learn about preventing sexual violence. He learned he loved working with groups on this issue and found it very rewarding. It gave him experience of how to talk about issues that are difficult to talk about, particular with men, without getting defensive. He did this work during his junior year and he still feels that he draws on the lessons and insights he learned about working in groups even now as a professor. During this time, he also wrote a paper drawing on his own experience and research to support the rape crisis center in conducting outreach with men. After the official internship semester ended, he stayed on as a volunteer, as part of his agreement, and continued developing and honing male outreach on sexual violence.

Matt's activism on sexual violence continued to blossom on campus. He developed and co-taught a course on interpersonal violence prevention and leadership, which became a popular class (and now has been institutionalized as a service learning course). Also, noting the holes in student affairs administration regarding sexual violence, he advocated for developing a paid staff position for an interpersonal violence prevention coordinator—someone who would be responsible for helping to coordinate resources, talks, etc. on preventing sexual violence across the campus community. This has also come to fruition since he has left UNC.

The rape crisis center was where he got his first job after graduation. He saw an office manager position open up during his senior year and knew, "I had to apply and interview. Once I had the internship experience —I knew I wanted to do more work on eliminating sexual violence and getting more men involved." He felt passionate about this work. In the interview, he was able to demonstrate that "I had internship experiences and the connections I made were, without question, putting the skills and lessons that I learned from my Women's Studies major to use." He was offered the position. As he was graduating without debt, he felt he could take an entry-level nonprofit job for a few years. Matt believed that taking an entry-level nonprofit position was a good way to use the class privilege he possessed of not having had to pay for school because of his parents' socio-economic status and ability to pay for his college education.

Matt worked in the rape crisis center for three years and was promoted several times: office manager, administrative services coordinator, and finally, community education coordinator. He completely enjoyed working in the community and talking with a variety of audiences, but over time he grew "very frustrated":

> I had only 45 minutes with students to dismantle rape culture—
> I thought how wonderful it would be if you had a semester—you
> can't do everything in a semester either, but you can get to know
> students, you can build on discussions and I thought that was
> amazing.

He loved teaching and facilitating, and could see pursuing the path of becoming a professor.

Early on in his undergraduate career, he had found a mentor, someone he identified as a "radical feminist mentor" who encouraged his work and supported him. With her encouragement, he developed his voice through writing for local newsmagazines and with her on topics including sexist language, the role of pornography in everyday culture, and teaching gender. He was torn between choosing a graduate program in Sociology or Women's Studies. He was, however, drawn to working with his mentor in Sociology and continuing the activism that he had begun in the North Carolina community. When he was accepted into UNC's Sociology program, he felt that it was a good fit

He loved deepening the work in sSociology with an emphasis on gender as a graduate student. His sense that he would excel in the classroom and enjoy working with students was confirmed. During his graduate career, he earned a teaching award, as well as the first university award to recognize a person making a significant contribution to women in the campus community. Matt finished his doctorate in 2008 and took a position as an Assistant Professor in the Department of Sociology and Anthropology at James Madison College, a small, private liberal arts college. He teaches a wide variety of courses, including "The Development of Sociological Thought and Method," "Microsociology," "The Sociology of Race and Ethnicity," and "The Sociology of Gender."

James Madison has a Curriculum in Women's Studies. Matt's course on "The Sociology of Gender" counts toward the Women's Studies minor—and he serves on the WMST advisory board. He says, "I get more radical every day." As a relatively new professor, he is interested in mentoring students, building a feminist community, and raising his daughter.

*Takeaways from Rebecca and Matt's Profiles*

- If you have an interest in Women's and Gender Studies prior to college, it may serve you throughout your academic career— Rebecca and Matt both had a longstanding interest in Women's and Gender Studies before they entered college. Once in college, they found themselves in classes that nurtured their interest in gender equality.
- Find an internship experience that is right for you. For Matt, his experiences as an intern and work on campus on the issues of sexual violence gave him a strong advantage when applying for an entry-level position at the rape crisis center.
- Allow yourself to be mentored. Matt and Rebecca both drew on mentors (from college networks and activist networks) who helped

them gain perspective in making career decisions and applying for
positions.

- Do not give up if your first position is not everything you dreamed
it was going to be. Cultivate interests outside of work—Rebecca's
interests did not align with her first position. But she continued
to pursue her interests through volunteering and community work.
Her activism kept her sane while she was not in her dream job.
Over time, the experiences gained as a long-standing volunteer and
activist gave her the expertise to move into positions that more
closely aligned with her interests.

*Evolvers*

*Rachel Burton: Industrial Maven*

Rachel first came to college interested in becoming a Nutrition Science
major, but she took an introductory course in Women's Studies because
of her interest in women's health issues and because someone had told
her there would be information on that topic in this course. While in the
course, "a big light bulb went off," and in her second semester she realized
she could combine Nutrition Science and Women's Studies. She liked
the idea of combining a liberal arts discipline with a science-based
discipline. Rachel wound up not finishing Nutrition Science, but finished
the Women's Studies major and became extremely involved in activist
issues.

During her college years, Rachel was very involved in several issue-
based groups on campus: an animal rights group, and a variety of women's
groups and organizations working on specific issues, such as sexist fraternity practices. She also undertook environmental activism off campus,
including direct action with organizations such as Greenpeace, Earth
First, and the Rainforest Action Network.

Her parents had questions when she dropped Nutrition Science, but
she was so involved with activities off campus that she did not really pay
attention to them. She also took a semester off (between sophomore and
junior year) and lived in a collective in Detroit. This move prompted her
parents to focus more on her major and how it was going to serve her in
the future, and she says it became a "big question." She always felt that

## NEW PATHS IN FARMING, ACTIVISM, AND SUSTAINABILITY

Roohol was able to lap into a cluster of interests that have been steadily dovoloping. There is a growing convergence among many people interested in the conneotiono between sustainability, "food justice," sustainable agriculture, and connecting to the land in secular and spiritual ways. Over the past 20 years, farming and building community through sustainable agriculturo have become attractive to graduating students. Women make up a growing porcentago of farmers. According to the U.S. Census of Agriculture (2012), the number of women who owned farms jumped 29 percent between 2002 and 2007. Many states have seen even larger jumps in the number of women farmers. One in 10 U.S. farms is owned by women. Men still own and run farms, especially those that are large scale, but "women tend to run smaller, more specialized enterprises selling heirloom tomatoes and grass-fed beef" to smaller niche markets (Aranti 2009). Women farmers have also benefited from the upsurge in the public's interest in buying local and organic produce from farmers' markets and through community-supported agricultural (CSA) programs.

Sometimes, farming communities are also places that encourage and foster spiritual growth. A former colleague of Cheryl's, Lisa Coons, is the Center Director for the Center for Earth Spirituality and Rural Ministry for the School Sisters of Notre Dame (SSND) in Mankato, Minnesota. According to the Center's website:

> The Center promotes and fosters awareness and ways of living that recognize and support the interconnection and interdependence of all life. In embracing people of all spiritual paths, the Center strives toward earth justice and sustainability through education, spirituality, sustainable agriculture, rural ministry, and political advocacy. One of the purposes of the Center is to model environmental stewardship on the SSND land itself through ecological awareness, ecosystem restoration, support of local food production, and environmentally sensitive maintenance practices.
>
> (Center for Earth Spirituality and Rural Ministry 2013)

If you are interested in farming and sustainable agriculture, a good place to start would be the American Farm Bureau's "Young Farmers and Ranchers Program" (American Farm Bureau Federation 2014).

"you can do anything you want with a Women's Studies major, it's just a matter of how you apply yourself."

She remembers that when she was getting ready to graduate and thinking about next steps, her visit to the career services office was not very helpful. After graduation, Rachel traveled overseas and began working on organic farms, pursuing her growing interest in sustainable agriculture (in England, Wales, Ireland, and Scotland). She also traveled to small farms and communities to learn how they organized on issues of the environment.

### FOR YOUR LIBRARY

Temra Costa (2010). *Farmer Jane: Women Changing the Way We Eat.* Layton, UT: Gibbs Smith.

Rachel came back to a rural community in North Carolina and deepened her interest in sustainable farming practices. She worked with a woman who owned a small organic farm, and Rachel notes, "She became a real mentor for me." Rachel took a tremendous leap and enrolled in a one-year certificate program in sustainable agriculture from a local community college. She worked part-time on her mentor's farm and then as a waitress and tried to stay active in environmental groups.

During the sustainable agriculture program, she got to know one of the teachers, a man who also taught the automotive mechanics class, and she mentioned that she had a broken transmission on a truck she owned. He said to her, "I'll show you how to fix it, if you buy the parts." Intrigued, she went to buy the parts: "It was a totally new arena." She spent the entire day with her teacher working on her transmission. At the end of the lesson, he said, "Girl, you're not half bad at this—you should think about doing this!" He convinced her to enroll in the automotive mechanics program.

As she evaluated his suggestion to return to school in a new subject area, she engaged in some self-reflection and goal planning. She currently had an excellent informal mentor (carpenter by trade and running her own farm) demonstrating hands-on and life skills concerning what it meant to be a female farmer. She surmised that her hands-on farming knowledge, combined with learning mechanical knowledge, would make a strong combination. She thought that if she wanted to pursue farming, it would be useful for the rest of my life whether I wanted to be a mechanic for the rest of my life and work on cars or if I just wanted to have the basic knowledge of engines and engine operation and maintenance [which] would be useful on farms.

She enrolled in the automotive mechanics program. Two other women were with her. One woman had a husband who was a truck driver, and she wanted to beef up her knowledge of engines and maintenance to help him. The other woman was generally interested in cars. Rachel was 25 at the time, and all the other members of the program were younger men:

> Early on there was a proving ground time period. It felt like the first semester, there was [a sense of being questioned] "How much do *you* really want to know about automotive technology? Are you just here to find a boyfriend?"

Rachel tried to cut through the hostility and suspicion: "I want to get dirty. I'm serious, not here to sit on sidelines and watch. And it was unacceptable for someone to do something for me." She tried to correct what she calls "tool grabbing" and the "let me just show you" attitude, where men in the class would dominate the tools and not give her or the other women an opportunity to use them and learn on their own. She had to instruct the male students, "Tell me, and then show me once." And, "I'm here to learn and I'm going to learn more than you." Luckily, the teacher was very supportive throughout the entire program, and she felt no intimidation or need to prove herself to him.

Rachel was able to pursue her training in automotive mechanics through what is now called the Carl D. Perkins Career and Technical Education Improvement Act of 2006. An earlier version, the Carl D. Perkins Vocational and Applied Technology Education Act ("Perkins Act"), refers to the federal law that funds vocational education programs at secondary and post-secondary institutions across the country. The Perkins Act contained provisions, dating from the 1970s, intended to help ensure that women and girls had equal access and opportunity to succeed in vocational education. A version of this grant was administered through the state of North Carolina in partnership with local community colleges. This grant supported women in pursuing training for a two-year degree in motorcycle mechanics, automotive mechanics, industrial maintenance, welding, and electric engineering. For Rachel, this meant that her books and tuition were paid for and she also received a set of mechanics tools when she graduated. If you are interested in these opportunities, you should talk with either a financial aid counselor at your current institution or an administrator at your local community college to see if there are programs funded within your state.

If her parents were skeptical of her interest in Women's and Gender Studies, they were even more skeptical of a two-year degree in automotive mechanics. After answering their questions and fixing her father's car, however (she said with a smile), it did not take long for them to see the utility of the degree. She even inspired her father, who was retired, to enroll in an automotive body program.

Her teacher and mentor helped her get her first automotive mechanic job at a local dealership for a year while she was finishing school. The move from student mechanic to the paid professional world of being an automotive mechanic was not easy for Rachel: "The transition from automotive classroom to automotive workplace was dramatically different in comfort level. The workplace was difficult to have a positive powerful learning experience."

At the two dealerships where she worked over a two-year period, there were very few women. If there were women there, they worked in very different positions than Rachel—mostly secretarial. Rachel was also keenly aware that the women who did work in the office were often relatives of the men who owned the dealership. She met no other female mechanics in her first two positions.

She faced sexism and heterosexism continually on her first job. A typical question from one mechanic was, "Are you a lesbian or carpet muncher?" She went through a hazing period with many of the male employees, who used the excuse that "we're teasing you because we like you." Although she was able to prove herself with several of the technicians, there were still technicians who would not work with her. Many women experience sexual harassment in the workplace, and women in the trades often face open hostility and discrimination such as this.

Rachel found that she was able to have a more a positive effect by being an automotive instructor at the community college. She was asked to do this by her instructor and taught full-time for three years—taking over his class often. Later, during this time, her first mentor also asked her to teach automotive high school classes. This was a gift for her:

> It was great; I learned even more working with him and beside him. First year was a challenge [with issues such as] not being a trained teacher, curriculum, dynamic of [being in my] late twenties and students were 17/18 and ready to get out of high school and stuck with a "newbie female instructor." Every year, though, more and more girls would come into the program because they heard through other students that there was a female instructor.

She could see a significant change as more and more women signed up to get these skills, and she felt comfortable in her class because they felt they would not "be picked on because people think they're hanging out with the boys." Rachel believes that paying attention to making women, as well as men, students feel comfortable creates a stronger classroom.

She was invited to teach night school, working with returning adults. Over time, as a teacher, she found more and more administrators who were supportive of her as an instructor of automotive mechanics. Sometimes, older male students would say, "I don't want to be in her class," but an administrator would back Rachel up.

The move to her current work in biofuels production and distribution was a natural outgrowth of her interests—a combination of sustainable agriculture, environmental activism, and new industrialism—and fit well with her skill set and self-confidence in working in often male-dominated work environments. Her interest in biofuels came from a different perspective, asking what was in fuels for cars, and from this she started researching alternative automotive fuels. Rachel then co-hosted a continuing education class on "biofuels," which was the first of its kind in the community. Every time she taught the class, it got bigger, with more people taking the class. Over time, as people began learning about biofuels, they wanted to know how and where to get them. Rachel teamed up with a few people to investigate, which caused this to grow into a bigger pursuit, leading to a substantial enterprise: "Let's make biofuels for ourselves." Her team then helped to induce demand for creating a distribution network—one tank at a time.

Rachel is co-founder of Piedmont Biofuels, a leader of biofuels in North Carolina. Piedmont Biofuels is a worker- and member-owned cooperative promoting and offering biodiesel fuel made from vegetable oil. They offer classes, consultations, and have also become a hub for issues of sustainable agriculture in the state. Her official title on her business card just states "In charge," but she explains that she is really the control manager for the biofuels plant and also the research director. She handles the understanding and handling of all the fuel issues (the making of the fuel and the quality of it in the laboratory). This brings her back to her roots in chemistry and nutrition science. She believes, "Nothing is ever wasted in one's development." Rachel also gives fuel quality presentations all over the world, writes grants, manages public funding, plays a key role in the day-to-day operations, and is also writing a book about her experiences in the sustainability field.

If she had not spent time in the Women's Studies arena, Rachel says:

> I may not have not gone down the auto pathway, because I may have not felt: this is something women don't do . . . but here's an opportunity to do it. I think there is definitely a connection between the fact I was a Women's Studies major and I went to pursue a nontraditional career and to understand and further my experience of being a woman in the workplace.

She feels her time in the automotive mechanic workplace was "just a different arena of understanding women's roles in society." She feels as if she is a model for other women who wish to pursue untraditional pathways using their degree.

### Kimberly Wilson: Tranquilista and Social Entrepreneur

Kimberly Wilson is a prime example of a person who is living her passion for Women's Studies and empowering women as leaders in new ways. She is a yoga teacher, entrepreneur (beginning at age 26), designer of eco-fashion, self-proclaimed do-gooder who runs a nonprofit that provides a space for yoga, creativity, and leadership for girls in grades 9–12, and lover of "all things fabulous." Although she came to Women's Studies toward the end of her academic career, she felt that it offered her a new way of thinking and living her life.

During her last year at the University of Oklahoma, she took her first Women's Studies course. The first thing she thought was, "Why did I

## OPPORTUNITIES IN TRADITIONAL AND VOCATIONAL TRADES

While your Women's and Gender Studies education provides you with the critical thinking tools to analyze gender and oppression in the world, perhaps you have always had a gift for working with your hands and creating beauty with hair, or repairing your car, or building a cabinet to hold all your textbooks from class. Rather than pursing a graduate degree, you may be more inclined to get your journeyman's (-person's) card, your cosmetologist license, or even a pilot's license. According to the Chicago Women in Trades (CWIT) website:

> Careers in the trades include carpentry, plumbing, welding, auto mechanics, and other high wage, high-skill blue-collar careers. These careers offer women insurance benefits, pensions, career advancement and challenging careers in addition to starting average wages of $12.00 an hour and the potential of making over $30.00 an hour!
>
> (Chicago Women in Trades 2010)

For more information, see United States Department of Labor (2009) and Thom (2002).

not know about this sooner?" In her community in Oklahoma, she knew very strict gender roles: "You get married, make babies, and stay at home." In theory, she did not see anything wrong with that as a personal choice; it was never, however, her interest, and she felt that women were not encouraged to seek other opportunities for professional and self-fulfillment outside of more traditional roles. Kimberly found that the Women's Studies and feminist community she discovered in her classes allowed her to think about her options as a woman. She loved the field's emphasis on activism, and this has been a recurring thread in the decisions she has made—and so has empowering women. She found it "so empowering to find a course of study that comported with the way one could live life."

After graduating with a degree in Psychology and a strong interest in Women's Studies, she moved to Washington, DC and enrolled in a paralegal program. She still did not know how she was going to use her interest in Women's Studies, but she kept looking for ways to make her work relevant to women. It was clear a few years into her paralegal job that she was just making it through, though it was paying the bills. She says she often thought, "There's gotta be more [to life] than to work your ass off for someone else."

She happened upon a book that helped her to ask questions about what was next. She worked through *The Artist's Way*, a famous book that promotes self-discovery through embracing one's creativity and passions in an everyday, practical way. Reflecting on things that she truly loved and loved to do planted a seed that was later to become her first business—Tranquil Space. Kimberly also did two important things that helped launch her business, her writing career, and her philanthropic work. She sought out further education and kept fine-tuning her inner vision.

Kimberly undertook a yoga teacher-training program after being a yoga practitioner for many years. She realized that there were not many yoga studios in Washington, DC that considered busy young women who needed a space to get connected to what they needed in their life and for the opportunity to become tranquil. This demographic was not being served, and she realized that she desired to create this space to serve women. She launched her yoga studio in the living room of her small DC apartment. The demand was so great that in just a few short years, she was able to launch Tranquil Space, a yoga studio listed in *travel + leisure* as one of the best in the world.

Kimberly also wanted to deepen her work in Women's Studies, so she searched out MA programs in Women's Studies and settled on the one at George Washington University. This program gave her a way to be focused on coursework, but had a lot of flexibility, and she was able to work on entrepreneurial leadership and interview many successful businesswomen. During her MA, she made it a point to study the structure of women-focused nonprofits and organizations.

### FOR YOUR LIBRARY

Julia Cameron (2002) *The Artist's Way: A Spiritual Path to Higher Creativity.* New York: Tarcher.

Kimberly Wilson (2006). *Hip Tranquil Chick: A Guide to Life On and Off the Yoga Mat.* Novato, CA: New World Library.

Kimberly Wilson (2010). *Tranquilista: Mastering the Art of Enlightened Work and Mindful Play.* Novato, CA: New World Library.

Through her postgraduate work, Kimberly soon wanted to document how she had come to create her vision of women's interests, yoga, and lifestyle, which she was embodying through her yoga studio and consulting work. She knew she had a book in her, but she decided to work with a writing coach to help the process. She worked for many years writing for local publications and newsletters. In 2003, she had a big "aha" moment:

> Observing the growing number of yoga books on the shelves, but realizing there were none about the city-dwelling diva living *la vida* yoga, I decided that was my story. I coined the book concept

## THE MA IN WOMEN'S STUDIES AT GEORGE WASHINGTON UNIVERSITY

Kimberly liked the flexibility of the MA program at George Washington University, which was designed for working professionals. Students have many choices of how to structure their MA program. Evening courses are available to accommodate working students, as is part-time study (six credit hours per semester). Students have the option of working on a practicum, independent research, or the more traditional thesis.

The MA in Women's Studies with a concentration in a liberal arts discipline or a topical focus offers students the opportunity to craft an individualized program of study in close consultation with faculty advisors. Students are expected to develop intellectual depth and a degree of expertise through a four-course concentration in either (a) a specific discipline such as Anthropology, Sociology, English, History, Philosophy (other disciplines are also possible, with permission), or (b) a topical area such as women and health, women and international development, race and gender (other areas are possible). There are ample opportunities for students with policy interests to include policy courses (such as Women and Public Policy, among others) in their program of study, either as part of their chosen discipline/field or as electives.

The disciplinary concentration works well for students interested in going on to a Ph.D. in a discipline and for those whose interests fit easily within disciplinary lines. Students are encouraged to find a faculty mentor in their disciplinary concentration. Alternatively, students may choose an MA in Women's Studies because their intellectual passions and career objectives are truly interdisciplinary. The topical focus option provides academic space for students with diverse interests.

(For more information, see www.gwu.edu/~wstu/programs/masters.htm)

"hip yoga chick" and took a local book writing course for aspiring authors to hone my idea . . . After many months I finished my proposal, researched like-minded agents, and sent query letters to a dozen of them.

(Wilson 2010: 26–27)

It took over a year, but she was able to find an agent and sold the idea:

I had six months to write and edit the book . . . *Hip Tranquil Chick* was released in 2006. By including the word *tranquil* in the title, I was able to associate the book with my businesses: my yoga studio, Tranquil Space; clothing line, TranquilT; and nonprofit, Tranquil Space Foundation.

In starting up her business and going back to graduate school, she evolved her interests and did not get intimidated in building a business even though she did not have a business background. She focused on her "desire to create community around this idea of stimulating the body and mind," and her sense of herself as "womencentric." During this time, she also facilitated women's circles, women's retreats, and mentoring women, one-on-one, who wanted to launch a business.

By following her interests through, she was able to open a well-regarded yoga studio and become a nationally sought-after speaker and author. Her book, *Tranquilista*, lays out her guiding philosophy, which helps people who have entrepreneurial interests get started with their ideas. She outlines a three-step process: spirituality, creativity, and entrepreneurship. This makes up her *Tranquilista* philosophy, which is about unlocking a woman's potential to make a difference through enlightened work and mindful play. In the next chapter, we will learn more about how she launched her nonprofit organization.

Her advice for those seeking a creative and/or entrepreneurial path is:

Really get clear on what it is you want, hone in on your passion. But, recognize that your passions may change, and that's OK— allow an evolution of your journey. If you're interested in a business think about what things you want in the marketplace that do not already exist. Never be shy about who you are. Never lose sight of who you are, what your passions are and make sure you have a community that does support that even if that is not at work.

*Peter Stuart: Untraditional Educational Counselor*

Peter Stuart describes himself as a person who came from a sheltered family, from a "suburban monoculture" without a lot of life experience before he entered Queen's College in Ontario, Canada, in 1990. He started off as a Math and Physics major, and he quickly discovered that while he liked and was good at these subjects, he did not feel challenged by them.

He had heard about gender issues from his mother, and although she would not necessarily describe herself as feminist, she often talked to him about the limited job choices she and her sisters faced. His mother is a nurse, and her five sisters all work in typically female-headed professions—as nurses, teachers, and secretaries.

He found himself attracted to Women's Studies and English classes, hoping to find new opportunities to problem-solve other than in his science and math classes. He says this about his first Women's Studies class, taken toward the end of his first year at Queen's College:

> Intro to Women's Studies just blew my mind. It completely opened my mind to a whole new way of studying the world. A really big thing that Women's Studies gave me was the words. It gave me the words and framework to describe things that were wrong. It gave me words to look at the power dynamics, and who benefitted and who were kept down in any situation I was in. I loved it!

By the end of the second year of university, Peter had changed majors and was studying to become a teacher. Once he decided to go into the teaching program, he chose his "teachable subjects" as English and Science. Although it was not offered as a "teachable subject" through the teaching program, he continued to take a number of cross-listed Women's Studies courses and declared it as a "medial subject." At the time at Queen's College, Women's Studies was organized as a "medial subject"– halfway between a minor and major through the Institute of Women's Studies. He loved the interdisciplinary nature of Women's Studies.

As Peter became more engaged in Women's Studies, he met other men who were also pursuing Women's Studies and he developed friendships with them. He also experienced some of the typical things that men face when they choose Women's Studies as an academic interest:

an assumption by some men that their interest is motivated by wanting to date women and questions of sexual identity.

Peter got asked often if he was gay: "This might have bothered me when I was younger but not by the time I was in university. We definitely talked enough about sexuality issues in class," which contributed to his comfort level. He also felt that there "were much bigger things to worry about than whether someone thought I was gay in a Women's Studies class." He felt welcomed, however, by the faculty and the majority of his women peers in Women's Studies classes.

His mother was very supportive about his interest in Women's Studies, but his father was not: "My dad thought it was funny and made dumb jokes about it and still does. He never told me I shouldn't be studying it. He just thought it was a typical silly thing that one studies at university."

These issues did not deter Peter from continuing in Women's Studies. He became actively involved both in student government and the December 6th Memorial Committee,[1] which worked on issues of sexual violence through programming events on campus. He also became very active in *SURFACE*, the monthly progressive newsmagazine that was designed to be a voice for marginal perspectives on campus. This magazine challenged the misogyny in the main campus news magazine and agitated for various issues on campus. Peter was co-editor of the news magazine and wrote articles for three years while at Queens. Co-editing and writing provided him with an opportunity to utilize his skill sets gained through English and Women's Studies.

He also was able to put his Women's Studies training into practice as he was developing his teaching skills. He often had to make visits to schools and do observations. He credits his "Women's Studies background in learning to teach and create an egalitarian classroom."

> I came into Women's Studies pretty blind and so I often used the lens about power structure—race, class, and gender and structure. No matter what type of oppression existed, we looked at who was benefitting here, [and] why? What structures were maintained and how can they be altered? In student teaching, I looked at how the traditional classroom is set up with bad kids in back and good kids in front and how teachers like it that way. That structure is set up for the benefit of the teachers. A lot of structure in the [average] classroom isn't questioned . . . [Because of] Women's Studies I could make active choices about who to

pay attention to, how to set up a class and how to focus on structural inequalities. I'd look at how the classroom was set up, who it was designed for, who it wasn't designed for, why and how could it be altered to make it work for more people.

When he graduated in 1995, he moved to Toronto, where he wanted to work with troubled high school kids in an urban area. He thought this would be a good way to apply his teaching and Women's Studies background. It did not turn out to be as straightforward a process as Peter hoped. He was underemployed for a while, because it was hard to get a job through the Public School Board. He became a tutor and through the tutoring job he met a few parents who had their children in a private school for special needs kids. They encouraged him to apply for a teaching position at the school.

At this point, Peter felt conflicted, because he did not see himself teaching in a private school. However, he was attracted to working with kids who needed particular kinds of experiences in the classroom. This was the first time he felt he had to be flexible with his broader values and goals. As it turned out, he taught at the private school for eight years. Over time, he says:

> [I] found it very difficult to teach in a private school setting. A lot of these kids were getting this support because their parents could afford it. Over time, it wore on me and even though I could focus on the fact that it was the kids who needed help, it was hard to overlook the money and politics and elitism.

He decided he wanted to work with adults, even though he was not sure how that was going to look. He got married and left Toronto to live in a smaller, less expensive city, near Kingston, Ontario. He briefly found a temporary position helping to retrain workers who had been laid off. He found that he did indeed really enjoy working with adults and kept his eyes open for other opportunities.

His mother-in-law had done some part-time teaching at the Federal Women's Prison in Kingston and told Peter that the school within the prison was hiring. Peter had never thought about teaching in prison or ever thought he wanted to be part of a correctional facility. He thought, though, that the position might be an opportunity to use his Women's Studies background, work with adults, and work in a totally new setting.

He was hired on a four-month contract and the staff was very happy to hire someone who had a background in Women's Studies. His Women's Studies background was viewed as an asset and an advantage. He began teaching Science and Math classes to inmates. Four years later, he is on staff full-time as an educational counselor. He loves his work. He believes he was meant to do this work:

> It's great. It's the job I was meant to do. I can use my Women's Studies background every day. The philosophy of women's correction in Canada is informed from a feminist perspective. Corrections itself isn't really a feminist organization, so in practice it's sometimes difficult to make the two work together; it doesn't always succeed, but at least the philosophy is there.

At any given time in the federal prison, there are about 160 women. As an educational counselor, Peter's work encompasses doing an assessment of women's previous work and educational history, and preparing them to obtain their high school diploma. He is also an informal mentor to his clients:

> People have an illusion that it [prison] is a difficult place to teach. That is an illusion. It is probably the easiest place to teach. You have got motivated students who understand the importance of education. You're working with people who want to get the most out of a horrible situation. The women really want to graduate because they know when they leave they will have to be very focused on finding a job, reconnecting with family, etc. and won't have as much time to focus on themselves.

Peter finds his work deeply fulfilling at this point in his life. He has been actively taking on informal leadership roles through the correctional facility. He looks forward to working on ways to improve school classes and facilities in the prison and provide new opportunities for his clients. He and his team of teachers share a broad vision of improving the school. He says that he never thinks, "This is as good as the school can be. There's just so much more to do."

Besides working full-time, he is also a very devoted parent. Being a "pro-feminist" parent is very important to him, and he credits his training in Women's Studies for shaping his understanding of how to raise a child in a gender-neutral way: "I'm shocked at how many parents do not question the gendering they do to their kids right at the beginning." Feminist community and political community are important to Peter, and he feels that he was very naive in thinking that he would find these easily once he graduated. He thought it would be easy to sustain intense conversations in the workplace, but he felt really "cut off" from the intellectual engagement after graduation. He has actively sought community through his work in the Green Party. He also has developed community through recreational sports and his love of hockey. He tried a few leagues looking for great sports and deep discussions and was not able to find this combination easily. So, he rejoined a hockey group that he had played in during his days in Toronto and drives an hour each way to it on the weekends:

> I rejoined the Gay Men's Hockey League in Toronto. I found that it's a great league to play hockey in but also because it's a hockey league formed from a political sensibility (and it's very accepting of straight guys) that there are more political discussions and people. I'm more politically aligned with [people in this league] than in other hockey leagues.

Peter has found a place for authentic expression in his work, home, and social life.

### Takeaways from Rachel, Kimberly, and Peter's Profiles

- Evaluate your ability to take thoughtful risks: Rachel, Kimberly, and Peter all took important risks in order to follow their inner vision.
- Do not be worried if you have several interests that do not all seem to fit together easily. They all had a cluster of eclectic interests that they nurtured through work, activism, and further schooling.
- Think about the kind of community you have now as an undergraduate and in what ways you will sustain it after graduation.

### Synthesizers

### Diana Rhodes: Policy Analyst, Coalition Builder, and Organizer

Diana Rhodes has an amazing ability to utilize her knowledge and skills from Women's Studies, along with the skills she has developed through her volunteer and unpaid labor in a variety of arenas: the arts and music scene and as a columnist for *Q Vegas*, as well as in grassroots activism and public policy advocacy.

How did a first-generation college student with an interest in the arts become interested in policy? Diana Rhodes graduated from the University of Nevada, Las Vegas, in 2006 with a dual bachelor's degree in Sociology and Women's Studies:

> I have to say that the feminist "click" happened when I was an undergrad. I had already declared my major in sociology because I had taken sociology courses at my high school in the community college program. I was 18 and I wanted to save the world and I didn't know how. I got interested in gender stuff through sociology, but I was still quiet and taking classes. At that time, [and] during my entire life, I was really quiet. I didn't like giving presentations. I never did public speaking. I just went to class and left. I took a Women's Studies class taught by Dr. Anita Tijerina Revilla in the Women's Studies Department at UNLV. Her classes were taught as experiential learning. It was a small class, but we sat in a circle, which was really huge [to me]. We all had to make eye contact with one another and it was less than a lecture type of environment but more of creating a dialogue and making sure everyone's voices were heard. This was a situation that I had never been in before and I realized how huge it was for me to be in that environment. I know at that time it was like pulling teeth to actually get me to talk, but I started taking Women's Studies courses and I had this "click" of everything I thought I knew. It actually had a name, a word, and a theoretical framework, and I was able to articulate what I felt inside. If I was angry or upset, I could know why something was wrong, if a dude said something to me, I would know how to articulate why I felt like it wasn't OK. That was around my sophomore year at UNLV and then I pretty much dove deep into Women's Studies after that. Soon after that time, I had decided that I identified as a feminist. I took as many WMST courses [as I could] and I became close with some of the Women's sStudies professors who helped me process things in a way that none of my other professors in any other department had done.

However, while some students may have been satisfied with this experience alone, it was the spark that ignited Diana into activism and creating community dialogue. Diana has a gift for bringing people together in a group who may not have necessarily interacted independently, ranging from academics to service industry workers, to those who work and perform in the independent arts and music scene. Whether she organizes feminist discussion groups at coffee houses, recruits members for the local "Feminist Drinking Club" or the "Feminist Drinking Caucus" (at NWSA), or facilitates meetings for Stand OUT for Equality, the Vagina Monologues, or Ladyfest, Las Vegas, Diana often initiates these groups as an outlet for her own interests and to satisfy elements of her intersectional identity (arts promoter, feminist, Asian-American, and self-described nerd).

After her first Women's Studies class, she says:

> My mind was going crazy and I was still processing all this stuff and trying to form my identity and figure out my experiences. But then it was the summer and all that rich dialogue [from class], all my peers were no longer in my life because classes were over. I didn't know what to do about it and so I decided to start my own consciousness-raising group because I had just learned about consciousness raising.

Diana says she had a deep desire to:

> create a community of people that actually gave a shit about what we were talking about or cared about, because a lot of my friends didn't. So I started a weekly feminist discussion group at a local, independently owned 24-hour coffee shop in China Town, which was really important to me to actually bring other people into this world that not a lot of people go into.
>
> The group started at 9 p.m. so people who worked retail or whatever were able to come later. I had advertised it in *City Life* [a free local Las Vegas arts scene periodical] and I MySpace messaged a few of my friends and fellow students and it [the feminist discussion group] was basically to talk about whatever we wanted to talk about. I wanted to get like-minded people together because I didn't want that dialogue to end [during summer break from college]. I just needed to keep it going for my own purposes, but also to create a community. I had my academic side but I also had my scene of subculture, punk rock, and independent music. Most of the people who came to the discussion group, week after week, were not academics, not actually even students [but] they were kids who worked at a record store and saw a flyer, they were young 15-year-old riot girls who had just learned about Bikini Kill [a group widely considered to be the pioneer of the riot grrrl movement] or they were straight

Summerlin [a suburb of Las Vegas] couples who just saw it in *City Life* and who thought the group might be interesting and [they could visit] a new coffee shop they'd never heard of.

The coffee shop's all-night atmosphere contributed to lots of arguments, debates, and chain smoking. Diana calls this her "bonding through vices" hypothesis. "Sometimes it would get heated between the academics versus the non-academics, and [during conversations] this whole kind of privilege and breaking down the privilege and class [structures] happened." The feminist group lasted a year and Diana had "created this weird community that I really appreciated, loved."

Her exploration of arts activism began almost immediately. Through a discussion initiated in her feminist discussion group, she helped organize Ladyfest Las Vegas, a two-day music and arts festival, highlighting women in the creative arts and held at UNLV in 2006.[2]

I learned a lot of stuff through Ladyfest. I'd never organized something like that before. I had never organized anything that big. What peaked my interest in nonprofit organizations and consensus-based decision-making was how this loosely based egalitarian group who was like "we don't do anything unless everybody agrees" shifts when you are throwing an event that costs money. There's a lot of logistical things that you need to think of. We had never done it so we had to figure it out as we went. It was a huge learning experience, lots of fights, a lot of dealing with having to become more bureaucratic, having to have consensus at meetings, making sure people followed through with what they said they were going to do.

During the time of Ladyfest, I did a bunch of fundraiser shows. A lot of my activism started off in the arts, so I would bring bands in and perform in shows. Most of my shows were women and/or queer bands. When I started working with bar owners and people who ran venues, it was funny in that, in my entire life before that, ever since I was 13, I was going to shows and local music shows and my boyfriend was in a band, my best friends were all in bands, all my friends owned record stores or worked at record stores and so I knew a lot of people. But as soon as I started doing what my other friends, guy friends, were doing, a lot of them turned their back to me.

Diana was dismayed that there were several people who did not understand the need for or value of creating and organizing a women-oriented arts and music festival. That initial lack of support, however, did not stop her and her loosely based group from putting on several very successful Ladyfest events.

Through her position at WRIN (a statewide research and education institute for women in Nevada and located at UNLV), Diana honed the skill of fundraising and deepened her interest in connecting communities. In her position, she put into practice the skills of building community she had utilized informally for the past several years. Diana actively worked at creating and maintaining relationships with community organizations, government officials, and lobbyists: "I had to go to a lot of events, corporate stuff, and I learned how to navigate all these worlds through that position." She learned how to lobby for WRIN at the state legislature (in order to receive funding) and interacted with representatives' senior staff in Carson City (Nevada's capital). The staff at WRIN is small, so she actively cross-trained in supervising, management of research projects, and events planning. Diana's entry into this line of work echoes a theme that is shared by several Women's and Gender Studies students. Women's Studies (the classroom, the concepts, and the faculty) gave Diana the encouragement she needed to voice her opinions and feel confident in doing so. She was then able to take on paid and unpaid positions that required effective communication skills.

Diana brought her Women's Studies knowledge, her community leadership gained working with WRIN, and her interest in public policy to activism during the monumental Proposition 8 ruling in California in the fall of 2008.[3]

> By early 2008, I had worked with the students [at the Gay and Lesbian Center of Southern Nevada]. I tutored students and helped some of the students get their GED, and that was my only involvement with the Center and with the queer community in early 2008. But when Proposition 8 happened, there were so many people who were so upset and emotional, I had to get involved. Candice Nichols, the director of the Center, put out an e-mail ... and said, "People are pissed, people are sad, people want to do something and people are calling me." Eight of us ... sat in the conference room at the Center and decided we should have a rally, for people to be able to express themselves about this event. We only had three days to do it because there were many national rallies going on in response to Prop 8.

We did it. We had a lot of speakers and we sent press releases out. [We were successful] because so many of us had so many skill sets and so many different populations that we could reach. There were approximately 2,000–3,000 people who showed up for the rally and it was amazing and beautiful. It wasn't something that necessarily happened all the time in Las Vegas. It was exciting to us and that group that organized that rally—the eight of us—decided to call ourselves "Stand OUT for Equality" and we became the policy wing group of the Gay and Lesbian Center. We started having other meetings and following up rallies or whatever the community wanted to do. [Eventually] we decided that we wanted to do a bill draft request for the legislature at the time, one for domestic partnerships, one for adding sexual orientation and anti-discrimination laws. Later, we took on an idea that an organization called "Nevada Women's Lobby" [developed], which is "Grassroots Lobby Days," where we get people to go up to Carson City and participate in a citizen's lobby event. We decided we were going to have "Equality Days," which would be a similar concept, but basically an LGBT citizen lobbying event in Carson City . . . which had never been done in Nevada.

The launch of Equality Days supported several legislative successes. The group realized that, working together with other groups across the state on different political issues, they "could have some success together, [and] we decided to create a coalition which meets every month for strategic planning."

The skills that Diana had developed from her Women's Studies background, her honors thesis research (see below), and her work experiences (at the Rape Crisis Center) allowed her to flourish in her role of Educational Program Director for New Leadership Nevada (administered through WRIN), a five-day residential leadership program for undergraduate women in the state of Nevada, which has been held since 2003. Cheryl first met Diana at this forum. In 2007, both Diana and Cheryl served as "FIRS" or Faulty in Residence for New Leadership. Previously, Diana had attended New Leadership as a participant in 2006. After their initial bonding at New Leadership, Cheryl was able to see Diana's poster presentation of her honors thesis research, "Deconstructing Beauty: Experiences of Asian American Women," at the 2007 NWSA annual conference. Later, Cheryl worked for Diana as a FIR and was also invited by Diana to present at New Leadership in 2009 and 2010 on values in leadership.

Diana says of her New Leadership experience:

New Leadership is where I learned a little bit about policy and
a lot about philanthropy. There was a panel on women and
philanthropy and I had never known what philanthropy actually
was. I had no idea there were rich people who want to give
organizations money just to do something because they're rich. I
had no clue that existed. A well-known female leader was on a
panel so I talked to her afterwards. I was talking about the
Ladyfest music festival, what we were doing, and she was like
"Great . . . send me the information. I'd like to learn more." So
I went home and sent her the press release that I had written,
and I sent her all that information and she says "GREAT . . .
where do I send the check to?"

This shocked her and opened her eyes up to new possibilities:

I had worked my ass off at all these shows and different venues
and bars, and I was fighting with bar owners when they ripped
off my bands and dealing with all this crap, and then some rich
lady sent me a check for $1,000? So that's when I started to learn
about philanthropy and this nonprofit world, which was really
interesting.

While Diana credits her click moment to her experiences in her
Women's Studies classroom, looking back she also realizes the influence
of her family on her feminist consciousness:

My mom always raised me as a strong, independent person.
    So my worlds have been in arts and music, policy, and all
around gender issues. I wear a lot of hats: my gay hat and my
APA [Asian Pacific Islander American] hat, punk rock hat and
my arts world hat . . . I feel like I have a lot of worlds I am
involved in. I think a lot of it shows [in] my own identity. I will
never say that the activism that I do or anything that I do is
completely altruistic. I don't do anything altruistically. There are
things that satisfy parts of me, like with WRIN I got to work
with more kinds of professional work and be that professional
person and with the Stand OUT for Equality, I got to do more
policy stuff and that was like my LGBT world and with
NAPAWF (which I was on the board), which is the National
Asian Pacific American Women's Forum [see www.napawf.org)],
that fulfilled a part of me that I had not necessarily had as much
access to before. Some of our politics weren't always the same

among the women who were involved in the organization, but being in a room with only APA women, working on APA issues was not something I had done before. That's huge for me and a big deal.

Diana, like many others in our survey, decided to go to graduate school to purse an MA at George Washington University in public policy with a concentration in Women's Studies. When asked about what skills she was specifically seeking she said:

Honestly, I'm not sure what skills I was looking for. . . maybe just a wider breadth of knowledge.

I left during the recession and economic crisis. Working for a state university, I found I was on the way to a furlough, and while there were other reasons involved, I just felt it was time to leave the state. I also found it was hard to find opportunities when not in the locale, as I was seeking employment in places like DC, NYC, and SF. I was finding that my field was increasingly becoming more professionalized and in order to find work, I realized I had to either move or get an advanced degree. So I did both. With my background in sociology and Women's studies, I wanted to continue with an emphasis in gender and sexuality with public policy. So I decided I needed the tools, education, and knowledge base to do so.

I specifically chose GWU because of the program's relationship with women's policy organizations and its emphasis on Public Policy and Women's Studies. I was excited to earn a Policy degree with a social justice lens. Now being in DC for a bit, I am finding how important institutional prestige can be.

During my time at GWU, I was encouraged to get an internship. Though I was in no position to go to an expensive graduate school and then get an unpaid internship. I found that totally crazy. But what found is that I became increasingly aware of the privilege that existed around me, since there were so many people who could attend an expensive school, live in an expensive city, and have an unpaid internship. I also found that prestige associated with higher education is much different on the East Coast than on the West Coast. I had an adjustment period with questions regarding academic pedigree. I had a background of attending commuter state schools (CSN and UNLV) and, for me, student life was not so much of a focus at UNLV as community life was. Needless to say, there was a definite adjustment period.

My background like many of my peers is as a first-generation student. We had to be specifically encouraged by our professors that we could actually go to grad school and that it was a normal cause of action. In fact, our faculty members helped many of us with the process—from applying to grad school, composing the personal statement, and studying for the GRE. And while I didn't go to grad school right after college, I had faculty members always willing to assist and mentor me.

Five years later, I went to another Women's Studies program and academic institution that operated so differently and had such a different history than UNLV.

While at GWU, I was able to secure a part-time job ... I needed an income to offset the other costs of grad school (even though I had managed to save some money prior to going to DC).

Diana took a part-time position at the Center for Women's Policy Studies, which developed into a full-time position that supported her as she finished her MA. The CWPS was founded in 1970, is a small national nonprofit organization, and is considered the first feminist policy organization in the United States. Diana's work included working with female elective officials who were either state legislative officials and/or female parliamentarians on international levels:

We worked in four major issue areas: reproductive rights, women and HIV, poverty alleviation (postsecondary education for low income women), and international trafficking of women and girls. In other words, we focused on policies that affected the human rights of women and girls. And we operated from an explicitly feminist and women's human rights framework.

The great thing was the Center served as a "niche" organization; they didn't do direct policy advocacy work. They also rarely worked with any of the other women's rights policy coalitions, as they wanted to remain true to never having a political agenda with its constituents. Again, our constituents were elected officials and so we were a trusted organization that didn't form relationships with them just to lobby them on particular pieces of legislation. Often I would get calls from women legislators seeking policy advice regarding a particular piece of legislation that NARAL or PPFA were lobbying for, but these legislators wanted non-partisan, feminist assistance.

There were five people on staff and I was the program and policy associate for almost a year and a half. When I finished my MA, I was offered a full-time contract. And funny enough, I found that my work experience, even at the grad school level, was more impactful than my classes. Working in the field had always been, and continues to be, the best learning experience. My academic credentials showed competence and gave me an edge in an increasingly professionalized environment, but the actual experience of being in the field is what I value most.

Diana currently works for Advocates for Youth, a national reproductive and sexual health/rights organization, based out Washington, DC. Their work is premised on the belief that all young people have the right to the education, resources, and tools necessary to make healthy and responsible decisions about their reproductive and sexual health. She is State Strategies Manager and manages their stated-based policy and mobilization initiatives. Their issues areas are a broad range of reproductive and sexual health that affect young people, with a primary focus on sex education and access to services. The policy areas she focuses on include sex education, youth access to services and care, including abortion, LGBT youth, and contraception access.

She says her work is:

> divided into two essential buckets: programmatic and state strategies. On the program side of things, I manage one major youth program called the Cultural Advocacy Mobilization Initiative, or CAMI for short. With this program, we partner with state-based organizations and work with them to build out youth activist networks to improve the sex education in their communities. Our partner organization hires a Youth Advocacy Coordinator whose job it is to recruit for, build, and maintain a 10-person youth activist council. Advocates for Youth, along with their Coordinator, train the council on organizing, mobilization, policy and advocacy, and other activist skills—to ensure they have the tools necessary to educate their communities and make policy change. We work with a diverse group of state partners and their landscape and strategies looks very different; for example, what works in Oakland, CA is very different from what works in Birmingham, AL. Throughout the year, I work with the Coordinators and Council to help with capacity building, strategic planning, policy analysis and other technical assistance. And while

we work to improve sex education across the country, we really "dig deep" in eight states through this particular project (CAMI). Youth activism is key in our work at Advocates because we understand that young people have the passion and power to make change, especially over policies and practices that affect their lives

So that's my programmatic work. The other part of my job is the State Strategies work. This includes working with national colleague organizations (such as PPFA, ACLU, and SIECUS) to build strategy around state policy initiatives. I work with my fellow national colleagues to organize an annual State Summit on sex education, where we convene up to 100 advocates and educators to share strategies and best practices, educate one another on upcoming trends, and cultivate strategic partner-ships—all with the goal of improving sex education in our nation's schools. Additionally, I provide technical assistance to state-based organizations, advocates, and coalitions across the country—mostly on policy and mobilization strategy.

Therefore, the two major areas of my work are: State Strategies —working with policy advocates—and CAMI—working with youth activists. Then half the time I'm trying to get the policy advocates to work with young people and our young people to be interested in policy.

In my current position at Advocates for Youth, I am able to combine my previous grassroots local advocacy and coalition work with my background working with elected officials and developing strategy and also my experience working with young people—in one position.

My previous work experiences give me a strategic lens in that I have worked with policymakers and understand how to approach decision-makers, also their particular challenges. At the Center, I worked with elected officials—connecting them to local advocates, (grasstops to grassroots)—and now I work with local advocates connecting them to each other and other stakeholders (grassroots to grasstops). It's a more holistic approach to the work.

Coming into a decade of this work now, Diana has thought about what makes this type of work sustainable:

I am finding even more so how important it is to live life fully. Activism, advocacy, academia, whatever it is—don't let one world swallow you up. "Work/life balance" is a cliché term, but it's important. My job and profession is great and I wouldn't trade it for the world—but it's not "who I am" and doesn't take over my life. I also participate in a local arts collective; I organize arts/music/food events in the community; I take classes and am constantly trying to learn new skills; I find new recipes and cook new meals when possible; I go hiking and camping when the weather's nice; I'm always coming up with new creative projects to work on; and I make sure to spend quality time with my partner and my friends in a meaningful and authentic way. I'm a feminist in every space I'm in, and it's important to recognize that those spaces don't always have to be "feminist activist" spaces—they can be an art gallery, the kitchen, or on the dance floor. Identity has become less and less important to me as of late, and being authentically ME has become more of a central goal. As a young professional, your job can become your life and your life can be spent at your job. Remember, there's a whole world to experience outside your office and e-mail!

*Takeaways from Diana's Profile*

- As Diana's profile indicates, while she had an inclination toward social activism, the Women's Studies classroom and environment allowed her to begin questioning the world around her and encouraged her to engage with her fellow classmates and her professors.
- Diana participated in a leadership program that honed her skills. If you have an opportunity to take part in a leadership program, you might want to consider it.
- Diana lived an understanding of intersectionality and created ways to work with multiple communities across a range of issues.

*Judi Brown: A Radical Feminist Infiltrator*

While not all feminists and Women's Studies graduates from Las Vegas are synthesizers, like the city in which they both were raised, Judi Brown and Diana Rhodes exemplify the elements of this category, which include adaptability, creativity, and innovation. Besides being friends and colleagues, much like those discussed by Jo Reger, who support social justice both in their personal and professional lives, each went on to pursue graduate degrees (and careers) in areas that fit their engagement with feminism.

## TIPS FROM DIANA

Besides taking Women's and Gender Studies courses, Diana suggests taking a Business course or a Finance course: "If your activism leads you to nonprofit work, or any other type of work with a business or organization, you need to be able to develop and follow a budget."

As enriching as Diana's experience has been as a synthesizer, she offers some cautionary words of advice:

If you are going into this activist world in any way, you must learn to say no to things. We want to do so many different things, so we'll say yes to conducting this workshop, and sitting on this committee, helping on that fundraiser, etc. All of it is great experience, but you get burned out really easily and it can lead to . . . being bitter. Say yes to the things you truly and actually believe in because otherwise you will spread yourself too thin and get burnt out and the things that you care about, the things that you want to make a difference in, suddenly become too much and you stop caring about them the way you used to. It stops being fun anymore and it becomes a chore. The passion dies once you become overwhelmed.

Cheryl first met Judi while Cheryl was serving as a Faculty in Residence (FIR) for New Leadership Nevada. Judi had just graduated UNLV with a duel baccalaureate in Women's Studies and Political Science. At the time of their first interview in the summer of 2010, Judi was working for the Public Education Foundation in special projects, which primarily entailed grant writing, events, and program management. She was also exploring graduate school programs in sustainability. Currently, as Cheryl has witnessed, Judi is able to infuse and apply her feminist principles into local community and international activism. She has also been able to take the skills she learned and honed both in the local Las Vegas independent music scene and the corporate world of private foundation and philanthropy, and emerge with a career in public administration.

According to Judi:

The field of sustainable public administration is not directly related to Women's and Gender Studies, but I took advantage of every possibility to incorporate my gender lens, whether by topics

I chose to focus on or working with organizations in similar fields. For me, sustainability as a framework synthesizes quite well with my own feminist framework; it calls for a paradigm shift in society to prioritize people and the planet as much as profits. The three pillars of sustainability are people, profit, and planet, meaning these should exist in harmony and not off-balance. For so long, the profit-driven model that has shaped our economy, particularly since the Industrial Revolution, has favored unchecked extraction of natural resources and exploitation of human capital. It has created this era of climate instability, which will continue to disproportionately affect Earth's most vulnerable communities. Applying the framework of sustainability to government policy and to the most powerful institutions of our time (corporations) allows for greater transparency as to how profits are affecting people and the planet.

So, one may ask how Judi became interested in feminism and Women's Studies, and how that led her to her current career. According to Judi:

I knew I wanted to study Women's Studies because it seemed to be the most important thing to me at the time. I can pinpoint at age 12 or 13 that I started claiming the label feminist, due to [the musical influence of the artist] Ani DiFranco. I was raised by a strong woman, but my mom never went to college, she stayed home and raised my brother and I. There were not the same recourses available for her in the community at the time, so this, along with being Catholic and having no real support from her family, my Mom got out of the relationship. When I was 12 and 13, I wanted to be independent, but mother was over protective. While I knew things happened to my mom, I never realized or internalized what had happened to her. I was listening to folk music and never thought to be an advocate for women. I was raised Catholic up until 16 (I went through a Confirmation and everything) and then I stopped. I thought about materials from church, like the Virgin Mary, and I felt like there was no real strong women's presence.

Yet I'm grateful for my religious background and can truly articulate my issues with it. I went to high school in Las Vegas and I never felt I was introduced to what I could do or study in college. I never was the person who knew what I wanted to do. I started college at CCSN (Community College of Southern Nevada (now CSN) at the West Charleston Campus where I started as a Biology major. During my first semester, I took an

"Introduction to American Politics" class with Dr. Ernst Bracey, an African-American professor and a Vietnam War veteran. He opened my eyes to the importance of politics in our lives. During high school, the importance of politics was not communicated in my AP Politics class.

As one can see, Judi was influenced in her feminism not only through the experiences her mother had with violence, but also through her engagement with popular culture and her religious upbringing. Additionally, the importance of politics in our everyday lives is a common thread in Judi's life growing up, as well as in her collegiate years and post-undergraduate career. Judi continued her education at UNLV and took an introductory Women's Studies class. She started reading feminist theory and also the feminist book *Cunt* by Inga Muscio (2002). She also connected to community activists and entrepreneurs. Judi says about this time:

> While I had always known I was a feminist and I was learning rhetorical tools to defend my Women's Studies and what I always knew, it was through my WMST classes and encounters with popular feminist theory books that I now I had the evidence to support it. I always loved music and in high school I watched live music, but rarely were there women. I started out looking for women in music, for example Slater Kinney. Now it's hard for me to believe that I got to do this (be in a band) . . . not until some women asked me to join them.

When asked about friends and family members' response to Judi's Women's Studies major and educational trajectory, like Diana, Judi's family is supportive of her not only as a first-generation college graduate, but also as a strong independent activist who has challenged gender norms and oppressive workplace situations. She has also served as a role model to others in the community:

> I know I have inspired a few women to major in Women's Studies. Women's Studies made me active in the community. For the first time since I've been in Las Vegas (since I was 9), I've felt a sense of community and that the folks in the classes were doing great things, it activated me. In high school, I didn't do anything. I was good at school, but I had no outside interests except that I have worked from age 14. My dad is a business owner. He has been an electrical contractor for more than 30 years. My mom always wanted me to go to college and not to be in her situation.

She felt trapped. She couldn't articulate what I could do with a degree or types of jobs, but she encouraged me and to this day encourages me with seeing situations in the office.

A reoccurring theme for Judi is that of someone who is able to occupy and negotiate different spaces and utilize the resources/concepts/skills from one world and put it into play in another. As mentioned previously, synthesizers have an ability to move among and between careers that involve working on gender directly and utilize their activism in both their paid and unpaid work. Synthesizers also are able to create new opportunities for taking risks with their vision. For Judi, her ability to move between often divergent social spheres, academic disciplines, and careers fields also intersects with her ability to find mentors and learn from opportunities (such as internships) what areas she excelled, and also which held her interest and fueled her feminist passions.

Like many students, by the time Judi was about to graduate, she was unsure how to blend her interests in WGST and political science. She also felt conflicted in her personal life, as she started dating someone (who would later become her significant other) who desired for them to remain in Las Vegas, which was not at the top of Judi's list:

I knew I needed to find something to do. I had interned with a campaign for a 2006 ballot initiative to change the existing laws in Nevada on marijuana. It was a lot of work and there were daily frustrations. It was perceived as a controversial issue, and I brought feminism into it. I didn't think nonviolent offenders should be in jail. It was from this experience that I discovered that I liked grassroots politics, but that it was lots of work, with not much gain and not something I wanted to do. I didn't want to be a staffer. Later, I took an internship at Harrah's Entertainment (now Caesar's Entertainment) in Community and Government Relations. At the time, it was headed by Jan Jones, who was the first female mayor of Las Vegas. This internship opened my eyes, as I didn't know that these offices existed within corporations, as well as in the gaming industry. Community reinvestment and diversity were all under the office. While the work I was given was not that interesting, the work of the office was interesting. It was when I started working for Harrah's Foundation, the non-profit arm of Caesar's Entertainment, that I realized my talents, such as writing and organizing special events. Thom Reilly was the executive director, and he is my mentor. It was in this job that I was able to learn how to review grant proposals and work with organizations to make their application stronger. I felt it was good work and we were giving money to good causes. At first I didn't want my paycheck coming from them, I wanted to be an activist and radical, but I also wanted to get paid.

During a subsequent interview in February 2014, Judi revisited where she was at in her life when she first agreed to discuss her journey in achieving a degree in Women's and Gender Studies, as well as her career trajectory and her plans for the future. As discussed previously, Judi not only applied for, but was accepted and successfully completed a graduate degree in public administration. While she did not choose to formally pursue an advanced degree in Women's and Gender Studies, her radical feminist perspective and activism were at the center of her education, as well as her capstone project and current employment position. While she currently resides in San Francisco, she maintains her close ties to Las Vegas, not only with family and friends, but with her educational mentors (e.g. Dr. Anita Tijerina Revilla), as well as her work mentors (Thom Reilly) and peer mentors (Diana Rhodes). Also of note is the influence of internships and capstone projects on Judi's career trajectories. Through her experiences, she is able to learn from a variety of organizational types and leadership styles, and also carve out new methods to achieve a workplace environment that reflects a personal standard of sustainability:

> It's really amazing how quickly transformation can take place. In preparation for responding to the essay questions for the updated *Transforming Scholarship* book, I took a look at what had been published about my life three short years ago, and reflected on how radically different it is now. Some things stayed on track; for example, I had mentioned wanting to go to graduate school for sustainability, and here I am—a recent graduate with a master's in Sustainable Public Administration and Policy from Presidio Graduate School in San Francisco, California. This also means that I am no longer living in southern Nevada, where I had spent most of my life.
>
> Having never moved away from home before, it was definitely a difficult decision to leave Nevada for graduate school. I put a lot of thought into it and questioned my motivations constantly. There is so much important work happening in Nevada, and much more that needs to happen—and the people who are doing it are also largely the people who helped shape the context for my own

previous academic and professional experience, some of which was nothing short of transformational. However, the type of work I wanted to do and the education that I needed to do were not available in Las Vegas. So I moved to San Francisco to pursue my MPA (Masters in Public Administration) in Sustainable Management from a young institution whose pioneering efforts have helped further sustainability in higher education through socially responsible business and policy/management degrees.

Sustainability through my lens is ecofeminism. When I first learned about sustainability as a framework, I saw it as an opportunity to practice more environmentally sound and socially equitable policies and procedures within organizations. It was an epiphany: sustainability and feminism. The narrative that I connected early on revolved around three pillars: ecology, economy, and people. When we look at companies and how much their stock is worth, we need to see how they are treating their employees. We need to have a way to hold firms accountable. For example, when we are ranking organizations and corporations, when we are assigning points with our methodology . . . vis-à-vis sustainability, it is important to note that there are no women on their boards or that they lack health benefits for trans* employees. It is a way to further my radical feminist agenda in a more radical way. For example, one of my undergraduate professor's perspectives influenced how I approached sustainability. Dr. Carol Mason's activist infiltration of pro-life space was so rad. She made herself so uncomfortable to fit in these spaces. It raised a question for me of how to infiltrate these spaces with all my different aspects. For example, I am a visibly queer women who understands the language of corporations. I can articulate my meanings and understand where they are at, but they do not always realize that I am infiltrating with my radical feminism.

As a radical feminist undergrad, I never would have imagined that I would be working in fields like impact investing/financial services and sustainable international development. I was definitely in more of a punk rock/DIY-influenced "burn it down" camp when it came to lamenting the seemingly intractable harm that capitalism has inflicted on the planet and its people, especially women. However, somewhere in the five years between my undergraduate and graduate degrees, I realized that for someone like me to have the greatest positive impact in my work, I needed to understand how all these powerful mechanisms operate. This is how I found myself surrounded by my sustainable business colleagues in their required class (and one that I took as an elective) called Capital Markets. In this class, we learned about the incredibly convoluted and corruptible global financial markets, which included a stock market simulation where students developed an investment strategy and made trades throughout the semester. Yup, that's right— this queer tattooed feminist vegan willingly signed up to understand how the market is manipulated on a daily basis to serve the needs of a very few who are privileged enough to master its nuances. The good news is that I've also learned ways that socially responsible investing can be used as a way of getting the Wal-Marts and Coca-Colas of the world to, in the simplest terms, just stop being evil. This, combined with increased public pressure around embracing sustainable practices, is what gives me hope that humanity can face the mounting challenges associated with an unstable climate.

I have been called a change agent by my former employer. For example, in 2011, grant applications were being sent in through paper. I had to facilitate the process and get buy-in from trustees to change the whole application process to bring the organization into the twenty-first century. I also realized I am an entrepreneur. I am building out a new phase of Judi Brown as a social entrepreneur.

My Women's Studies degree helped me to navigate the highly privileged space that is higher education in the Bay Area. Many of my colleagues (mostly white) came from various places of privilege, particularly socio-economic, and in classroom discussions, debates or within teams, I always made it a point to check our assumptions. I became known as the champion of social sustainability, as I often found the "people" pillar less popular than "planet" and "profit." I came prepared with the skills to both acknowledge and dismantle systemic forms of oppression, and discuss how reinforcement of those oppressions at the micro-level impedes sustainable development at the macro-level. I heard many of my colleagues pay lip service to the concept of diversity without trying to understand systemically why more people of color weren't participating in the sustainability movement. I helped educate both classmates and members of administration on how institutional barriers have barred participation, and that for the school to be accessible to marginalized communities, it would have to set up scholarships for that purpose. This was an initiative I helped spearhead in my role as President of Student Representatives in my third semester.

It was often quite difficult for me to understand, accept, and then begin to transform a space of such privilege. Although the institution I chose for my advanced degree was mission-driven and, therefore, attracted a lot of like-minded individuals, I still struggled to not feel like an alien. I have learned to meet people where they are at, even if getting there sometimes meant accidentally engaging in inelegant and perhaps inarticulate (especially when alcohol-fueled) debates with my colleagues about unearned privilege and the fact that reverse racism does not exist. I decided to head up the school's queer club, called Q Sustainability, as a way to help my colleagues bridge the gap between social exploitation and environmental degradation. I held workshops on gender-neutral pronouns, put together a panel on what the queer rights movement might look like post-DOMA, and infused social justice concepts into everything I took on. One would think this wouldn't be much of a challenge in the historically activist Bay Area, but again, when well-meaning people come together to save the world but have not yet learned their positionality (because they didn't take Women's Studies!) and how their place relative to other communities in the world affects their ability to do the work, there are oftentimes difficult conversations that need to be had. I have discussed with a receptive administration at the school the possibility of adding more about privilege and social justice to the curriculum. I feel that if everyone in my cohort showed up to school already knowing what we Women's and Gender Studies students know, then we'd be able to get to our world-saving work much sooner.

One of the reasons I was attracted to Presidio Graduate School was that it places high value on Experiential Learning, which means every semester students have the opportunity to work with a live organization and provide some sort of deliverable. For example, I was able to work with the City of Berkeley on developing a valuation model that projected the city's unfunded liabilities in deferred maintenance and employee pensions for a public finance class. These projects sort of exist in lieu of internships. In my third semester for a research methods class, I learned about an organization called Zawadisha working with women entrepreneurs in Kenya on a more intelligent form of micro lending that provides infrastructural support to address sociocultural barriers to women's empowerment in addition to access to capital. I ended up doing my capstone project on this organization's model and was able to travel to Kenya with the founder to meet the women, visit their businesses, and learn from them how they define empowerment. My capstone project led me to co-create a Theory of Change and a three-year Adaptive Strategy alongside its founder. I now work with the organization part-time with the title Director of Mission Advancement, where I assist with fund development, cultivating partnerships, and generally evangelizing the work whenever possible. In a lot of ways, this work represents the culmination of all my previous education, activism, and experience. With this work, I am doing praxis, and I am living out the general thesis through which I entered the field: that raising the position of women and girls around the world will save the world.

Yet, when I was working on my capstone project, I also wanted to make sure that I was being true to myself and my feminist principles. I set up a call with Dr. Anita Trijina Revilla to run through what I was proposing and check myself. When making my proposal, I had concerns about all this business and its terms, all these gross terms. The whole idea was to flip all these things on its head. I feel that international programs have failed, in that they haven't addressed folks where they were at an "I know more than you" approach and the concept of experiential knowledge ran through my whole project. I wanted to make sure that I was being real in my feminist integrity and radicalism and that I was not relying on existing power structures. It is within my job to know who my "home base" folks are. These are those folks who get it. Among our Presidians there is a tendency within social circles to speak to folks as if they are white, when they are not. I had to make sure I am living social justice principles and this process helped me check myself and use the language I wanted to use and determine if it the language is appropriate. It was really helpful to have that feedback and—ultimately—validation.

In addition to my work with Zawadisha, I also work part-time as an impact investing analyst for a company in downtown San Francisco called HIP Investor, Inc. HIP stands for Human Impact + Profit and they're one of the companies who are attempting to ignite that paradigm shift to more responsible investing. I've been working on rating municipal bonds for impact, a project I started with HIP in the Capital Markets class I took as an elective. I also continue to manage a corporate foundation, Caesars Foundation, which I started doing part-time when I started grad school in the fall of 2011. When I got back from Kenya in November, I started working with a woman who learned about my work with Zawadisha and reached out to me to help her start a nonprofit that showcases the work of organizations and individuals in the self-reliance movement.

I have learned that I am not a person who wants a job—I am a social entrepreneur. I like to work on various projects at the same time, recognizing the alignment between them all. I place tremendous value on the ability to make my own schedule and be flexible with how, when and with whom I do work. Years ago, I would have been terrified at the thought of not having one employer that took care of my healthcare and retirement benefits. Now, I would much rather work out of a coffee shop or an entrepreneurial coworking space than ever set foot in another cubicle. This year, I plan to start my own business, consulting with a wide variety of institutions and organizations that prioritize human impact and climate stability. I am not a person of financial means, and I've taken on an absurd amount of student debt, but as scary as that all is, being independent is much more important to me and much closer to my own self-actualization.

What has provided freedom and clarity for me is realizing that there is no such thing as my dream job. My dream is to simply apply the skills and concepts I've acquired to both saving the world while simultaneously making it a better, safer place for women. Going back to when I was reviewing what Cheryl and I discussed a few years ago, what I found interesting was my own bright-eyed idealism about the nonprofit job I had landed, which ended up being an incredibly challenging experience. I worked in that role for a year and a half, under abusive management and having witnessed unethical behaviors at the highest level of the organization. Once again, my disillusionment around initially thinking I had found or even created a job that would be both fulfilling and utilize my talents, but also allow me to work in some facet of social justice had turned into a disappointing and even traumatizing experience. I can look back on all that now and see how much I learned.

*Takeaways from Judi's Profile*

- Judi was able to recognize that she wanted some integration between her politics and professional life, and was able to seek out employment opportunities based on that recognition.
- She was able to hone in on what she did not like about the internship experience, and recognize that she had talents and interests in a different aspect of the organization.
- She was willing to try to bring her full and authentic self to spaces that intimidated her.
- Judi was also willing to take risks personally, but professionally as well. About risk, she notes:

At a time with so much at risk, sometimes the greatest risk you can take is to believe in yourself. I definitely credit my Women's Studies education with helping me get here, even if it took almost 10 year and resulted in countless heartbreaks along the way. If you end up somewhere comfortable and everything is easy, you won't learn. And I never want to stop learning.

## POINT OF VIEW CONTRIBUTOR FOR CHAPTER 6

Jo Reger is an Associate Professor of Sociology and Director of the Women and Gender Studies Program at Oakland University. Her research areas of interest are gender, social movements, and qualitative methods and theory.

 ## YOUR TURN: EXERCISES

Now that you have spent some time reading the profiles, we invite you to reflect on how they can serve you as you decide what is next after graduation. Here are some questions to get you started:

1. Whose story did you identify with? Why?
2. What resources are you developing that will help you?
3. Take a moment and revisit the role of mentors in the profiles. Some were cultivated, and others stumbled upon. What is the role of professional mentors in your life now?
4. Looking at Rebecca and Matt's stories, do you have interests that are being expressed through internship programs or activism that you could pursue in a career?

## Notes

1. On December 6, 1989, Mark Lapine shot 14 women in an engineering school in Montreal. He did this because he believed that women were overtaking men in engineering. This incident became known as the "Montreal Massacre" and had a defining effect on generating national attention on gendered violence. Peter was in his last year of high school when this event happened, and by the time he got to university, he, along with many other students, found themselves primed to take on issues of sexual violence on campuses.
2. Ladyfest started in 2000 in Olympia, Washington. It is a community-based, not-for-profit global music and arts festival for female artists that features bands, musical groups, performance artists, authors, spoken word and visual artists, and workshops. It is organized by volunteers. All the proceeds are donated, and the Ladyfest events that have happened around the world are independently organized (see http://ladyfestten.com).
3. Proposition 8 (or the California Marriage Protection Act) was a ballot proposition and constitutional amendment passed in the November 2008 state election. The measure added a new provision to the California Constitution, which provides that "only marriage between a man and a woman is valid or recognized in California" (see www.courtinfo.ca.gov/courts/supreme/highprofile/prop8.htm).

# 7
# TRANSFORM YOUR WORLD
## PREPARING TO GRADUATE AND
## LIVING YOUR FEMINIST LIFE

For many students and their families, graduation is often synonymous with getting a job. "What are you going to do with your degree?" is the common refrain heard at gatherings and events around graduation time. Although these occasions are intended to celebrate the rite of passage from college and university life, there is often a subtle undercurrent reminding the graduate of the responsibilities and duties that lie ahead.

If you are a junior, you might be reading this chapter to discern what steps you need to take to prepare for employment. If you are graduating, you may be wrestling with a variety of questions, including some concerning employment, and some about living the values shaped by your education. For example: How will you create and sustain feminist intellectual and social communities once you graduate? How do you integrate ideas about equality into intimate partner relationships and parenting? How will you maintain a balance between work and home? While this chapter may not be able to answer all these questions for you, at least you'll become familiar with how other Women's and Gender studies graduates have grappled with them. Balancing your feminist ideals and Women and Gender Studies education presents challenges and opportunities that make us stronger and smarter citizens in our complex global world.

We should also note that, historically, women have faced additional challenges when entering the workforce and creating a life that is self-directed. One aspect of gender socialization is that of encouraging women to prioritize others' needs over their own. In Adrienne Rich's essay "Claiming an Education," she argues it is imperative that women remain actively engaged in the work of self-definition:

> Responsibility to yourself means refusing to let others do your thinking, talking, and naming for you, it means learning to respect and use your own brains and instincts . . . responsibility to yourself means that you don't fall for shallow and easy solutions . . . you refuse to sell your talents and aspirations short . . . it means that we insist on a life of meaningful work, insist that work be as meaningful as love, and friendship in our lives.
>
> (Rich 1979: 26)

Sometimes when we are searching for direction in our professional lives, we listen to others rather than ourselves. We narrow our vision of ourselves due to fear of economic or family pressures, and rely on conventional methods when seeking jobs because it seems easier or more acceptable. We encourage you to take responsibility for yourself in setting aside time to think about your long-term goals and about what you would really most like to experience or accomplish as part of the working world.

In this final chapter, we provide you with some insights about how best to live a life that incorporates the skills, knowledge and values you gained through your degree. The first section focuses on preparing for employment. We will address some general strategies that would apply to students of all academic backgrounds, but with special attention to issues specific to WGST students. We think it is important for Women's and Gender Studies graduates to take the very critical thinking and creative skills that are so fundamental to this interdisciplinary field of study and apply them to finding or creating job opportunities. And the good news is that you have done some of the preliminary work in Chapters 5 and 6! The second section of this chapter focuses on learning how to care for yourself after you graduate and ways to build and sustain community. We want to stimulate your thinking about what resources you can cultivate to continue lifelong learning and leadership after you obtain your degree and not burn out while doing so. Transforming the world is hard work and self-care is a critical component! As the airlines always remind us in their pre-flight safety message, we must put on our own oxygen mask before helping others—in order to transform the world, you must take care of yourself first.

## What is Next for Me? Four Questions

Urged on by fellow students and parents, you may find yourself thinking about and asking what is next for you. These are important questions to wrestle with, and they often take hold by the end of the junior year. Dr. Robert Pleasants, whom you met in the Introduction, provides a powerful method for reflecting on the future:

> Women's Studies departments are often safe spaces for personal exploration, for political awareness, and for figuring out an excit-ing nexus between the two. But what happens after graduation, when majors emerge from the college bubble and reenter the "real world"? For many, the prospect is intimidating: it can be difficult to sustain feminist awareness and find fulfilling employ-ment. In helping my students navigate this transition, I encourage them to reflect—starting with themselves and working outward. Specifically, I ask my students four simple questions when they graduate:
>
> 1.   Who do you want to be? If you're graduating, take some time to ask yourself this important question. Chances are, you have probably asked it dozens of times during the last four years, likely with dozens of answers. But graduation can offer a unique opportunity for determining who you want to be for the rest of your life. Depending on where you move or what you do after graduation, you could face a brand new beginning, which can be exciting, terrifying, and confusing all at once. And if you're a feminist in a non-feminist world, it can be particularly tough. To hold on to what you have learned and live up to your ideals can take effort, but the rewards are worth it. If you want to be a feminist, I encourage you to commit and keep seeking out feminist knowledge. But you can't sustain this commitment alone, which brings me to my next question.
>
> 2.   Who do you want to be *with*? The first years after college are an interesting time of re-evaluating friendships and forming new ones, so what better opportunity to surround yourself with people who are interested in gender and social justice issues?

I shudder to think who I would be if I hadn't begun a relationship (literally on graduation day) with a feminist woman. We've been together ever since. An important part of our relationship has always been challenging ourselves, inspiring one another, and holding each other accountable. I encourage you to find people you like and who are like you, but also seek out people who are different in ways that challenge you. Find people who *inspire* you.

3. What will you do? The previous question might leave you wondering, "How do I meet people who care as much as I do about gender equality?" Simple: volunteer. There are feminist organizations almost everywhere in need of volunteers. In addition to doing rich, fulfilling work at these organizations, I guarantee you'll have fun and meet new friends. Oftentimes, the organizations with the most intense training can provide the most enlightening and fulfilling experiences, giving you a perspective you simply can't get in a classroom. Volunteering is also a great way to explore career options if you're still wondering what you want to do with your life.

4. How can you change the world? Yes, I know. This is the big, tough question. In addition to the ideas listed above, there are ways to work for social change by looking at the bigger picture. You can find a career at a grassroots feminist organization, work at a local women's center, or work or volunteer at an organization focused specifically on societal-level women's rights—NOW, Ipas, National Abortion Rights Action League (NARAL), Amnesty International are just a few of the more prominent organizations that come to mind. Or if you decide on graduate school, you can study gender issues and advocate for equity in almost any discipline. Even if your career itself isn't explicitly feminist, any of the actions listed in the questions contribute to a better society, because all social change begins with individuals. What will your role be?

Dr. Pleasants raises four important questions Women's and Gender Studies students should think about while transitioning from student to graduate. We suggest that you make time to reflect on these questions in a sustained way. You may want to write your thoughts down, in a designated journal, while you consider what is next. For some people, the question will be a relatively straightforward one—law school, a social work program, working in the family business. But for most of us, these questions involve serious self-reflection. We encourage you to make time to think about what your vision looks like. Writing your answers down creates clarity, specificity and provides a record that you can reflect on many years after you graduate. For others, you may want to set up (or continue) an informal support group of friends and fellow WGST graduates to share your ideas, fears, suggestions, and even available work and volunteer opportunities.

## Section 1: Preparing

### Getting the Help You Need

We think preparing for the workplace involves three key actions. The first is recognizing your skills. The second is to learn skills that will create a good fit for the workplace. In Chapter 4, you learned what skills many graduates possess after their Women's and Gender Studies training, and in Chapters 5 and 6 you explored the different kinds of career pathways graduates pursue. So, by now you have some ideas about what kinds of skills you have and what types of work you are prepared to do. The third action is for you to mobilize helpers in this process. In preparing for employment, it is important to gather helpers along the way. People that you might consider asking for help and support include mentors, advisors in formal academic advising programs, internship supervisors, coworkers, and peers. If you are actively involved in a community organization, you may be able to ask the members for help. Later in this chapter, we revisit the role of mentors, a discussion begun in Chapter 2.

### Understanding Career Assessment, Aptitude, and Personality Tests

In addition to Dr. Pleasants's four questions that open the chapter, we would also like you to consider a fifth question that is practical to consider: What kind of workplace are you best suited for? You may or may not know the answer to this question. If you do not know the answer, there are resources out there that can help. One way to find out more about yourself is to take career assessment tests. We live in a culture where we take fun career aptitude tests all the time online. You have probably been tempted more than once to find out what kind of "rock star" you are on Facebook. There are a number of career assessments and aptitude tests that you may want to investigate to see what types of jobs are out there, and which ones may match your personality type, your skills, and/or your interests. These tests are usually low-cost or free. According to Hodges (2010), the majority of these tests involve a questionnaire that take less than 30 minutes to complete. You can take many of these tests online or you might be able to utilize your campus office of career services for access to these tests.

Some tests that Susan Doyle, author of *Internet Your Way to a New Job* (2009), suggests you may want to explore Myers-Briggs (MBTI), Career Key, Keirsey Temperament Sorter, Discover your Perfect Career Quiz, and the Princeton Review Career Quiz. The first three fee-based instruments ask questions to gain an idea of your personality type or temperament and may link these to characteristics of others in certain occupations. The last two assessments generate the best career path for you based on your responses to a series of questions about yourself.

Based on your responses to certain activities, ideas, or situations, these tools suggest types of careers, fields, and work settings in which you are most likely to excel. By taking one of these assessment tests, you can hopefully get a better idea of who you are, what you like, and in what situations you will thrive. Rather than believe that you must change yourself to work well with a particular person, situation, or organization, it may be helpful to realize that you may not be a good fit in certain work environments.

Increasingly, employers use a variety of employment tests either as part of a pre-screening process or to examine a sense of fit between the candidate and the position. Some of these tests directly assess your potential fit with the job (including measures to predict your performance

## SOCIAL MEDIA SAVVY

We offer a word of caution about posting your scores from on-line quizzes and other materials on social-media websites. We live in a time where you can post many things about yourself (and often others post pictures and comments about you as well). Be aware that employers can and do their own research on potential employees vis-a-vis social-networking sites. Be smart about your image and how you want to present yourself to the world. You may also consider constructing non-public sites, which allow you to share material that fits your personality, interests, and identity with friends who ideally respect your non-public persona.

and your longevity) and your personality, whereas others examine your cognitive abilities, emotional intelligence, your legal and financial background, or your health (physical, mental, substance-use history, etc.) (Doyle 2010). While the scope of questions that you may be asked may seem intrusive or excessive, these tests are generally accepted, as long as they are properly administered in a non-discriminatory way. Moreover, after you land your position, you may find yourself being asked to take a test for consideration of advancing to a new position. Employment tests are also used in some employment situations to assess leadership potential. If you find yourself in an applicant pool in which you are asked to take one (or all) of these types of tests even before being considered for a position, you must weigh the emotional, mental, and time costs of these tests. While some tests may be good indicators that an organization or business wants to match the talents and personalities of their workers with the demands of the job and the work environment, other pre-/post-employment screening practices may seem unnecessary and conflict with your beliefs. They might also be a strong indicator of an environment with which you may ultimately be uncomfortable. Because of this, you may want to discuss these issues with current employees (if possible), your career advising center, your professors, and your peers. Below, Cheryl discusses what she learned taking a personality test:

> One of the best opportunities I had was to take the Strength Finders personality assessment while I was enrolled in a Women's Leadership Institute offered by the Mankato YWCA. This test was different from others. Rather than pointing out weaknesses, it analyzes strengths and gives you an idea of what you can bring to an organization. Other tests, such as the Myers Briggs, can also give you some personal insight into your inner motivations, as well as the types of environments and management styles that work best for you. This self-knowledge and the ability to convey this to employers will set you apart from other applicants in the competitive job market.
>
> When I applied for my current position, I experienced the world of pre-employment screening tests. When I first received the phone call from human resources that I had been selected to continue in the search process, I was ecstatic. Because I had been working in higher education for almost 10 years at that point, I expected a series of conversational interviews with supervisors and HR staff. Instead, I was informed that I would be taking a

standardized test with other applicants and that my score on the test would determine whether or not I would be selected for a formal interview. Walking into the testing room, I was reminded of my anxiety when I took standardized tests to evaluate my aptitude as part of the process for applying to undergraduate and graduate degree programs (SAT, ACT, GRE). The CPS Human Resources Professional and Paraprofessional Entry Level Analyst exam is a time-limited test divided up into four sections: reasoning/analytical ability, math and statistics knowledge, written communication, and interpersonal skills. Going into the test, I felt fairly confident of my knowledge in these areas. Afterward, I was amazed that I made it into the interview group considering I had not done well on the math and statistics section. I also wished I would have had some time to prepare for the exam rather than take it cold. After I was hired, I was required to take some additional tests such as medical screening (tuberculosis tests) and an assessment of my general medical health to secure my employment.

For more information on the test Cheryl took, see www.cps.ca.gov/ ExaminationServices/TestRental/Professional/pp_EntryAnalyst.asp.

### Lessons from Cheryl's Experience

If you are selected to interview for a job, ask if there are any pre-employment tests required. Your human resources liaison might be able to give you the name of the exam. If so, see if there are any study guides or practice tests available online or in your local public library or campus career services office.

Aptitude and pre-employment screening tests are only one part of the screening process. Remember to take care of yourself and mentally, physically, and emotionally prepare for the interview. Be prepared to apply your knowledge in an interview situation. You may be interviewed by a hiring committee, which means that you need to focus, adequately answer multiple questions, and hopefully remember the names of the committee members. Or you may have a one-on-one interview. Either way, you may want to practice and pre-script answers to possible questions, pace yourself, and remember that you have practiced many of these skills in the classroom.

### Career Fairs and Career Services

Some Women's and Gender Studies departments and programs provide specific career and job fair events during the semester. This is an excellent place to network and gain professionalization skills. As we suggested in Chapter 2, a natural place to seek help after checking with your program is your college or university career services office. Your career services office can be an incredible resource for helping you with the basics of navigating online resources, developing resumes, and connecting you to alumni who may be interested in assisting you. Many universities pay for e-folio resources (to develop online resumes, portfolios, etc.) so that you can use this long after you graduate.

Your career services office may direct you to professional association websites to check for information on employment in the field. They may also direct you to blogs, depending on your interest. There are blogs for medical students, nursing students, law students, nontraditional students, and many more—many universities have their own student blogs set up. You can search through www.blogfinders.com to find out what others are saying about their experiences in a particular profession.

Your career services office may also offer coaching services that provide a one-on-one connection. A coach may help you review your strengths and skills, offer feedback on goals, and help you develop an individual plan for meeting your goals. Coaching may be useful for students who already have professional jobs or are making major job changes.

More than 40 percent of respondents to our survey primarily utilized their career services office to help them with employment options. This

## USING SOCIAL MEDIA TO BUILD NETWORKS

Social media plays an increasingly important role in helping job seekers find employment. Did you know that 75 percent of all jobs are landed through networking? It is true, and that is where social media can help. As Linda Conklin writes in "Nothing Works Like a Network," employers like using shortcuts to find qualified employees, and one way they do that is through using LinkedIn. Companies often use automated systems that search for key words and phrases to identify open positions. You can sign up for free with LinkedIn (a business oriented social networking service) and use the Network tab to find fellow alumni and the organizations where they work. You may be able to create a connection and seek information about that organization. Taking time to learn and utilize LinkedIn can help you build your professional network (Conklin 2013).

was a good first step for many; however, a majority of students find they need to think outside the box in searching and applying for jobs.

Looking for a new or different job allows a person to step outside their current situation and imagine original possibilities for personal and intellectual growth. Taking an alternative career path also allows for the development of new social networks and the potential for an increase in income. Conversely, looking for a new job makes one really assess one's toolkit; those resources that need to be developed. It also takes time, patience, and some resources.

Many students find entering the professional job market to be daunting, but just like any other project, it is actually quite manageable through time management and organization. In fact, most of us have some employment experience before graduating, employed in one way or another before we first entered the "formal" job market.

### Internships and Externships

As discussed in Chapter 2, internships are often a common feature of Women's and Gender Studies programs and undergraduate education in general. One of the best ways to find out what types of employment interest you is through an internship or externship. Internships can help you to find out what you want from a job and what you do not want. This is also a great time for one to gain skills and build resumes with vital information that can set a person apart from other applicants in the job market. Through internships, you can also meet people who become mentors. If you are unable to get a position with the organization you interned with, the experience can open other doors and expand your social networks.

Approximately 45 percent of our survey respondents replied that they completed an internship during the course of their undergraduate degree program. This percentage is close to the data collected from a 2008 survey by the National Association of Colleges and Employers (NACE). The NACE survey found that 50 percent of graduating students had participated in internships (Greenhouse 2010). In this survey of the more than 400 respondents who answered the question of whether they received college credit for their internships, almost 60 percent received college credit. Many of the survey respondents interned at social justice organizations, such as domestic violence shelters and women's health organizations, but others completed internships for museums and archives, state and local government departments (e.g. Department of Transportation), market research and lobbying firms, high schools, and symphonies and philharmonics.

Here are a few comments from our survey respondents about what they gained from their internships:

- "I developed a close and important relationship with my supervisor, who continued to mentor me after the internship ended . . ."
- "[I] learned how to present at conferences, many topics [on] sexuality and gender, peaceful alternatives, counseling, networking skills, and much more."
- "I learned a ton about the type of work that interested me and also discovered there are areas of women's health and rights that are less interesting to me."
- "[I] learned the intricacies of working in a nonprofit organization. Gained confidence and broadened my horizons . . ."

Michele notes of her own experience with an internship:

During the summer between my sophomore year and junior year in college, I participated in a program called the Minority Leaders Fellowship Program. Through that program, I had an opportunity to undertake a summer-long internship at the main office of the National Organization for Women in Washington, DC. I was thrilled to work in this historic feminist organization. I remember soaking in everything about the organization. I worked on two projects. One was documenting and disseminating the work by Southeast Asian women in the US who were working on issues of reproductive rights, domestic violence, and literacy in their communities. This task provided me an opportunity to become more familiar with the work of these communities in the US and globally. The second project was assisting the staff on the various projects they undertook on reproductive rights campaigns. This included working on press releases, preparing materials for fundraising events, reviewing legal cases happening around the country, and preparing materials to distribute at various events. These were all skills that I would draw on for research in my last two years of college and later graduate school. It was one of my first professional positions, so I learned a lot about the social norms that govern offices. An internship experience can provide skill development, but it can also provide a sense of community. Being in that environment solidified my feminist identity at the time, helped me to feel less isolated at college, and helped me hone my research and writing skills. These laid the foundation for my later work on my senior project (see the Introduction) and graduate school. Although I wound up going to graduate school rather than the nonprofit world, I had a sense that I could also enjoy working for a nonprofit organization whose mission I valued.

Besides interning for a local nonprofit, or securing a summer, fall, or spring semester internship with a local organization, you may also want to consider doing an international internship. If you are unable to participate in a study-abroad experience, an internship for an international company or nongovernmental agency may not only give you the work experience you seek in a field you are interested in, but also allow you to practice one of the language skills you gained during the course of your education.

You may also want to explore "externships" as a way to develop your foundation of skills. While the concept of an internship may be quite familiar to you, the term "externship" may be new. According to the Career Development Center at the University of Arkansas, an externship might be described as an "internship lite" (http://career.uark.edu/template). Rather than lasting the course of a semester, an externship may only last for a few days and is more informational than experiential. While internships are done during the formal education process, some externships are conducted after graduation.

Externs may observe and interview professionals in the organizations whose careers interest them, but rarely do these opportunities offer academic credit or pay. Yet, externships are a great way to get some insight into a career pathway without committing an extensive amount of time or labor. Externships not only afford students the opportunity to consider a career, but may be the deciding factor on whether to apply for a competitive internship or find another career field altogether.

Cheryl notes of her own experience with externships:

> I took this route after I finished my undergraduate degree. While browsing the career services at a university near my family's home, I found an ad announcing an externship at the Children's Museum

of Indianapolis. While the experience illuminated the fascinating world of working for a museum, it also made me realize this was not the field for me. But it did answer my question of whether or not I had the potential to educate others. The opportunities I had to lead tours of school age kids and keep their attention were turning points for me for continuing my education and wanting to teach.

## Mentors

Mentors can play an important role in helping to prepare you for postgraduate success process. We discussed mentoring briefly in Chapter 2, and here we emphasize that if you have not sought help from a mentor, now is a time to do so. Mentors can provide a good sounding board for thinking through career and employment options. They can ask adept questions that might help you see your skills in a new light. For example, when Cheryl was first going on the academic job market while finishing her Ph.D., she was able to learn the culture of this process through discussions with her formal advisor and her colleagues, as well as utilizing the resources of her university and professional association. Your mentor is an excellent person to ask for support, help, and guidance during this process. If you are also considering asking them to be a reference or write a letter of recommendation, it is useful to start by asking, "Can you recommend me strongly?"

## Asking for a Letter of Recommendation

For most jobs, you will be asked to supply references or letters of recommendation. This is very important, and there are some things you will want to consider when deciding who and how to ask.

Professors typically are swamped with requests from students beginning in October through early January because of the deadlines of graduate, medical, and law school applications, as well as scholarship applications. It will not always be possible to provide a month's notice for a letter of reference, but the more time you give your recommender, the better. We encourage you to be organized and polite when you ask a faculty member, mentor, graduate student, and/or former employer for a letter of reference.

One thing as you prepare to transition beyond college is to recognize that there will be periods where you'll feel overwhelmed and periods

## ETIQUETTE FOR A LETTER OF RECOMMENDATION

- Try to provide all important information succinctly in one e-mail.
- Give specific time frames about when the reference is due, the address and proper contact information, or the appropriate link for an online form. When asking for a letter from a professor with whom you took a class, remind him or her of the courses you took with them, the semester and year, and any outstanding coursework (tests, research papers, etc.).
- For former employers, remind your former employer of the kinds of skills your job entailed, send a current resume and a few sentences about why this employment opportunity is of particular interest.
- Send a copy of the job description.
- Give at least four weeks between your request and the deadline.
- If the letter of recommendation cannot be submitted online, send a pre-addressed stamped envelope to your professor or former professor. Not only does it save time for your recommender, but it saves the cost of postage.
- Send a thank you e-mail or handwritten note to your recommender.
- Let your recommender know if you wind up getting the position! They will enjoy knowing they played a role in your success. Your success may lead to opportunities to come back to the department and to serve as a role model or a resource for other students. This may include speaking in classes or on panels, or serving as a mentor.

that you want to procrastinate. That's normal. It is important to be creative in thinking about how to make a living, and to realize that often it is by trial and error that we learn how to apply our inner strengths and external skills in the workplace. The journey of how to apply your Women's and Gender Studies training in the workplace is interesting and unique. The temptation when seeking employment is to think of shooting an arrow out toward one's dream position. And sometimes graduates do find the perfect position their first time out. For most, however, finding out what one enjoys doing and is good at is more of an ongoing process of self-discovery, establishing relationships, and being flexible and creative in employing self-assessment tools rather than a one-time experience.

## Section 2: Caring for Self and Community

Integral to the process of supporting your postgraduate process is the care and maintenance of oneself. Like the popular adage "it takes a village to raise a child," we cannot discount the importance and development of support systems in our lives. For many, our support systems are composed of family, friends, intimate partners, mentors, peers, and spiritual advisors. Other areas that help us lead healthy and productive lives include access to healthcare (mental, physical, dental), healthy relationships (intimate partner, as well as friendship networks and the people who raised us), legal services (consumer issues, immigration/ citizenship issues, divorce and family custody, estate planning and criminal matters), financial planning, saving and debt management, continuing education and professional development, as well as spiritual self-reflection and participation in communities of faith. In order to care for yourself, it is important to know not only what services are available for your care, but also how to utilize them. Therefore, prior to graduation, we suggest reviewing the many resources you have utilized in the past, referrals you may not have needed during your educational experience but you found potentially useful and develop your own referral list. This can provide a strong foundation for the types of services you may need if and when you leave your hometown or college community for another state or country. This may also serve as a great resource for others who are making similar journeys to new and exciting places. We discuss several dimensions of caring for yourself and your community.

### Know Your Rights: Workplace Issues

Key areas that feminism has made strides in are on issues of workplace equality, including raising awareness about the issue of sexual harassment. As you think about current and future employment, it is important that you know what your rights are in the workplace. In *Taking on the Big Boys: or Why Feminism is Good for Families, Business, and the Nation* (2007), Ellen Bravo, the director of the film *9 to 5*, discusses a host of issues in which feminism is intricately involved in both our public and private lives. From pay equality and access to gender-dominated occupations, to part-time and temporary employment, Bravo reminds Women's and Gender Studies students of two major areas in which we need to remain aware and vigilant while on the job; sexual harassment and the right to organize. Not only do these issues affect us personally—as many readers may be victims of workplace harassment or report labor violations—but these issues collectively allow larger systems of oppression to continue.

## Sexual Harassment

The federal statutes on sexual harassment are defined as:

> unwelcome sexual advances, requests for sexual favors, and other verbal and physical conduct of a sexual nature will constitute harassment when: submission to such conduct is made either explicitly or implicitly a term or conditions of a person's employment; submission to or rejection of such conduct by an individual is used as a basis for academic or employment decisions affecting that individual; such conduct has the purpose or effect of unreasonably interfering with an individual's academic or work performance or creating an intimidating, hostile, or offensive academic or work environment.
>
> (Code of Federal Regulations 1980)

Unfortunately, we may have been exposed to these systems of oppression throughout our educational career. Some of the major findings of the 2006 American Association of University Women Report, "Drawing the Line: Sexual Harassment on Campus," include:

- Sexual harassment is common on college campuses and is most common at large universities, four-year institutions, and private colleges.
- Men and women are equally likely to be harassed, but in different ways with different responses. Female students are more likely to be the target of sexual jokes, comments, gestures, or looks. Male students are more likely to be called gay or a homophobic name.
- Lesbian, gay, bisexual, and transgender individuals are more likely to be harassed.
- Different racial and ethnic groups experience sexual harassment in similar, but not identical, ways.
- Men are more likely than women to harass. Both male and female students are more likely to be harassed by a man than a woman.
- For many students, sexual harassment is a normal part of college life.

- For many students, their attitude about their college experience is negatively affected by the harassment.
- Experiences in college shape lifelong behaviors and attitudes that are continued in the workplace and larger society.
- Sexual harassment will continue as long as it is not taken seriously.

This report suggested that while sexual harassment may have been learned and perpetuated throughout our educational experiences, it is little wonder then that sexual harassment continues into other institutional settings, such as the military, the workplace, and religious institutions. Many myths still exist about sexual harassment. According to Bravo (2007: 101), they include:

- Sexual harassment is a thing of the past.
- Sexual harassment is subjective.
- Often, sexual harassment is trivialized as an issue of taste or of someone "not being able to take a joke" rather than behavior of a sexual nature at school [or] at work that is unwanted, unwarranted, offensive, creates a hostile or uncomfortable work environment and makes it difficult for employees to effectively do their work.

## Unions

As for labor organization and unionizing, there are a lot of myths and stereotypes that Bravo believes exist about workplace justice causes and organizations. You and your family may have already participated in an organized labor environment, or you may be interested but have not yet had the opportunity to join. Conversely, you may have been approached and decided not to join a union at your current job due to costs, questions about union benefits and participation, or for other reasons. While union organization has illuminated class issues across the globe, the role and impact of women and minorities in demanding access to better wages and safe, non-exploitative workplaces is often minimized. For example, Bravo points out how black laundresses organized a union in 1866 in Jackson, Mississippi, for better wages shortly after emancipation. She also discusses how issues of maternity leave benefits and childcare resources were voiced for working women by unions (the AFL and CIO) decades before the US enacted federal policies on these matters. Currently, recent workplace justice activism has in large part been enacted around issues ranging from the informal economy, home healthcare, welfare and workfare, and female immigrants (Cobble 2007). An analysis of issues of gender, race/ethnicity, sexuality, age, and ability are at the very core Women's Studies graduate intellectual and economic lives. In addition, many Women's and Gender Studies students apply their Women's Studies degree working for unions and for other local, state, and federal organizations that ensure worker safety and protections. Some of the myths that are often associated with collective action and worker activism include:

- Unions are not for women and minorities.
- Union membership takes workers' wages rather than fighting for them.
- Unions are obsolete in current professionalized business environments.
- Unions limit businesses' ability to be competitive and offer low prices for customers.
- Union membership has been decreasing due to rejection from workers.

*Health and Well-Being*

Access to quality and culturally appropriate healthcare has been a long-standing issue for feminists. The ability to make informed decisions about one's physical body and mental health has been a rallying point for the women's movement, ranging from issues regarding access to safe and reliable birth control and abortion, gender sensitive counseling and therapeutic models, and most recently access to hormone therapy and gender surgery. Yet these issues are far from resolved and are constantly changing due to changes in policy and law and the corporatization of the medical industrial complex, as well as the medicalization of bodies. As you transition from student to the workplace, healthcare may become an issue to be attentive to regarding what employment you seek and understanding benefit packages.

In the United States, healthcare, is undergoing a major structural shift with the enactment of the Affordable Care Act (also known as Obamacare). Under this legislation, it is expected that citizens of the United States will become enrolled in some form of insurance plan. It is expected that this will enable many Americans who formally did not have

## REPRODUCTIVE RIGHTS AND JUSTICE

As discussed in Chapter 2 by Carol Mason, reproductive justice is an area that is still controversial. Women's and Gender Studies students may question their own personal beliefs and attitudes on this topic if it becomes an issue in the workplace. For example, perhaps you identify as "pro-life" personally, but will work at a place that ensures access to birth control (and abortion) for everyone. Perhaps you will work for a private, faith-based organization (or the U.S. Military), for which your ability to access birth control/abortion is limited. You may wish to obtain a permanent form of birth control (vasectomy or tubal ligation) and you cannot access this method due to your age, income, or insurance carrier. Perhaps you wish to adopt a child, but are curtailed due to your sexuality or your relationship status.

Because of these issues, it is important to become familiar with the reproductive health laws and regulations in your particular country, state, organization, and insurance or medical carrier.

the means to have access to healthcare the opportunity to do so. Yet access to care does not mean that the type of care one receives will necessarily be feminist or responsive to one's life situation. Therefore, it is important to seek out competent, respectful and supportive healthcare providers.

As discussed earlier in the book, activism surrounding securing the rights of individuals and oppressed minority groups in society has been a hallmark of second and third wave feminist movements. These issues often recognized as the products of the feminists are some of the most controversial both politically and on a personal level.

### Financial Considerations

It is time to talk about money. Thinking and talking about money as graduation approaches can feel challenging. In this section, we encourage you to think about your future in fiscally responsible ways. Walking along the journey to our ideal situation takes time and strategic planning. We highlight some key areas that will be useful for you to consider as you think about the role of resources and graduation (or changing positions).

There is the assumption by many that college is a time for young adults to extend adolescence, and sow their wild oats by indulging themselves—feeding their heads during the day (through reading theoretical treatises or sitting in lectures/seminars) and engaging in hedonistic pleasures at night. It is often perceived that students do not work or, if they do work, it is temporary until one achieves the career position their college degree has prepared them for. This, however, is not the reality. Many students work either on-campus or off-campus jobs or work during the summer in order to help with some of the expenses of attending college. Others obtain loans, scholarships, or other sources of funding that may require time or service after finishing one's degree. Many students may offset these costs with military or other types of service (AmeriCorps or Peace Corps). Americans are working longer and later than previous generations due to structural constraints (such as changes in social security eligibility and rising retirement ages), as well as through a desire to stay in the workforce for social, personal, and economic reasons.

Increasingly, the pressure of life after college is affected by the amount of debt students amass through the course of their education. Debt may not only influence the type of employment you seek, but affects your life experiences and changes for years to come. Your student loan debt may be influenced by the type of institution you attend (private or public, community college, or Research I-type university), your institution's tuition and fees, and the type of loan you obtain. Almost two-thirds of four-year undergraduate students graduate with debt. Student loans average in the tens of thousands of dollars and upwards (Kantrowitz 2010).

### Building and Sustaining Feminist Communities

It is true that even if you pursue graduate education, the classroom will never feel the same. This is also true about friendships and community life. The intensity of shared social and intellectual space that defines the undergraduate college experience changes dramatically after graduation. You will need to actively cultivate community to serve your broad intellectual, social, political, and perhaps spiritual needs. There are many ways to think about the kind of intentional communities that you want to develop and occupy after graduation.

For Matt Ezzell, building (and sustaining) feminist community has been a high priority since finishing his Ph.D. in Sociology. He worked very hard as an undergraduate and graduate student at building a strong feminist community and set of allies. Now that he is an assistant professor, he acknowledges that building feminist community is more challenging, given his often seventy-hour-a-week job as a professor. Still, he sees it as essential:

> [F]eminism is a process, not an endpoint. It is an ongoing exercise struggle and process of self-engagement and practice of self-reflexivity. I think for a lot of folks, if you don't have feminist community it is so difficult to sustain this critique. It's not an academic exercise for me.
>
> If you want to do this [feminist] work it's incredibly rewarding, [and] if you do this in an organized way, you will find feminist community. You can't do this by yourself.

You may find yourself wanting to begin (or to continue) being part of a faith-based or spiritual community after you graduate. Feminists and issues of religion and spirituality have not often been easy companions, because American second-wave feminism saw itself as a highly secular movement. Karlyn Crowley, Associate Professor at St. Norbert College, ruminates on spirituality, feminism, and the challenges of building community.

## POINT OF VIEW

### THE HOLISTIC FEMINIST SUPERPOWERS NEEDED TO BUILD COMMUNITY

#### Karlyn Crowley, St. Norbert College

After majoring in Women's Studies in the first cohort at my small, liberal arts college, Earlham, in 1990, I knew that I wanted to go to graduate school. But then I went and lived in an intentional Quaker spiritual community, Pendle Hill, for a year. And it changed my life. But I'm getting ahead of myself. I have had many spiritual paths in my life and always one political one before I could name it—feminism. Sometimes they intersected and sometimes they flat out didn't. For part of high school, I identified as a born-again Christian. That I can say that out loud in this book may be a shock to some of you and a relief to others. Perhaps just skimming the words "born-again Christian" in a Women's and Gender Studies book made you recoil from the flashing red lights emanating from those three little words. For others, you might have flinched from the shock of recognition and perhaps even felt sheepish about your religious closetedness as a feminist.

See, I like that moment—where something makes me so uncomfortable that I have a visceral, bodily reaction to flee. Feminism taught me to stay. Let me explain. Part of what Women's and Gender Studies has given me as an intellectual gift is the ability to identify a gap, a problem to be solved, something uncomfortable to be parsed. One of those enduring questions for me is: How do the spiritual and the political interact? What's their chemistry? I have asked that question for some time in my personal life and intellectual life. For me, Quakerism was a place where my spirituality and politics congealed. Had I not gone to graduate school in Women's and Gender Studies and Literature, I might have gone to divinity school. This persistent quest to answer these questions led to exploring Wiccan rituals, Buddhism, and meditation, among other practices. And when it came time to write a dissertation, I was in the produce aisle at the natural grocery and a professor turned to me over the spinach and said, "What do you spend most of your time thinking about?" She followed up with, "What would you study or read regardless?" And I thought—oh I read books on spirituality and I think about feminist stuff. Oh—I should think about them together. Why doesn't anyone think about them together? That began my book, *Feminism's New Age: Gender, Appropriation, and the Afterlife of Essentialism* (2011), where I investigate white women's commitment to New Age spiritual practices and feminism—are they congruent, in conflict, or both? I ask: How do white women build spiritual community when, from the outside, it looks racist, appropriative, and naive? Is it? Or is the story more complicated?

The story is more complicated. But let me shine big pointing arrows on this point first: when you have an idea, an intuition, or hunch about a problem to be solved, particularly one that needs feminist analysis, then *listen to yourself!* Because those hunches are in the vein of Adrienne Rich and the early feminist notion of the value of experience, particularly women and marginalized people's experience. I shared the story of my personal and intellectual paths intersecting to make two points:

- Pay attention to what you care about. Answer the question the professor in the produce aisle asked me: What do you think about, talk about, write about in your spare time? What feminist intervention needs to be made there?
- Welcome your complicated feminist self. Give ze a birthday party. Don't fight against these tangled, even mangled, components of your identity and imagine they don't "fit" in feminism. Examine and knit them together making new art, a new aesthetic. And yes, I'm using a 1970s feminist metaphor, but I said knit, not weave.

Relatedly, then, what have I learned about how feminists do spirituality and community? It depends. Not surprisingly, white women often long for more community, particularly through cross-racial connection, thus the boon in white women's participation in New Age spiritual practices such as Native sweat lodge rituals based in racial appropriation. Women of color often create their own separate communities in response to institutionalized racism. White women are frequently baffled by not getting an invitation to join communities of color; women of color are often exhausted by white naivete, at best, and white racist harm, at worst, in these contexts. Meanwhile, Women's and Gender Studies, as a field, is aggressively secular and frequently unaware of the racialized valence of that secularity. Women and peoples of color continue to protect their traditions and build an alternative Women's and Gender Studies genealogy based in integrated spiritual activism.

Some of this description is segregated and grim—is there potential for multiracial political and spiritual community? What do we know from feminist intellectual scholarship that can heal this frequent division: look hard and long at a problem and identify it. Name it. Learn its history. Do your homework. Then make an anti-racist intervention for justice sake.

What am I saying? I'm saying that communities are messy, hard, worth it, and need spiritual and political healing. You are the one to do that healing. And Women's and Gender Studies gives you the tools—the ability to do intersectional analysis, the ability to do meta-critique of your own standpoint, the ability to not gloss over whitewashed histories, but to ask harder questions about true history, and the ability to stay, hear hard words and truths, and not be afraid.

These are your holistic—spiritual—feminist superpowers. Use them.

## Transform Your World

There are a multitude of ways that graduates in Women's and Gender Studies try to live their vision and enact social change. In the sections that follow, we explore some ways that graduates have created meaning in their personal and professional lives that extend their commitment to gender issues.

## Stay Involved: Clubs, Networks, Organizations

You may find yourself after graduation staying near your former institution, or, conversely you may move away. If you are staying in the same area, we suggest that you really push yourself to move beyond the college and/or university contacts that you may have developed. While it is very important to keep these ties, we think it is also useful to find other anchors that will help begin your professional and broader social network.

Conversely, moving to a new city can feel both exhilarating and daunting. You will also need to develop your networks there. There are several excellent organizations that help to fill that gap, and these are places where you can meet people committed to empowering women and girls in various ways. If you did an internship for a national non-profit, for example, you may decide to find a chapter of that national nonprofit where you are moving and decide to volunteer in your new place of residence.

The graduates surveyed are an actively engaged group in global civil society. They are involved in professional, social, and political organizations. They are also involved in clubs, loose affiliations, collectives, networks, and informal groups. Their interests span a wide array of interests, causes, and concerns. The top organizations that most graduates belong to are: professional, (explicitly) feminist, and women's organizations. The diversity of organizations and causes is quite breathtaking, ranging from Volunteer Simplicity Groups to the Human Rights Campaign. Graduates were not only active in well-defined organizations, but, continuing the trend they showed as undergraduates, they had often created groups, clubs, and organizations to meet their needs. Many respondents indicated that they belonged to a variety of clubs, groups, and organizations. Membership and affiliation continues graduates' commitment to improving society and applying what they know outside of a formal classroom. In our survey, we created some basic categories that tried to capture the range of organizations a person might belong to or be active in. Below, we highlight a few of our findings on membership and belonging of Women's and Gender Studies graduates:

- 57.8 percent of all graduates were active in a professional or work-related organization (e.g. American Bar Association).
- 21.9 percent of all graduates were active in a women's organization (e.g. American Association of University Women).
- 27 percent of all graduates were active in explicitly feminist-identified organizations (e.g. National Organization for Women).
- 10 percent of all graduates were active in social networking organizations (e.g. Jaycees).
- 24 percent of all graduates were active in health and/or fitness-related clubs, leagues, and organizations (e.g. softball league).
- 12 percent of all graduates were active in faith-based organizations (e.g. Salvation Army).

- 7 percent of all graduates were active in family-related organizations (e.g. Parents, Families and Friends of Lesbian and Gays, P-FLAG).
- 20 percent of all graduates were active in social clubs (e.g. Stitch 'n Bitch).
- 27 percent of all graduates were active in other groups, clubs, associations, organizations, and networks not indicated by our survey categories (e.g. a theater collective or the ACLU).

Joining networks, organizations, and clubs provides the potential for support, mentoring, skill-building, and sometimes just plain fun and relaxation! Deciding if you would like to become a member of organizations, groups, or clubs will be an important decision as you navigate life post-graduation.

You may find yourself also interested specifically in activism. There are many important emerging issues to devote time and energy working on. One that we think is important is immigration, and we asked Anita Tijerina Revilla to talk about why this is a feminist issue.

## POINT OF VIEW

### FEMINISM AND CITIZENISM

Anita Tijerina Revilla, University of Las Vegas, Nevada

I am an activist scholar, a feminist, queer Chicana who grew up in poverty and was raised by an amazing single mom who was widowed at the age of 30. I have also been a student at some elite institutions in this country, including Princeton, Columbia, and UCLA. Today, I am a professor and the director of Women's Studies at UNLV. This path has intensely impacted the way I view the world and the process in which my critical consciousness has developed. I enjoy being a professor and researcher. Still, it has been important for me to root my personal and professional work in my vision of social justice, which is ever expanding. This began with a realization of the deeply internalized racism and classism that I had experienced as a young Tejana (Mexican American born and raised in Texas). I was systematically taught to be ashamed of my Mexican-ness, brown skin, and poverty. It took many years for me to reclaim my Tejana identity. Once I was able to take pride in my own identity, I became ferociously committed to a plan of social change. I studied African American Studies, American Studies, and Latin American Studies, along with my degree in Religion. Later, I pursued and received master's and doctoral degrees in education because it was my belief that if I wanted to change the world, I could best do it by being a teacher or teaching teachers. Eventually, this led me on my path to Women's Studies, which essentially is a university degree rooted in social justice and civil rights struggles.

As a fourth-generation Tejana, I was raised to be anti-Mexican. My family, who was born and raised in Texas for over 100 years, believed themselves to be better than immigrants from Mexico. Often, I heard them use words such as "wetbacks" or "*mojados*"—warning us never to marry a Mexican because they might be marrying you just to gain citizenship. I was in graduate school before I fully understood the experiences of undocumented immigrants living in the US. My activism with Chicanas/Latinas in Los Angeles led me to become an immigrant rights activist, a citizen ally to non-citizens, and an activist scholar of the immigrant rights movement. Today, immigrant rights activism is my foremost focus of study in Las Vegas, as I have been studying and participating in it for the past eight years. Specifically, I follow the lives and experiences of feminists and queer activists who have served as leaders in the local movement. These young people have expanded my knowledge of immigration tremendously. Together, we have identified a type of discrimination that is targeted at people who do not have citizenship in the nation in which they reside. We call this citizenism and define it as a global system founded on the subordination of non-citizens (Rangel-Medina and Revilla 2011). We believe citizenism is more expansive than racism. For it also includes layers of classism, imperialism, and colorism, and it is a global phenomenon targeting all people who do not have access to citizenship in the nation state in which they reside. It has created a system of advantages that unfairly privileges U.S. citizens, and reinforces unearned and unjust citizen privileges. Citizenism lends itself to the belief in and practice of citizen superiority/supremacy. Furthermore, it results in social, economic, political, and legal discrimination against undocumented immigrants. Citizenism is the active criminalization of marginalized laborers who are living in the US for the purpose of economic survival.

We live in a nation that overwhelmingly scapegoats immigrants and manipulates the general population into an ignorant stance of hatred/fear toward non-citizens. It is a layered and complex issue. Therefore, I have outlined some fundamental points of information related to the immigrant rights struggle:

1. Immigrants have historically been recruited to the US as cheap and exploitable labor by U.S. corporations.
2. They contribute to our economy as laborers, consumers, and human beings.
3. Many immigrants are economic refugees (fleeing their countries so that they can economically survive/live).
4. The economic crises in their countries are often being fostered/designed by U.S. globalization (i.e. U.S. companies profit from the developing countries'

labor; they create their businesses in depressed economies, shut down local businesses and destroy their natural resources). This creates unemployment and poverty in those nations. Thus, the US is intimately connected to the lack of resources in developing nations.

5. Furthermore, the US has funded and supported political/economic wars in many of the countries where undocumented people come from; therefore, the US is directly responsible for creating more economic and war refugees. They flee to the "powerful" country that is responsible for their dislocation.

6. The majority of Latinas/os who migrate without authorization are of indigenous heritage. Therefore, they are directly connected to this land—North, South, and Central America. They have been migrating for generations. It is their human right. They belong to this land, and they should have the freedom to cross "borders" that were created by people in power to dominate and oppress.

7. The laws that are in place were socially/legally/politically constructed to oppress working-class, poor, brown, and indigenous people who migrate for the purpose of economic survival. Therefore, these immigration "laws" are manifesting as contemporary segregation, Jim Crow, sharecropping, and racial profiling. The laws are unjust, and as Martin Luther King, Jr. suggested, we have an obligation to contest unjust laws. We cannot wait for folks to realize or learn that the laws are discriminating/inhumane laws created to maintain an exploitable workforce.

8. Furthermore, the children of undocumented migrants were brought to the US without consent, but very much for their survival. Their families sacrificed so that they could eat, live, work, survive, and prosper. As a nation, we must honor this sacrifice of both their parents and the children.

9. We must not pretend that undocumented people are being treated in humane ways. Citizens are acting like they are superior to immigrants in much the same way that white people believed themselves "superior" to folks of color during the eras of slavery and segregation.

It is my firm belief that a feminist vision of social justice must include the struggle of immigrant rights. A feminist vision that falls short of this is merely reinforcing discrimination and exploitation of a very vulnerable population. As feminist activists and scholars, we must ensure that our visions and actions for social justice fully integrate this struggle. Otherwise, we are quite simply part of the citizenist project.

## Give Back

After graduation, you might consider how closely you want to stay affiliated with your program. We would encourage you to think about the multiple ways that you might support your program, either through making a donation, mentoring current students, or coming back to share your story of success. In fact, as you consider financial issues as highlighted in the previous section, part of your budgeting and expenditures may be to think about how much money you would like to earmark for the organizations and causes you believe in and want to support. For many of us, we were able to achieve our undergraduate degree through the contributions of those who proceeded us, either directly (e.g. scholarships), or through the funds raised and maintained by a variety of feminist organizations.

Once you graduate with your interest in Women's and Gender Studies, consider supporting your institution, specifically your Women's and Gender Studies unit. It is never too late to start a tradition of giving, and you can start out by committing to as little as $10 a year.

Giving back gives you a say in the direction the program or unit is going. It also continues to support the continued viability and visibility of Women's and Gender Studies programs at the institutional level— well-endowed programs are noticed throughout various administrative levels (i.e. development office and dean's office).

Additionally, you may be called on to support your program if it comes under fire. As we have explored throughout this book, although Women's and Gender Studies is globally flourishing, it still has its fair share of critics and detractors. So, the other reason why it is important that you stay connected is so that you can lend your voice to support the unit if it comes under institutional or external threats. Since the first edition of this book, we have seen many units face various challenges based on shrinking resources in higher education and ideologically motivated attacks. Well-written and engaging letters from alums can make the difference. For an excellent example, see Judy Brown's letter in support of the women's studies program at the University of Nevada, Las Vegas (see Berger and Radeloff 2011).

Keep in touch and make sure that they have your e-mail address.

### Start a Nonprofit Organization

We met Kimberly Wilson in the previous chapter. She began her yoga studio on a shoestring budget and turned her passions for empowering women into a successful career as yoga teacher, motivational speaker, and author. She is always looking for ways to serve women and girls that highlight issues of creativity and leadership. After several successful years as a business owner, she wanted to do more for the community. At first, she and her team began a program for at-risk teenage girls to come to her yoga studio for weekend workshops. She and her team, however, wanted to create more structure and visibility for empowering women. Over several years, she created a foundation, the Tranquil Space Foundation, to do more work in the community than her for-profit-based business could.

Tranquil Space Foundation focuses on expanding opportunities for girls and women to develop their inner voice through yoga, creativity, and leadership activities. Its signature program, TranquilTeens, provides workshops for girls in grades 9–12 through partnerships with schools and community organizations. The foundation has also recently added Tranquil Women to support women in the DC area. Tranquil Space also gives money to women-focused organizations that resonate and align with its overall mission.

## STAY CONNECTED: FEMINIST MEDIA: MAGAZINES, BLOGS, WEBSITES, OH, MY!

How will you continue to stay active and abreast of issues once you graduate? Once you leave college, you will not have the luxury of finding out about the latest feminist-inspired play or women's activism happening in Peru. You also will find that your friends will be busy with their lives, and you may find yourself separated. If your institution does not have an alumni network, offer to start one. There is a wealth of feminist magazines (*Ms.*, *Bitch*, and *Bust*, for instance) and many feminist blogs (i.e. The Crunk Feminist Collective, Jezebel, the f-bomb (UK), etc.) to choose from to stay informed. There is no reason not to stay connected to your interests.

After graduation (or even while in school), you may have a desire to put your interests into action through creating a nonprofit organization/foundation. It can sound daunting, but remember, nonprofit organizations can dramatically range in size from two people to 2,000. See Kimberly's *Tranquilista* (2010) for an excellent overview on starting a nonprofit.

For others, while you may not start your own nonprofit or blog, you may try to exemplify the application of your feminist principles in your personal and professional life. One powerful area to achieve this goal is through parenting, as Kathie Cashett, whom you met in Chapter 5, explored in her Spotlight

---

### 🔍 SPOTLIGHT: CATHERINE "KATIE" CASHETT

The role of parenting in modern life and a historical and complicated analysis of motherhood may be a familiar theme in your classes. We found, however, a frank discussion of feminist parenting is much less common (though often wondered about by some) discussion among graduates. From our survey, we learned that many graduates who chose to parent felt that their WGST education helped them to make conscious decisions about parenting styles, division of labor among partners, whether to be a single parent, or adopt, etc. Many also noted in our survey the difficulty of being a parent and raising a child in accordance with their feminist ideals. Katie, a Women's and Gender Studies graduate, provides us insights into her experience.

My background and beliefs in feminism have had a tremendous impact on my mothering, from resisting pink clothing for my newborn daughter to giving my son dolls, from the decisions I made regarding childbirth to the ways in which my husband and I balance the job of caring for our children. Of course, now my 7-year-old daughter has chosen to paint her room pink and my 4-year-old son is obsessed with anything that moves—cars, balls, and trains. I support their choices and their interests and continue to communicate the kinds of messages that support a more gender-neutral parenting such as all colors are for all kids (not just pink for girls and blue for boys) and all toys are for all kids. My daughter enjoys games with cars and my son throws on the occasional tutu, and recently my husband has taken to wearing pink socks to reinforce these messages. While neither of our parents would have identified as feminists when they were raising us, they were influenced by the ideas of a more equitable domestic and parenting sphere and we both had good role models to draw from in our own childhoods.

My husband was born and raised in Mexico and has in his father a wonderful example to follow since he was involved with cooking, cleaning, and parenting and did not allow his sons to shirk their duties in the family. My husband is a true co-parent who shares in the multitude of responsibilities—cooking, cleaning, communicating with teachers, ferrying kids to appointments and lessons, packing lunches, helping with homework, and reading bedtime stories. We work as a team, which is important for our kids to see as they grow up. My husband also gained from his family a strong sense of cultural identity, which we in turn try to pass onto our children. Feminism is at the heart of my goals as a parent to raise my children to be kind, respectful, and inclusive and to take strength and pride in their bicultural and bilingual upbringing.

Work and life balance remain a challenge. My Women's Studies education prepared me in some senses for what challenges would lay ahead, but there is more work for feminists to do in terms of supporting families. In my seven years as a parent, I have worked part-time, been a stay-at-home mom, worked full-time and telecommuted. I have hired nannies and sitters, worked from home, used daycare centers and in-home childcare, organized a cooperative preschool, and relied on friends and family. In my experience, flexible part time work is ideal—and incredibly difficult to obtain at a rate that supports or even partially supports a family.

This is where feminism has succeeded, but where there is more work for feminists to do is in the broader social and political domain to enact changes in policies and laws that allow families to thrive.

I hope by the time that my children are considering starting families there are better options in terms of workplace flexibility, childcare, and other social supports for parents.

This is something that all feminists, be they parents or not, can work towards. Supporting families is a profoundly feminist action and one that can affect all of us for generations.

## KATIE'S TIPS: FEMINIST PARENTING

Katie offers some resources she has found useful in fusing "feminism and parenting."

*Tatterhood and Other Tales* by Ethel Johnston Phelps (Feminist Press at CUNY, 1979)

*The Amelia Bloomer Project* produces an annual list of recommended feminist literature for children from birth to age 18 (ameliabloomer.wordpress.com).

*A Mighty Girl* not only has recommendations for reading, but also for toys and movies for "smart, confident, and courageous girls" (www.amightygirl.com).

Feminist parenting blogs include Viva la Feminista, Blue Milk, and Lesbian Dad.

*MomsRising* chronicles grassroots activist work on issues affecting families such as paid maternity/ paternity leave, paid sick days, and flexible work (www.momsrising.org).

*It is OK to Shift Gears*

We think it is important not to get into a trap about thinking what might be a "good feminist" job, as sometimes happens to graduates. As Rebecca Mann stated in the previous chapter, any job can be a feminist job depending on the mindset that you bring to it. For some people, a feminist job means working face to face with women and/or girls in a direct service capacity. For others, a feminist job means working in a feminist organization, and for others still, it means making a difference through daily interactions in which we seek change regarding issues of oppression. Our study suggests that graduates find themselves living their ideals in a myriad of ways. Yet, in your journey to find an applied and or meaningful work environment, you may encounter situations in which your boss or your colleagues are not as supportive as you would expect them to be. Feminism, as we have previously explored, conceptually means a lot of different things to different people. Therefore, you may practice or believe in a different type of feminism than others. Unfortunately, this also means that the "enlightened" and progressive workplace you envisioned possibly varies greatly from your day-to-day experience. For example, in *Fast Girls: or Teenage Tribes and the Myth of the Slut*, Emily White (2003) shares her perspective of being hired at what she thought would be an empowering and progressive organization, and instead experienced a hostile workplace in which internalized sexism abounded.

This experience of working in an uncomfortable workplace was echoed by Judi Brown, who you met earlier:

> I worked for a health information technology organization for about a year. I thought the experience would be great, but the CEO and the woman who ran my department were sexist. I knew I had to leave the job after working there for three months. Plus, the job wasn't challenging, but I was paid a lot of money to do that.

While Judi continued to work for the organization in order to make ends meet and support her partner, a graduate student at the time, she was actively looking for other opportunities to fuse her feminist ideals and activist principles. One of the resources that ultimately helped her find one of her positions was a conversation with one of her mentors:

I called my mentor in tears (fifth time) asking about job possibilities. He [had] heard that my current employer was looking
for an assistant. I wasn't really excited about being an assistant;
I was really disheartened with having my dual baccalaureate and
not [being] able to utilize my education and talent on the job. I
met with the President and CPO and she spoke with me for
about 20 minutes. She told me that even if the position was open,
I had more to offer than the position entailed. She valued my
community involvement and my artistic abilities. I was eventually
brought into the organization in January 2010 for a position as
"Special Projects Coordinator." Primarily, this job involves grant
writing, events, and program management. The job is challenging,
and I have to make things up as I go along, but it fits with the
organization. The CPO/President prides herself in running the
foundation like a think tank. She has a strong personality and
she took a chance on me, gave me an office, and even a MacBook
Pro. Every day, something is different and at the end of the day
I know I am working to impact and change the lives of children
in our community. If you feel good about the work you are doing,
you don't mind doing the 10- to 15-hour days.

As Judi's experience shows, through time, diligence, and social networking, you can change jobs or careers. Our suggestion upon encountering
a negative experience at your first place of employment is to weigh your
options and have an escape plan at the ready. You may find that you can
enact changes and create dialogue in your organization due to your
Women's and Gender Studies training. If not, you may have to come to
the realization, after some difficult internal dialogues and consultations
with friends and family, that either you are not the right fit for the job at
this time, or that you may have to accept the situation as it is and move
onto another opportunity, either of your own creation (see Jennifer
Pritchett's story in Chapter 5) or for another organization or entity.

## Conclusion

It has been our pleasure to travel with you on the wonderful journey that
you have taken with this book. We hope you now can fully imagine what
we always say to students pursuing a Women's and Gender Studies
education—Women's and Gender Studies can go anywhere and belongs
everywhere!

We have provided many of the tools, skills, and resources that will support you to take your place in a long line of Women's and Gender Studies graduates who have traveled the same path. There is so much opportunity that awaits you. We believe that the world needs your courage, vitality, insights, and creativity in order to make many of the changes that you have thought about in your classes. Stay true to your values, affirm your truth, and know your contribution is important.

## POINT OF VIEW CONTRIBUTORS FOR CHAPTER 7

**Karlyn Crowley** directs the Women's and Gebnder Studies program and is an Associate Professor of English at St. Norbert College. Her scholarship is primarily in two areas: Women's and Gender Studies and Gender, Religion, and American Literature and Culture.

**Anita Tijerina Revilla** is Associate Professor and Director of Women's Studies at the University of Nevada, Las Vegas. Her research focuses on student movements and social justice education, specifically in the areas of Chicana/Latina, immigrant, feminist, and queer rights activism.

## YOUR TURN: EXERCISES

### 1. SEEK OUT EXEMPLARS

As you are thinking about the five "What is next?" questions posed at the beginning of this chapter, select two or three people whose careers you admire and research their trajectory. Some of them may have had opportunities and resources not available to you (e.g. family money/social connections, living in a specific historical moment, etc.), but use your best critical analytical skills to map out what aspects of these careers are replicable and set some goals of your own—and tell your family and friends about it!

### 2. RESEARCH YOUR RIGHTS

It is important for us to know our rights when we feel threatened or vulnerable on the job. Unfortunately, it is one thing to know you have rights, but another to know where to go for help and resources (people and organizations) that may be able to provide assistance. Hopefully, you will never need to use the information from this assignment, but it could help you, your colleagues, or your family in the future. Consider this exercise an important part of your preparation for employment opportunities. Below, we have posed pertinent questions about what your rights are in the workplace. You can use some of the websites and books listed in this chapter and/or the References to help guide you.

- What is legal and not legal for potential employers to ask you during an interview?
- What are your basic rights in terms of sexual harassment and labor organizing?
- Who do you contact if you feel you have experienced sexual harassment, a hostile workplace, or discrimination based on union membership?
- Do you live in a right-to-work state? If so, what does that mean?
- Where might you go for more information?
- What are the local, state, and national organizations that can help?
- If you are not living in your country of origin, what are your rights in the country in which you work?

## 3. CLAIM YOUR FEMINIST SUPERPOWERS

We have spent much of this chapter asking you to consider the ways in which you will take care of yourself and build communities that support your intellectual and social growth. As Dr. Crowley (2011) notes, creating community is a relational process that takes work, and is "messy." First, we encourage you to write down about both the kinds of communities that you want to connect to (i.e. in person, virtual), along with what kinds of axes (e.g. peer friendship, recreational, political, etc.), and create a plan for how to start building those connections the first six months out of school. Second, take some time to reflect on what your unique "feminist superpowers" are, and how you might use them in the next phase of your life.

# APPENDIX
## A RESEARCH NOTE

In order to gain information about the types of career and employment paths people who graduate with a concentration in Women's and Gender Studies have pursued during the past 15 years (1995–2010), we employed a multiple-method approach for data collection. Prior to initiating the research, Institutional Review Board approval was obtained concurrently through the University of North Carolina at Chapel Hill (Study #10-0107) and Minnesota State University, Mankato (Study #5504). Research participants consisted of adults (18 years of age or older) who graduated with a major, minor, or concentration in Women's and Gender Studies from a college or university either in the United States or internationally. Those who participated in the study were informed on the research mandates of confidentiality, voluntary participation, and the ability to exit the study at any point through the web page prior to beginning the survey questionnaire. Participants implied consent by proceeding to the survey.

### The Survey
Data about Women's and Gender Studies undergraduates were obtained through the use of two research methodologies. The first research method employed was an online survey using Survey Monkey (www.survey monkey.com). The survey was launched on February 9, 2010, and was

closed on August 21, 2010. Participants were selected through a conve-
nience or snowball sampling approach. Respondents were informed of
the survey either through an e-mail that was sent to the undergraduate
department and program heads of active Women's and Gender Studies
departments and programs from which they graduated, or through notices
posted on our behalf through various organizations and individuals on
the social networking site Facebook.

There is no standardized list of all Women's and Gender Studies
programs and departments globally. We primarily relied on the lists of
programs and departments maintained through NWSA's website, which
are all located in the United States. We sent an e-mail to every institution
listed that offered any Women's and Gender Studies curricula at the
undergraduate level. We also had our research assistant conduct multiple
online searches of Women's and Gender Studies programs outside of the
US. She heavily relied on the Women's Studies Programs, Departments,
and Research Centers' website (http://userpages.umbc.edu/~korenman/
wmst/programs.html). This website is maintained by Joan Korenman,
Professor Emerita of English, and Affiliate Professor Emerita of Women's
Studies at the University of Maryland, Baltimore County (UMBC).

Because it was important to us to represent as many non-U.S. schools
as possible, we also asked programs, centers, and departments outside the
US to send information about their program and their students. Department chairs and program heads received a letter that explained our
research, included our IRB numbers, and contained information to send
to their alumni. By contacting all active programs and departments, a
purposive non-random sample was obtained.

Department chairs and program heads were asked to send an e-mail
with the survey (as a link), with a brief note from us, to the alumni of
the program. Besides the survey link, participants also received information
about the opportunity to be invited to a Facebook group called "Women's
Studies Students: School and Career."

Multiple e-mails were sent (if we received no response), and many
phone calls were made to programs and departments to encourage as wide
a participation rate of institutions as possible. We received many e-mails
from faculty and staff members that said one of following three things:
(1) the major or minor was no longer offered; (2) the department or unit
had no working alumni list and was not able to create one in a timely

manner; and (3) the information that they ever offered a program was incorrect. As we went through the process, institutions were marked off our list as unable to participate. Occasionally, in the case of reason (2), the director or program head was able to send a request to the college or university's development director to ask that our material be forwarded through whatever alumni lists the development office might have on file. We frequently asked former students, colleagues, and associates if they would directly post our link to the survey on their personal Facebook pages. We also asked colleagues to help us spread the word to programs and departments that were unresponsive.

Ultimately, more than 1,000 participants initiated the study, and more than 900 completed it. Graduates in this survey represent over 125 institutions. The major areas of the survey included general demographic questions (e.g. age, sex, gender, racial/ethnic identity, country of origin, religious background and current practices, parental education, current marital and family status, mentors), the characteristics of the participant's undergraduate degree experience (highest degree, year that undergraduate degree was completed, age at beginning and end of degree, other degrees obtained, type of degree—major, minor, concentration—name and location of college or university for the Women's and Gender Studies degree, international educational opportunities, internships, and involvement with on/off campus activism activities), and life after graduation (contact with department or program, involvement with organizations and/or activism, opinion of preparation for the job market, assessment of the top skills and concepts learned as part of the degree, any advice for potential Women's and Gender Studies students).

### The Interviews

The second research method employed was a short, open-ended interview (either face to face or via telephone) with survey participants who contacted the authors of this study through the e-mail address posted at the end of the survey. At the end of the online survey, respondents were given the opportunity to contact the principal investigators if they were interested in being interviewed about their experiences of being a Women's and Gender Studies graduate. The e-mail address listed was to our research assistant. The research assistant would then forward names of potential interviewees to us. Interested participants were sent a letter electronically regarding their participation in the study and their time availability, as well as a request for the participant to indicate three topic areas they were interested in providing more information about than was provided in the survey. The respondents were then asked to provide in the subject line of their response e-mail "Women's and Gender Studies Graduate Interview." As the survey is anonymous, these respondents were asked to provide the authors some demographic and locating information, such as name, the name of the institution in which they graduated with their Women's and Gender Studies degree, and their current employment position.

During the course of the interview, respondents were also asked to elaborate on one or several subject areas from the survey. Women's and Gender Studies students may have been asked questions ranging from tips for faculty about advising, mentoring, or providing career advice to Women's and Gender Studies students; social networks and other information important for the respondent's first position that utilized their Women's and Gender Studies major or minor; what was special and unique about their Women's and Gender Studies classroom experience; what information did the respondent wish they knew or planned for prior to graduation; what had changed in the participant's viewpoint of living their feminism/Women's and Gender Studies ideals since leaving school; what insight or "ahas" were gained from the respondent's internship or service learning opportunities; how had the respondent applied skills and concepts from their degree into any research projects or career experiences; and who were the participant's mentors and unexpected allies since graduation. We used these interviews to select the graduate profiles highlighted in Chapter 5.

## The Facebook Page and Informal Interviews

Our intention for the Facebook group was to create an online community for people interested in feminism, women's issues, and former Women's and Gender Studies students. We created it as a space for discussion, networking, and general camaraderie. So the group consists of many people who took our survey, people who did not meet our graduation requirement (graduated too early—before 1995—to take the survey), and some faculty and staff members who were interested in our research. Before long, as we were writing drafts of several chapters, we found

ourselves asking this agreeable group questions about themes in the book
(e g "What's unique about the Women's Studies classroom?") and receiving prompt feedback on our ideas. We found this experience facilitated
a novel and engaging way to solicit advice and support from a community
of experts while writing. They kept us inspired!

Besides survey participants and the Facebook group, we both actively
contacted colleagues and former students for comments and information
regarding international education, business ownership, civic education,
and human resource issues. Prior to being interviewed, participants gave
verbal consent. We also spoke informally to employers and Women's and
Gender Studies program and department heads.

# REFERENCES

Aaron, J. and Walby, S. (Eds.) (1991). *Out of the Margins: Women's Studies in the Nineties.* Bristol, PA: Falmer Press.

Adamson, B. (2013). "I'm a Male Nurse—So What?" Retrieved April 30, 2014, from http://everydayfeminism.com/2013/06/male-nurse-so-what.

American Association of University Women (2006). *Drawing the Line: Sexual Harassment on Campus.* Washington, DC: AAUW.

American Association of University Women (2013). *Women in Community College: Access to Success.* Washington, DC: AAUW.

American Farm Bureau Federation (2014). "What is the Young Farmers & Ranchers Program?" Retrieved April 30, 2014, from www.fb.org/index.php?action=programs.yfr.home.

Andreeva, N. (2009). "HBO Signing Up for Women's Studies." *Reuters*, April 15. Retrieved November 13, 2009, from www.reuters.com/article/televisionNews/id USTRE53E11720090415.

Aranti, L. (2009). "A New Crop of Farmers." *The Washington Post*, June 28. Retrieved June 28, 2009, from www.washingtonpost.com/wpdyn/content/article/2009/06/27/AR2009062702386.html.

Association of American Colleges and Universities and Hart Research Associates (2013). "It Takes More than a Major: Employer Priorities for College Learning and Student Success." Retrieved April 30, 2014, from www.aacu.org/leap/documents/2013_EmployerSurvey.pdf.

Baxandall, R. and Gordon, L. (Eds.) (2001). *Dear Sisters: Dispatches from the Women's Liberation Movements.* New York: Basic Books.

Berger, M. (2004). *Workable Sisterhood: The Political Journey of Stigmatized Women with HIV/AIDS.* Princeton, NJ: Princeton University Press.

Berger, M. and Guidroz, K. (Eds.) (2009). *The Intersectional Approach: Transforming the Academy through Race, Class, and Gender.* Chapel Hill, NC: University of North Carolina Press.

Berger, M. and Radeloff, C. (2011). *Transforming Scholarship: Why Women's and Gender Studies Students are Changing Themselves and the World,* 1st ed. New York: Routledge.

Bochner, S., Furnham, A., and Ward, C. (2001). *The Psychology of Culture Shock,* 2nd ed. New York: Routledge.

Bolles, R. (2014). *What Color is Your Parachute? A Practical Manual for Job-Hunters and Career Changers.* Berkeley, CA: Ten Speed Press.

Boston Women's Health Collective (2005). *Our Bodies, Ourselves: A New Edition for a New Era,* 4th ed. Oneonta, NY: Touchstone Press.

Bourgeois, T. (2007). *Her Corner Office: A Guide to Help Women Find a Place and a Voice in Corporate America,* 2nd ed. Dallas, TX: Dallas Books.

Boxer, M. J. and Stimpson, C. R. (2001). *When Women Ask the Questions: Creating Women's Studies in America.* Baltimore, MD: Johns Hopkins University Press.

Braithwaite, A., Heald, S., Luhmann, S., and Rosenberg, S. (2005). *Troubling Women's Studies: Pasts, Presents, and Possibilities.* Toronto: Sumach Press.

Bravo, E. (2007). *Taking on the Big Boys: or Why Feminism is Good for Families, Business, and the Nation.* New York: The Feminist Press at CUNY.

Brooks, K. (2009). *You Majored in What? Mapping Your Path from Chaos to Career.* New York: Viking.

Buchholz, R. A. (1991). "Corporate Responsibility and the Good Society: From Economics to Ecology; Factors which Influence Corporate Policy Decisions." *Business Horizons,* 34(4): 19–31.

Buckingham, M. and Clifton, D. (2001). *Now, Discover Your Strengths.* New York: Free Press.

Bureau of Labor Statistics, U.S. Department of Labor (2009). "College Enrollment and Work Activity of 2008 High School Graduates." Bureau of Labor Statistics news release. Retrieved February 26, 2010, from www.bls.gov/news/release/hsgec.nr0.htm.

Bureau of Labor Statistics, U.S. Department of Labor (2010). "Occupational Outlook Handbook, 2010–2011 Edition, Job Opportunities in the Armed Forces." Retrieved August 1, 2010, from www.bls.gov/oco/ocos249.htm.

Bureau of Labor Statistics, U.S. Department of Labor (2012). "Number of Jobs Held, Labor Market Activity, and Earnings Growth among the Youngest Baby Boomers: Results from a Longitudinal Survey." Retrieved April 30, 2014, from www.bls.gov/news.release/pdf/nlsoy.pdf (Chapter 3, p. 121).

Bureau of Labor Statistics, U.S. Department of Labor (2014a). "Industries at a Glance; Educational Services: NAICS 61." Retrieved April 30, 2014, from www.bls.gov/iag/tgs/iag61.htm.

Bureau of Labor Statistics, U.S. Department of Labor (2014b). "Industries at a Glance; Health Care and Social Assistance: NAICS 62." Retrieved April 30, 2014, from www.bls.gov/iag/tgs/iag62.htm.

Bureau of Labor Statistics, U.S. Department of Labor (2014c). "Industries at a Glance; Information: NAICS 51." Retrieved April 30, 2014, from www.bls.gov/iag/tgs/iag51.htm.

Bureau of Labor Statistics, U.S. Department of Labor (2014d). "Occupational Outlook Handbook, 2012–13 Edition, Business and Financial Occupations." Retrieved February 1, 2014, from www.bls.gov/ooh/business-and financial/home.htm.

Bureau of Labor Statistics, U.S. Department of Labor (2014e). "Occupational Outlook Handbook, 2012–13 Edition, Protective Service Occupations." Retrieved February 1, 2014, from www.bls.gov/ooh/protective-service/home.htm.

Buzzfeed (2013). "22 Things Women and Gender Studies Majors Understand." Retrieved October 20, 2013, from www.buzzfeed.com/juniperbug/22-things-only-womens-and-gender-studies-majors-f59x.

Byrd, P. R., Cole, J., and Guy-Sheftall, B. (Eds.) (2009). *I Am Your Sister: Collected and Unpublished Writings of Audre Lorde.* Oxford: Oxford University Press.

Cameron, J. (2002). *The Artist's Way: A Spiritual Path to Higher Creativity.* New York: Tarcher.

Campbell, S. and Orr, J. (2010). "The Corporate Seduction of Feminism." Retrieved April 30, 2014, from www.socialistreview.org.uk/article.php?articlenumber=11109.

Carson, R. (1962). *Silent Spring.* New York: Houghton Mifflin

Carter, J. (2007). *Double Outsiders: How Women of Color Can Succeed in Corporate America.* St. Paul, MN: JIST Books.

Center for Earth Spirituality and Rural Ministry (2013). "School Sisters of Notre Dame." Retrieved April 30, 2014, from www.ssndcentralpacific.org/Partner/Partners-In-Mission.

Center for Gender Studies University of Basel (Switzerland) (2014). "Post Graduate Programs Basel (2014)." Retrieved April 30, 2014, from https://genderstudies.unibas.ch/en/research/phd-program-gender-studies.

Chanda, G. (2011). "Alum Spotlight: Vanita Gupta in conversation with Geetanjali Singh Chanda." *Yale Newsletter WCSS & LGBTS*, 2(1) (Fall). Retrieved April 30, 2014, from http://ris-systech2.its.yale.edu/newsletter/wgss/vol3/gupta.html.

Chicago Women in Trades (2010). "Women in Skilled Trades Project." Retrieved August 1, 2010, from www.chicagowomenintrades.org/artman/publish/article_252.shtml.

Christ, C. (Ed.) (1992). *Womanspirit Rising: A Feminist Reader in Religion.* New York: HarperOne.

Civil Liberties and Public Policy (2014). "2014 Conference: From Abortion Rights to Social Justice: Building the Movement for Reproductive Freedom." Retrieved April 30, 2014, from http://clpp.hampshire.edu/conference.

Cobble, D. (2007). *The Sex of Class: Women Transforming Labor.* Ithaca, NY: Cornell University Press.

Code of Federal Regulations (1980). Title 29: Section 1604.11a. 45 Federal Register 74677, November 10, 1980.

College and Career Readiness Career Center (2014). "Science, Technology, Engineering & Mathematics." Retrieved April 30, 2014, from http://ccr.mcgraw-hill.com/category/career-center/science-technology-engineering-mathematics/.

Collins, P. H. (1993). "Toward a New Vision: Race, Class, and Gender as Categories of Analysis and Connection." In T. Ore (Ed.) (2008). *The Social Construction of Difference and Inequality*, 4th ed. Columbus, OH: McGraw-Hill.

Collins, P. H. (2007). *Black Feminist Thought*, 2nd ed. New York: Routledge.

Conklin, L. (2013). "Nothing Works Like a Network." *Carolina Alumni Review*, September/October, p. 60. Retrieved April 30, 2014, from www.carolinaalumni review.com/carolinaalumnireview/20130910/?pg=63&pm=2&u1=friend#pg63.

Connell, R. W. and Messerschmidt, J. (2005). "Hegemonic Masculinity." *Gender and Society*, 19(6): 829–859.

Costa, T. (2010). *Farmer Jane: Women Changing the Way We Eat*. Layton, UT: Gibbs Smith.

CPS HR Consulting (2014). "Professional and Paraprofessional Entry Level Analyst Test Rental." Retrieved April 30, 2014, from www.cpshr.us/testrental/pp_entryanalyst. html.

Crowley, K. (2011). *Feminism's New Age: Gender, Appropriation, and the Afterlife of Essentialism*. New York: SUNY Press.

Daly, M. (1993). *Beyond God the Father: Toward a Philosophy of Women's Liberation*. Boston, MA: Beacon Press.

Dean Dad (2012). "Why Men Should Take Women's Studies." *Confessions of a Community College Dean*. Retrieved October 8, 2013, from www.insidehighered.com/blogs/ confessions-community-college-dean/why-men-should-take-women%E2%80%99s- studies#sthash.k4rtNp0M.dpbs.

Dever, M. (2004). "Women's Studies and the Discourse of Vocationalism: Some New Perspectives." *Women's Studies International Forum*, 27(5–6): 475–488.

Dicker, R. and Piepmeier, A. (Eds.) (2003). *Catching a Wave: Reclaiming Feminism for the 21st Century*. Northeastern, MA: Northeastern University Press.

Doyle, S. (2010). "Career Tests—Taking a Career Test." Retrieved August 1, 2010, from http://jobsearch.about.com/od/careertests/a/careertests.htm.

Doyle, A. (2011). *Internet Your Way To a New Job: How to Really Find a Job Online*, 3rd ed.. Cuppertino, CA: Happy About Publishing.

Duffy, S. and Kan, S. (2013). "Business Schools Should Act on Women's Entrepreneurial Potential." *Financial Times*. November 21. Retrieved May 28, 2014 from www.ft.com/ cms/s/2/d2ac6ff0-4e0b-11e3-8fa5-00144feabdc0.html#axzz30sltgKLl.

Enke, A. (Ed.) (2012). *Transfeminist Perspectives in and Beyond Transgender and Gender Studies*. Philadelphia, PA: Temple University Press, 2012.

Fabello, M. (2014). "So You Want a Feminist Job." Retrieved April 30, 2014, from http://everydayfeminism.com/2014/01/you-want-a-feminist-job.

Faludi, S. (1992). *Backlash: The Undeclared War Against American Women*. Norwell, MA: Anchor.

Flavin, J. and Paltrow L. M. (2013). "Arrests of and Forced Interventions on Pregnant Women in the United States, 1973–2005: Implications for Women's Legal Status and Public Health Journal of Health Politics." *Policy and Law*, 38(2). Retrieved April 30, 2014, from http://jhppl.dukejournals.org/content/38/2/299.full.pdf+html?sid= b0811f36-d4e4-4b51-a830-e175e6eee40c.

Frank, A. J. (2007). "What I'm Doing With My Women's Studies Degree." *Ms. Magazine*, Summer. Retrieved April 30, 2014, from www.msmagazine.com/spring2007/womens studies_letters.asp.

Freedman, E. (2002). *No Turning Back: The History of Feminism and the Future of Women*. New York: Ballantine Books.

Friedan, B. (1963). *The Feminine Mystique*. New York: W. W. Norton & Company.

Friere, P. (2001). *Pedagogy of the Oppressed*. New York: Continuum.

Garrett, C. D. and Rogers, M. (2002). *Who's Afraid of Women's Studies?* Lanham, MD: AltaMira Press.

George Washington University (2014). "Guide to Graduate Study." George Washington University: Colombian College of Arts and Sciences Women's Studies Program. Retrieved April 30, 2014, from http://programs.columbian.gwu.edu/womensstudies/graduate/guide.

Goffman, I. (1959). *Presentation of Self in Everyday Life*. New York: Doubleday.

Gosfield, J. and Sweeney, C. (2014). "No Managers Required How Zappos's is Ditching Old Corporate Structure for Something New." Retrieved April 30, 2014, from http://theartofdoing.com/no-managers-required-how-zapposs-is-ditching-old-corporate-structure-for-something-new/#sthash.CE0W80LM.dpuf.

Greenhouse, S. (2010). "The Unpaid Intern, Legal or Not." *New York Times*, April 2. Retrieved August 2, 2010, from www.nytimes.com/2010/04/03/business/03intern.html#.

Griffin, G. (2005). *Doing Women's Studies: Employment Opportunities, Personal Impacts, and Social Consequences*. London: Zed Books.

Griffin, G. (2009). "The 'Ins' and 'Outs' of Women's/Gender Studies: A Response to Reports of its Demise in 2008," *Women's History Review*, 18(3) (July): 485–496.

Guy-Sheftall, B. (2009). "Forty Years of Women's Studies," *Ms.*, Spring, pp. 56–57.

Hemmings, C. (2011). *Why Stories Matter: The Political Grammar of Feminist Theory*. Durham, NC: Duke University Press.

Henderson, M. G. and Johnson, E. P. (2005). *Black Queer Studies: A Critical Anthology*. Durham, NC: Duke University Press.

Hesse-Biber, S. N. and Leavy, P. L. (2007). *Feminist Research Practice: A Primer*. Thousand Oaks, CA: Sage.

Hobson, J. (2012). "Hot Topics in Women's Studies." *Ms. Magazine* (Fall): 41.

Hochschild, A. (1979). "Emotion Work, Feeling Rules, and Social Structure," *American Journal of Sociology*, 85, pp. 551–575.

Hochschild, A. (1983). *The Managed Heart: Commercialization of Human Feeling*. Berkeley, CA: University of California Press.

Hodges, J. (2010). "a) Doctor b) Builder c) Cop d) HELP!" *The Wall Street Journal*. Retrieved April 30, 2014, from http://online.wsj.com/news/articles/SB100014240527 4870413380457519801174591847.

Hollibaugh, A. (2000). *My Dangerous Desires: A Queer Girl Dreaming Herself Home*. Durham, NC: Duke University Press.

hooks, b. (1984). *Feminist Theory: From Margin to Center*. Boston, MA: South End Press.

hooks, b. (2000). *Feminism is for Everybody: Passionate Politics*. Boston, MA: South End Press.

Howe, F. (Ed.) (2000). *The Politics of Women's Studies: Testimony from the Thirty Founding Mothers*. New York: The Feminist Press.

Jones, A. (2013). "Tips for Marketing Yourself During the Job Hunt." Retrieved April 30, 2014, from http://idealistcareers.org/tips-for-marketing-yourself-during-the-job-hunt/.

Jones, A. (2014). "Join the Idealist Careers LinkedIn Boot Camp!" Retrieved April 30, 2014, from http://idealistcareers.org/join-the-idealist-careers-linkedin-boot-camp/.

Kantrowitz, M. (2010). "The Smart Student Guide to Financial Aid," FinAid Page, LLC. Retrieved February 26, 2010, from www.finaid.org/loans/.

Kesselman, A., McNair, L., and Schniedewind, N. (2008). *Women Images and Realities: A Multicultural Anthology*, 4th ed. Columbus, OH: McGraw-Hill.

Kim, E. (2013). "Being a Woman in a Male-Dominated Field, with Patricia Valoy." Retrieved April 30, 2014, from http://everydayfeminism.com/2013/09/episode 20/.

Kimmel, M. (1994). "Masculinity as Homophobia. Fear, Shame, and Silence in the Construction of Gender Identity." In P. Rothenberg (Ed.) (2003). *Race, Class, and Gender in the United States: An Integrated Study*, 6th ed. New York: Worth.

Kimmel, M. (1996). "Men and Women's Studies: Premises, Perils, and Promise." In N. Hewitt, J. O'Barr, and N. Rousebaugh (Eds.) (1996). *Talking Gender: Public Images, Personal Images, and Political Critiques*. Chapel Hill, NC: University of North Carolina Press.

Kimmich, A. (2009). "Undergraduate Programs." *Ms.*, Spring: 62.

Kirk, G. and Okazawa-Rey, M. (2010). *Women's Lives: Multicultural Perspectives*, 5th ed. Columbus, OH: McGraw-Hill.

Kolmar, W. and Bartkowski, F. (2010). *Feminist Theory: A Reader*, 3rd ed. Columbus, OH: McGraw-Hill.

Koyama, E. (2003). "Transfeminist Manifesto." In R. Dicker and A. Piepmeier (Eds.) (2003). *Catching a Wave: Reclaiming Feminism for the 21st Century*. Boston, MA: Northeastern University Press.

Langenberg-Miller, E. (2007). "What I'm Doing With My Women's Studies Degree. *Ms. Magazine*, Summer. Retrieved April 30, 2014, from www.msmagazine.com/spring 2007/womensstudies_letters.asp.

Levin, A. (2007). "Questions for a New Century: Women's Studies and Integrative Learning." A Report from the National Women's Studies Association. College Park, MD: NWSA.

Lorber, J. (1994). *Paradoxes of Gender*. New Haven, CT: Yale University Press.

Lorber, J. (2012). *Gender Inequality: Feminist Theories and Politics*. New York: Oxford University Press.

Lorde, A. (1982). *Zami: A New Spelling of My Name*. Trumansburg, NY: Crossing Press.

Lorde, A. (1984). *Sister Outsider*. Trumansburg, NY: Crossing Press.

Lovejoy, M. (1998). "You Can't Go Home Again: The Impact of Women's Studies on Intellectual and Personal Development." *NWSA Journal*, 10(1): 119–38.

Luebke, B. and Reilly, M. (1995). *Women's Studies Graduates: The First Generation*. New York: Teachers College Press.

McCaughey, M. (2009). "Sticks and Stones." *Ms.*, Spring: 70.

McIntosh, P. (1988). "White Privilege and Male Privilege: A Personal Account of Coming to See Correspondences through Work in Women's Studies." Working Paper 189. Wellesley, MA: Wellesley College Center for Research on Women.

MacNeil, N. (2012). "Entrepreneurship is the New Women's Movement." *Forbes*. Retrieved April 30, 2014, from www.forbes.com/sites/work-in-progress/2012/06/08/ entrepreneurship-is-the-new-womens-movement.

Magezis, J. (1997). *Women's Studies (Teach Yourself)*. Columbus, OH: McGraw-Hill.

Maparyan, L. P. (2011). *The Womanist Idea*. London: Routledge.

Martin, E. C. and Sullivan, J. C. (Eds.) (2010). *Click: When We Knew We Were Feminists*. Berkeley, CA: Seal Press.

Mason, C. (2002). *Killing for Life: The Apocalyptic Narrative of Pro-Life Politics*. Ithaca, NY: Cornell University Press.

Mason, C. (2012). "What to Do When They Say Holocaust," *On The Issues Magazine*, Winter. Retrieved April 30, 2014, from www.ontheissuesmagazine.com/2012winter/2012winter_Mason.php.

Massa, C. (2011). "Students and Faculty Discuss Feminism and Greek Life" CUINDE-PENDENT.com. October 11. Retrieved January 2014 from www.cuindependent.com/2011/10/12/students-and-faculty-discuss feminism-and-greek-life/28422.

Messer-Davidow, E. (2002). *Disciplining Feminism: From Social Activism to Academic Discourse*. Durham, NC: Duke University Press.

Messner, M. A. and Sabo, D. F. (1994). *Sex, Violence, and Power in Sports: Rethinking Masculinity*. Trumansburg, NY: Crossing Press.

Meyers, N. (director) (2003). *Something's Gotta Give* [motion picture]. Columbia Pictures Corporation.

Minnesota State University, Mankato (2008). "Advising, General Education and Cultural Diversity." In *Undergraduate Bulletin 2008–2009*. Mankato, MN: Minnesota State University. Retrieved November 15, 2009, from www.mnsu.edu/supersite/academics/bulletins/undergraduate/2008-2009/generalinfo/generaleduandhonors.pdf.

Morgen, S. (2002). *Into Our Own Hands: The Women's Health Movement in the United States, 1969–1990*. New Brunswick, NJ: Rutgers University Press.

Muscio, I. (2002). *Cunt*, 2nd ed. San Francisco, CA: Seal Press.

Nasri, G. (2014). "6 Personal Philosophies that Shaped Successful Entrepreneurs." Retrieved April 30, 2014, from www.fastcompany.com/3024831/bottom-line/the-personal-philosophies-that-shape-todays-successful-innovators.

National Advocates for Pregnant Women (2009). "How Personhood USA & The Bills They Support Will Hurt ALL Pregnant Women." *YouTube*. Retrieved April 30, 2014, from www.youtube.com/watch?v=-3X4_p3yAC8&feature=c4-overview-vl&list=PL0161452866BB7549.

National Center for Education Statistics (2007). "Digest of Education Statistics (Annual Report)." Washington, DC. Retrieved September 14, 2009, from http://nces.ed.gov/das/.

National Institute of General Medical Sciences (2013). "Medical Scientist Training Program National Institute of Health." Retrieved April 30, 2014, from www.nigms.nih.gov/Training/InstPredoc/Pages/PredocOverview-MSTP.aspx.

National Science Foundation, Division of Science Resources Statistics (2009). "Doctorate Recipients from U.S. Universities: Summary Report 2007–2008. Special Report NSF 10-309." Arlington, VA: NSF. Retrieved August 1, 2010, from www.nsf.gov/statistics/nsf10309.

National Women's Studies Association (2007). "Mapping Women's and Gender Studies Data Collection: Executive Summary." College Park, MD: NWSA. Retrieved August 1, 2010, from www.nwsa.org/projects/mapping.php.

Nichols, M. (director) (2003). *Angels in America* [motion picture]. Avenue Pictures Productions.

Økland, J. (2010). "How it Happened that a Country's Public Debate was Focused on Gender Studies for Months on End." May 10. Retrieved September 30, 2010, from www.gender.no/Open_dialogue/Gender_blog/8420.

Paltrow, L. (2013) "40 Years after Roe v. Wade: Reproductive Justice in the Age of Mass Incarceration." Lecture Flyer. Retrieved April 30, 2014, from http://advocates forpregnantwomen.org/main/programs/public_education/lynn_paltrow_speaking_ opportunity_40_years_after_roe_v_wade_reproductive_justice_in_the_age_of_mass incarceration.php.

Patel, J. (2012). "9 Reasons To Choose A Corporate Job Over A Startup." Retrieved April 30, 2014, from www.fastcompany.com/1825592/9-reasons-choose-corporate-job-over-startup.

PBS (2013). "Spelman College Charts a New Path by Encouraging Women in STEM Studies." Interview transcript. Host: Gwen Ifill. Interviewee: Dr. Beverly Daniel Tatum. Retrieved April 30, 2014, from www.pbs.org/newshour/bb/education-july-dec13-spelman_12-09.

Pharr, S. (1988). *Homophobia: A Weapon of Sexism.* Berkeley, CA: Chardon Press. Retrieved April 30, 2014, from www.csusm.edu/sjs/documents/homophobiaaweaponofsexism condensed.pdf (updated in 1997).

Pipher, M. (2006). *Writing to Change the World.* New York: Riverhead Trade.

Rangel-Medina, E. M. and Revilla, A. T. (2011). "Las Vegas Activist Crew." In M. Berta Ávila, A. Tijerina Revilla, and J. López Figueroa (Eds) (2011), *Marching Students: Chicana and Chicano Activism in Education, 1968 to the Present* (pp. 167–187). Reno, NV: University of Nevada, Reno Press.

Rich, A. (1979). "Claiming an Education." In S. Shaw and J. Lee (Eds.) (2009) *Women's Voices/Feminist Visions: Classic and Contemporary Readings,* 4th ed. New York: McGraw-Hill.

Rivera, C. (2006). "A Women's Studies Graduate Goes to Africa." In A. Kesselman, L. D. McNair, and N. Schniedewind (Eds.) (2008). *Women: Images and Realities: A Multicultural Anthology,* 4th ed. New York: McGraw-Hill.

Rosen, R. (2000). *The World Split Open: How the Modern Women's Movement Changed America.* New York: Penguin Press.

Roy, J. (2009). "Community College Programs." *Ms.,* Spring: 62.

Schneider, C. (2009). "Foreword." In E. L. Dey, C. Barnhardt, M. Antonaros, M. Ott, and M. Holsapple (Eds.) (2009). *Civic Responsibility: What is the Campus Climate for Learning?* Washington, DC: Association of American Colleges.

Scott, J. W. (Ed.) (2008). *Women's Studies on the Edge.* Durham, NC: Duke University Press.

Segal, P. (director) (2000). *Nutty Professor II: The Klumps* [motion picture]. Universal Pictures.

Shrewsbury, C. (1993). "What is Feminist Pedagogy?" *Women's Studies Quarterly,* 21(3–4): 8–16.

Silius, H. (2005). "The Professionalization of Women's Studies Students in Europe: Expectations and Experiences." In G. Griffin (Ed.) (2005). *Doing Women's Studies: Employment Opportunities, Personal Impacts, and Social Consequences.* London: Zed Books.

Slavin, L. (2013). "How to Weather Post College Unemployment." Retrieved April 30, 2014, from http://everydayfeminism.com/2013/06/post-college-unemployment (originally published on http://feminspire.com/how-to-weather-post-college-unemployment).

Sontag, S. (2001). *Illness as Metaphor and AIDS and Its Metaphors.* New York: Picador.

Stafford, Z. (2012). "How Feminism Made Me a Better Gay Man." Retrieved April 30, 2014, from www.huffingtonpost.com/zach-stafford/how-feminism-made-me-a-better-gay-man_b_1393114.html.

Stevenson, A., Elliot, J., and Jones, R. (Eds.) (2001). *The Oxford Color English Dictionary,* 2nd ed. Oxford: Oxford University Press.

Stewart, N. A. (2007). "Transform the World: What You Can Do with a Degree in Women's Studies." *Ms.,* Spring, pp. 65–66.

T, J. (2012). "It's Not Feminism That Hurts Men." 21 May. Retrieved May 28, 2014 from www.thefword.org.uk/features/2012/05/its_not_feminism_that_hurts_men.

Thom, M. (2002). "Tradeswomen Unite: A Movement Goes National." *Ms. Magazine,* Summer. Retrieved April 30, 2014, from www.msmagazine.com/summer2002/thom.asp.

Thompson, S. (2002). "Becoming a Feminist Physician." In A. Kesselman, L. D. McNair, and N. Schniedewind (Eds.) (2008). *Women: Images and Realities: A Multicultural Anthology,* 4th ed. New York: McGraw-Hill.

Tong, R. P. (2008). *Feminist Thought: A More Comprehensive Reader.* New York: Westview Press.

Turner, N. A. (2007). "What I'm Doing With My Women's Studies Degree." *Ms. Magazine,* Summer. Retrieved April 30, 2014, from www.msmagazine.com/spring2007/womensstudies_letters.asp.

United States Department of Labor (2009). "Quick Facts on Nontraditional Occupations for Women." Retrieved April 30, 2014, from www.dol.gov/wb/factsheets/nontra2008.htm.

University of Arkansas Career Development Center (2008). "Externships/Job Shadowing." Retrieved August 1, 2010, from http://career.uark.edu/Students/Externships.aspx.

University of Auckland (2014). "Women's Studies." Retrieved April 30, 2014, from www.arts.auckland.ac.nz/en/about/subjects-and-courses/womens-studies.html.

University of California Berkeley (2003). "How to Get a Job in Politics." Retrieved April 30, 2014, from https://career.berkeley.edu/Article/030418a.stm.

University of California Berkeley (2014). "Career Center." Retrieved April 30, 2014, from https://career.berkeley.edu/Info/AboutUs.stm.

USA Jobs Resource Center (2014). "Determining the Right Career Path for You." Retrieved April 30, 2014, from https://help.usajobs.gov/index.php/Determining_the_Right_Career_Path_for_You.

U.S. Army (2014). "Army Medicine: About Army Allied Health." Retrieved April 30, 2014, from www.goarmy.com/amedd/allied-health/medical-service-specialist-corps.html.

U.S. Census of Agriculture (2012). "2007 Census of Agriculture: Women Farmers." Retrieved April 30, 2014, from www.agcensus.usda.gov/Publications/2007/Online_Highlights/Fact_Sheets/Demographics/.

U.S. Department of Education, National Center for Education Statistics (2007). "Integrated Postsecondary Education Data System (IPEDS)." Retrieved November 10, 2009, from http://nces.ed.gov/ipeds/.

Uwujaren, J. (2012). "Gainful Unemployment: 5 Acts of Self Care While Job Hunting." Retrieved April 30, 2014, from https://everydayfeminism.com/2012/12/gainful-unemployment/.

Valenti, J. (2007) Full Frontal Feminism: A Young Woman's Guide to Why Feminism Matters. Emeryville, CA: Seal Press.

Vitae (2014), "Find Jobs: Vitae" (search engine). Retrieved April 30, 2014, from https://chroniclevitae.com/job_search/new?cid=chenav

Walker, T. (2000). "A Feminist Challenge to Community Service: A Call to Politicize Service Learning." In B. J. Balliet and K. Heffernan (Eds.) (2000) The Practice of Change: Concepts and Models for Service-Learning in Women's Studies. Washington, DC: American Association for Higher Education.

Wantland, R. (2005). "Feminist Frat Boys? Fraternity Men in the (Women's Studies) House." NWSA Journal, 17(2) (Summer): 156–163.

Wecker, M. (2011). "How to Go to Medical School for Free." US News and World Report. Retrieved April 30, 2014, from www.usnews.com/education/best-graduate-schools/top-medical-schools/articles/2011/10/14/how-to-go-to-medical-school-for-free-2.

Weigman, R. (Ed.) (2002). Women's Studies on Its Own: A Next Wave Reader in Institutional Change. Durham, NC: Duke University Press.

West, C. and Zimmerman, D. (1987). "Doing Gender." Gender and Society, 1: 125–151.

West, L. (2013). "If I Admit that 'Hating Men' is a Thing, Will You Stop Turning it into a Self-Fulfilling Prophecy?" Jezebel. Retrieved April 30, 2014, from http://jezebel.com/5992479/if-1-admit-that-hating-men-is-a-thing-will-you-stop-turning-it-into-a-self-fulfilling-prophecy.

White, E. (2003). Fast Girls: Teenage Tribes and the Myth of the Slut. Berkeley, CA: Berkeley Trade.

Wilson, K. (2006). Hip Tranquil Chick: A Guide to Life On and Off the Yoga Mat. Novato, CA: New World Library.

Wilson, K. (2010). Tranquilista: Mastering the Art of Enlightened Work and Mindful Play. Novato, CA: New World Library.

WMST-L (nd). "Women's Studies vs. Gender Studies." Retrieved April 30, 2014, from http://userpages.umbc.edu/~korenman/wmst/womvsgen.html#TopOfPage.

Women's Sports Foundation (2009). Women's Sports Foundation Education Guide: Special Issues for Coaches of Women's Sports. East Meadow, NY: Women's Sports Foundation. Available for download at www.avca.org/includes/media/docs/WSF-Special-Issues-Womens-Sports.pdf.

Zellinger, J. (2012). "Campus Confidential: A Feminist Rushes A Sorority," The Frisky. February 23. Retrieved January 2014 from www.thefrisky.com/2012-02-23/campus-confidential-a-feminist-rushes-a-sorority/.

# INDEX

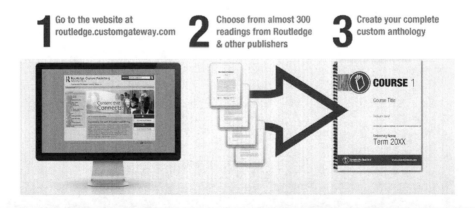